Political Economies of Energy Transition

Global climate solutions depend on low-carbon energy transitions in developing countries, but little is known about how those will unfold. Examining the transitions of Brazil and South Africa, Hochstetler reveals how choices about wind and solar power respond to four different constellations of interests and institutions, or four simultaneous political economies of energy transition. The political economy of climate change set Brazil and South Africa on different tracks, with South Africa's coal-based electricity system fighting against an existential threat. Since deforestation dominates Brazil's climate emissions, climate concerns were secondary there for electricity planning. Both saw significant mobilization around industrial policy and cost and consumption issues, showing the importance of economic considerations for electricity choices in emerging economies. Host communities resisted Brazilian wind power but accepted other forms. Hochstetler argues that national energy transition finally depends on the intersection of these political economies, with South Africa illustrating a politicized transition mode and Brazil presenting a bureaucracy-dominant one.

KATHRYN HOCHSTETLER is Professor of International Development at the London School of Economics and Political Science. Her book *Greening Brazil: Environmental Activism in State and Society* (co-authored with Margaret E. Keck, 2007) received the Lynton Caldwell Prize from the Science, Technology, and Environmental Politics section of the American Political Science Association.

Business and Public Policy

Series Editor:
Aseem Prakash, University of Washington

Series Board:
Sarah Brooks, Ohio State University
David Coen, University College London
Nathan Jensen, University of Texas, Austin
Christophe Knill, Ludwig-Maximilians-University, Munich
David Konisky, Indiana University
David Levi Faur, Hebrew University, Jerusalem
Layna Mosley, University of North Carolina, Chapel Hill
Abraham Newman, Georgetown University
Leonard Seabrooke, Copenhagen Business School
Mike Vandenberg, Vanderbilt University
Edward Walker, University of California, Los Angeles
Henry Yeung, Singapore National University

This series aims to play a pioneering role in shaping the emerging field of business and public policy. *Business and Public Policy* focuses on two central questions. First, how does public policy influence business strategy, operations, organization, and governance, and with what consequences for both business and society? Second, how do businesses themselves influence policy institutions, policy processes, and other policy actors and with what outcomes?

Other books in the series:

Political Economies of Energy Transition

Wind and Solar Power in Brazil and South Africa

KATHRYN HOCHSTETLER
London School of Economics and Political Science

CAMBRIDGE
UNIVERSITY PRESS

Shaftesbury Road, Cambridge CB2 8EA, United Kingdom

One Liberty Plaza, 20th Floor, New York, NY 10006, USA

477 Williamstown Road, Port Melbourne, VIC 3207, Australia

314–321, 3rd Floor, Plot 3, Splendor Forum, Jasola District Centre, New Delhi – 110025, India

103 Penang Road, #05–06/07, Visioncrest Commercial, Singapore 238467

Cambridge University Press is part of Cambridge University Press & Assessment, a department of the University of Cambridge.

We share the University's mission to contribute to society through the pursuit of education, learning and research at the highest international levels of excellence.

www.cambridge.org
Information on this title: www.cambridge.org/9781108826808

DOI: 10.1017/9781108920353

First published 2021
First paperback edition 2024

A catalogue record for this publication is available from the British Library

ISBN   978-1-108-84384-3   Hardback
ISBN   978-1-108-82680-8   Paperback

Contents

Figures

Tables

Acknowledgments

Like all lengthy book projects, this one has depended on the assistance of many people in many places over many years. Among them, I'd like to single out Peter Evans who transformed the project with a casual suggestion that I add a comparison with South Africa to my proposed study of energy transitions in Brazil. I would never have thought of this cross-regional comparison on my own, but the book itself shows how fruitful the suggestion has been.

Adding a book-length study of a new country was a daunting prospect, and I am especially grateful to a group of researchers of and/or in South Africa who helped guide my initial approach. These included Romy Chevalier, Ivor Chipkin, Jonathan Crush, Neva Makgetla, Sue Parnell, Gay Seidman, and Harald Winkler and others at the Energy Research Centre of the University of Cape Town. Brazil was more familiar territory, as I have been traveling there for research since 1989. In Brazil, Rebecca Abers, José Augusto Pádua, and Eduardo Viola were especially important in helping me think through this project. I was grateful to discover that South Africans in the climate and energy sectors were every bit as generous and thoughtful as I have found Brazilians to be over many years. These pages could not have been written without their willing participation as interviewees and guides to the renewable energy sector, and their insights appear throughout the book. Needless to say, none of these individuals or groups are responsible for the conclusions that I drew from our conversations or any errors that I might have made.

This book built on earlier projects, among them those with coauthors Genia Kostka, Manjana Milkoreit, Ricardo Tranjan, and Eduardo Viola, all of whom have helped shape my thinking on these topics. Manjana and Ricardo were also highly valued research assistants at an even earlier stage, along with Sean Jiaming Low, Devon Mase, and Samantha Wisnicki. I thank them all for their insights and hard work. The earlier work was funded by a Standard

Research Grant from the Social Sciences and Humanities Research Council of Canada, research funds from the Balsillie School of International Affairs and the University of Waterloo, with the London School of Economics and Political Science funding final stages of the research.

Over the years, many people provided comments on the book's chapters in various forms and I am grateful for all their useful suggestions and advice (they are alphabetized by first name, Brazilian style): Al Montero, Alina Averchenkova, Alisha Holland, Alison Post, Almut Schilling-Vacaflor, Antoine Maillet, Anthony Pereira, Antonio Botelho, Audie Klotz, Cathy Boone, Charlotte Halpern, Christian Brannstrom, Dimitris Stevis, Ed Amann, Elisabeth Jay Friedman, Jonas Wolff, Ken Shadlen, Laura McDonald, Mat Paterson, Matt Amengual, Matthew Lockwood, Mimi Keck, Natalya Naqvi, Peter Kingstone, Peter Newell, Pritish Behuria, Rebecca Abers, Ricardo Grinspun, Robert Wade, Sarah Brooks, and Veronica Herrera. Many more offered helpful comments during presentations in eleven countries. I am especially grateful to Emily Tyler who read the whole manuscript at a late stage and saved me from at least a few important errors of fact and interpretation. The two reviewers for Cambridge University Press also offered many very useful suggestions and prodded me to greater theoretical ambition and precision in particular. They definitely made the book a better one. Of course, none of these readers are responsible for the times when I failed to take on their wise suggestions. Finally, at Cambridge University Press, Aseem Prakash and John Haslam deserve thanks for bringing this book into existence, with Aseem showing remarkable enthusiasm and support over too many years of research and writing.

This book is dedicated to my parents, Daniel and Arie Hochstetler. They grew up mostly without electricity in the Old Order Amish Church, so it has been a long journey for both them and me to my academic career and this book about wind and solar power. At the same time, this book has its roots in my love of reading, travel, learning, and talking to strangers – all of which I learned from them – so perhaps the journey was not so disruptive after all. I would like to thank them and all my family and in-laws for supporting me through my odd routes through life. I thank Roger most of all; there from the beginning and here even now. He could not have been more supportive of this book and my work, wherever it took me.

Abbreviations

Please note that all the departments are South Africa and all the ministries Brazilian.

ABDI	*Agência Brasileira de Desenvolvimento Industrial*, Brazilian Agency of Industrial Development
ABEEólica	*Associação Brasileira de Energia Eólica*, Brazilian Association of Wind Energy
ABIMAQ	*Associação Brasileira da Indústria de Máquinas e Equipamentos*, Brazilian Machinery and Equipment Industry Association
ABINEE	Associação Brasileira da Indústria Elétrica e Eletrônica, Brazilian Electrical and Electronics Industry Association
ABRACE	*Associação Brasileira de Grandes Consumidores Industriais de Energia e de Consumidores Livres*, Brazilian Association of Large Industrial Energy Consumers and Free Consumers
ABSOLAR	*Associação Brasileira de Energia Solar Fotovoltaica*, Brazilian Photovoltaic Solar Industry Association
ANC	African National Congress
ANEEL	*Agência Nacional de Energia Elétrica*, National Electricity Agency
BEE	Black Economic Empowerment
BNDES	*Banco Nacional de Desenvolvimento Econômico e Social*, Brazilian National Economic and Social Development Bank
CCEE	*Câmara de Comercialização de Energia Elétrica*, Council of the Electricity Market
CDE	*Conta de Desenvolvimento de Electricidade*, Electricity Development Fund

CEBDS	*Conselho Empresarial Brasileiro para o Desenvolvimento Sustentável*, Brazilian Business Council for Sustainable Development
CER	Centre for Environmental Rights
CNPE	*Conselho Nacional de Política Energética*, National Council on Energy Policy
COFINS	*Contribuição para o Financiamento da Seguridade Social*, Contribution for the Financing of Social Security
CONAMA	*Conselho Nacional do Meio Ambiente*, National Environmental Council
COSATU	Congress of South African Trade Unions
CPT	*Comissão Pastoral da Terra*, Pastoral Land Commission of the Catholic Church
CSIR	Council for Scientific and Industrial Research
CUT	*Central Única dos Trabalhadores*, Unified Workers' Confederation
DEA	Department of Environmental Affairs
DEAT	Department of Environmental Affairs and Tourism
DPE	Department of Public Enterprises
DTI	Department of Trade and Industry
EIA	environmental impact assessment
EIUG	Energy Intensive Users Group
EPE	*Empresa de Pesquisa Energética*, Energy Research Enterprise
Eskom	Electricity Supply Commission (also Escom, historically)
FBE	Free Basic Electricity
FINEP	*Financiadora de Estudos e Projetos*, Fund for Studies and Projects
FiT	feed-in tariff
GDP	gross domestic product
GHG	greenhouse gas (emissions)
GIP	green industrial policy
GW	gigawatt
ICMBio	*Instituto Chico Mendes de Conservação da Biodiversidade*, Chico Mendes Institute for Conservation of Biodiversity

ICMS	*Imposto sobre Circulação de Mercadorias e Serviços*, Tax on the Circulation of Merchandise and Services
IDC	Industrial Development Corporation
IEMA	*Instituto de Energia e Meio Ambiente,* Institute of Energy and Environment
INEP	Integrated National Electrification Programme
IPCC	Intergovernmental Panel on Climate Change
IPP	independent power producer
IRENA	International Renewable Energy Agency
IRP	Integrated Resource Plan
ISA	*Instituto Socioambiental*, Socioenvironmental Institute
ITTCC	Industry Task Team on Climate Change
kWh	kilowatt hour
LTMS	long-term mitigation scenarios
MAB	*Movimento dos Atingidos por Barragens*, Movement of those Affected by Dams
MCT	*Ministério de Ciencia e Tecnologia*, Ministry of Science and Technology
MDIC	*Ministério de Desenvolvimento, Indústria e Comércio Exterior*, Ministry of Development, Industry, and Foreign Trade
MEC	Minerals-Energy Complex
MMA	*Ministério do Meio Ambiente*, Ministry of Environment
MP	*Medida Provisoria*, Provisional Measure
MST	*Movimento dos Trabalhadores Rurais Sem Terra*, Landless Rural Workers' Movement
MW	megawatt; sometimes MWh (megawatt hour) or MW installed capacity
NDC	Nationally Determined Contribution (to the Paris Agreement)
NEDLAC	National Economic Development and Labour Council
NERSA	National Energy Regulator
NGO	nongovernmental organization
NIMBY	not in my back yard
NUM	National Union of Mineworkers
NUMSA	National Union of Metalworkers of South Africa
OUTA	Organisation Undoing Tax Abuse

PAC   *Programa de Aceleração do Crescimento*, Program for
      Growth Acceleration
PADIS   *Programa de Apoio ao Desenvolvimento*
      Technológico da Indústria de Semi-conductores,
      Program of Support for the Technological
      Development of the Semi-conductor Industry
PIS   *Programa de Integração Social*, Program of Social
      Integration
PITCE   *Política Industrial, Tecnológica e de Comércio*
      Exterior, Industrial, Technology, and Foreign Trade
      Policy
POCE   *Plataforma Operária e Camponesa para Energia*,
      Labor and Peasant Energy Forum
PPCDAm *Plano de Ação para a Prevenção e Controle do*
      Desmatamento na Amazônia Legal, Plan for Action to
      Prevent and Control Deforestation in the Legal
      Amazon
ProGD   *Programa de Investimento em Geração Distribuida*,
      Program of Investment in Distributed Generation
Proinfa   *Programa de Incentivo às Fontes Alternativas de*
      Energia Elétrica, Program of Incentives for Alternative
      Energy in Electricity
PSDB   *Partido da Social Democracia Brasileira*, Brazilian
      Social Democratic Party
PT   *Partido dos Trabalhadores*, Workers' Party
PV   photovoltaic (a kind of solar power)
RDP   Reconstruction and Development Program
REDZ   Renewable Energy Development Zones
REFIT   renewable energy feed-in tariff
REIDI   *Regime Especial de Incentivos para*
      o Desenvolvimento da Infraestrutura, Special Regime
      of Incentives for Infrastructure Development
REIPPPP Renewable Energy Independent Power Producers
      Procurement Programme
SACP   South African Communist Party
SAFTU   South African Federation of Trade Unions
SAPVIA   South African Photovoltaic Industry Association
SARI   South African Renewables Initiative
SAWEA   South African Wind Energy Association

SEA   strategic environmental assessment
SEEG   *Sistema de Estimativas de Emissões e Remoções de Gases de Efeito Estufa*, System of Estimates of Greenhouse Gas Emissions and Removals
SOE   state-owned enterprise
UNCED   United Nations Conference on Environment and Development
UNFCCC   United Nations Framework Convention on Climate Change
WWF   Worldwide Fund for Nature; there is a WWF-Brasil and a WWF South Africa

1 Political Economies of Energy Transition in Brazil and South Africa

Wind and solar power are growing at remarkable rates worldwide, driving new industries worth many billions of dollars every year. These developments have eased a possible transition to a lower-carbon energy system, itself crucial for addressing global climate change. Yet as wind and solar power are growing beyond minimal levels, they are becoming increasingly disruptive to existing electricity systems and economies. The analytical starting point for this book is that a renewable energy transition requires a large-scale political economy transition. That is, successful energy transitions mean changing a series of political and economic arrangements even as they also demand new physical infra-structure and patterns of electricity consumption. Incumbent sources of electricity are locked in "through a complicated series of interlocking payments, patronage, and tax arrangements" (Victor and Heller 2007a: 274) that often contributes to making them both cheaper sources of electricity and politically entrenched. This book is about the potentially disruptive power of renewable electricity and the polit-ical and economic challenges associated with its expansion in middle-income and developing countries.

Almost all existing studies of renewable energy focus on advanced industrialized countries or China (e.g., Aklin and Urpelainen 2018; Geels 2014; Gilley 2012; Karapin 2016; Lewis 2013; Moe 2015). Often motivated by concerns about global climate change, these countries led the way in developing the sector, introducing many innovations and enabling a sharp drop in costs. Renewable energy has been an economic and environmental game changer for the early adopters. This book turns from advanced industrialized countries to cover the development of wind and solar power in Brazil and South Africa, two important emerging economies. With India, Mexico, and others, their investments in wind and solar power are starting to catch up with those of the first generation of developers of nonhydro forms of renewable energy (Frankfurt School-UNEP

1

Centre/BNEF 2019: 14).[1] Most of the future growth in the sector will come in middle-income and developing countries, as will much of the future greenhouse gas (GHG) emissions. This book takes on the critical question of whether renewable energy can be an economic and environmental game changer for such countries as well, using the Brazilian and South African cases to illuminate the dynamics that arise.

Economic growth is important for all countries, but it is an especially high priority in middle-income and developing countries. In a low-carbon energy transition, economic growth is decoupled from GHG emissions, meaning that an economy can grow even as GHG emissions fall. This can happen as the economy draws on energy inputs that are less carbon intensive (like wind and solar sources of electricity) and as a result of related transformations in the socioeconomic model (Geels 2014; Meadowcroft 2009). If a low-carbon transition is feasible, it could transform some of the long-standing tensions between environmental and economic development goals. Thus, this book allows for a reconsideration of the relationship between environment and development in two emerging powers, a generation after the Brundtland Report popularized the claim that sustainable development was possible (World Commission on Environment and Development 1987).

Economically, policies promoting wind and solar power were some of the most common governmental responses to the 2008 financial crisis. This modern economic sector, promising strong future demand, good manufacturing jobs, and lots of room for innovation, appeals to many countries as a growth sector (Aggarwal and Evenett 2012; Hess 2012). Because it can operate at a small scale, solar power can also bring to unserved consumers and communities everything from electric light to cell phone charging to medical clinics. Environmentally, three-quarters of the GHG emissions that cause climate change come from the extraction, refining, and industrial use of fossil fuels, with the electricity sector accounting for 31 percent

---

[1] Brazil also produces other forms of renewable energy, especially hydropower and biofuels. It has a petroleum industry, too, and both countries have actual (Brazil) and potential (South Africa) natural gas resources. For tractability, this book focuses only on wind power and photovoltaic solar power, so it is not a full account of energy transition. It also focuses primarily on grid-scale electricity because it is most common in these countries, although Chapters 2 and 4 discuss distributed solar generation.

of all global emissions in 2014.[2] Clean, renewable electricity – including solar and wind power – could replace fossil fuels, generating minimal GHG emissions and fewer of the other environmental impacts of power installations. It is no wonder that expanding renewable energy is central to the UN's Sustainable Development Goals and the Paris Agreement on Climate Change.

At the same time, there are equally evident problems with the transition to these new sources of electricity. Broader use of renewable energy will require expensive changes in existing electricity grids, as well as the displacement of powerful entrenched actors in traditional electricity sectors (Aklin and Urpelainen 2018; Geels 2014; Ting and Byrne 2020). As existing electricity sources are shut down, the communities and workers who depended on them will lose out (Healy and Barry 2017; Swilling, Musango, and Wakeford 2016) – even as the quantity and quality of new jobs are not always as advertised. Market forces are unlikely to push a low-carbon transition when fossil fuels are still readily available and their costs can be externalized. Instead, government support is needed, at least to start the transition, risking expensive rent-seeking (Pegels 2014a: 3–4). Despite striking declines since 2009, the market costs of renewable sources of electricity have usually been higher than those of the fossil fuels they would replace (Schlömer et al. 2014: 1332–1333). Further, the typically small installations of wind and solar power can have significant negative effects on local conditions – birdlife, economic activities, and so on – leading to community opposition (Avila 2018).

Notwithstanding the challenges outlined, 164 countries had some kind of renewable energy target by 2015 (International Renewable Energy Association 2016a: 8). Governments around the world are promoting wind and solar power (e.g., Aggarwal and Evenett 2012; Aklin and Urpelainen 2018; Barbier 2010: 6–10; Hochstetler and Kostka 2015; Kim and Thurbon 2015; Lewis 2013; Mazzucato 2015; Moore 2018; Nahm 2017; Pegels 2014b; Unruh 2002; Wu 2018; Zysman and Huberty 2014). But how are states intervening, and why are they intervening as they are? Will those interventions be successful, and on what terms? Which other actors help to determine outcomes, in cooperation with or against states? Cross-cutting all of this is the "just

---

[2] www.climatewatchdata.org/ghg-emissions?breakBy=sector&chartType=per centage.

transition" question: Who will pay the costs and receive the benefits of energy transition? I argue that answering these questions for Brazil and South Africa requires investigating four political economies of renewable energy: those of climate change, industrial policy, distribution and consumption, and siting. These are all potential drivers of renewable energy expansion or delay, each reflecting the problem structure of a different policy sector related to renewable energy.

To briefly introduce the themes of each political economy, Chapter 2 examines the role of wind and solar power plans in the climate action commitments of Brazil and South Africa, looking directly at how such plans reflect the balance of forces between actors who favor low-carbon and high-carbon economic models. Chapter 3, on industrial policy, sees low-carbon transition as a problem of developing the firms and industries that can generate electricity from non-fossil fuel sources. Chapter 4 asks whether and how renewable electricity can meet the needs of both household and industry consumers, paying attention to price, physical access, and quality concerns. Although most of the book is about grid-scale wind and solar power because that is where Brazil and South Africa have focused their policies, this chapter addresses the question of distributed (small or household-level) generation as well. In Chapter 5, I examine the siting challenge: renewable electricity plants, like all physical infrastructure, must be sited in particular locations, where their impact on local ecosystems and communities may generate support or opposition.

Explanations of wind and solar power adoption usually focus on only one or perhaps two of these dynamics. Yet they simultaneously present different packages of incentives and disincentives for wind and solar power generation that interlock to sometimes reinforce and sometimes oppose each other. A powerful coalition to support climate action may lose out to coalitions worried about protecting existing industries and minimizing costs, for example, or could get an additional boost from them. Understanding national renewable energy outcomes requires looking not just at a fuller array of policy sectors implicated in renewable energy but also at their intersection. Always important, these observations are especially critical for middle-income and developing countries where the economic drivers are particularly important and may or may not coincide with the climate change motivations that drove many early adopters.

All of these are critical questions for major emerging powers like Brazil and South Africa. These two countries are now among the top emitters of GHG globally, but they reached that status decades after the current industrialized powers did and are still catching up economically. They have been rapidly building out their electricity infrastructures, both to support their expanding (they hope) economies and to bring historically excluded citizens onto national electricity grids (Abromovay 2010; Leite 2009; Winkler 2009). Their decisions about the electricity sources that will power their next decades of economic growth are central to current uncertainty about whether global GHG emissions targets can be met – and are also potentially important models for their regions and other later-rising countries (Downie and Williams 2018; Masters 2011). As Brazil and South Africa always rank as some of the most unequal countries in the world, they face particularly compelling questions about who will pay the costs of energy transitions.

Figure 1.1, which shows the amount of wind and solar power procured for the national grid in Brazil and South Africa between 2002 and 2019, tracks intriguingly different outcomes that also suggest that there is no single political economy of energy transition. Wind power generation in Brazil started earliest and is by far and away the most

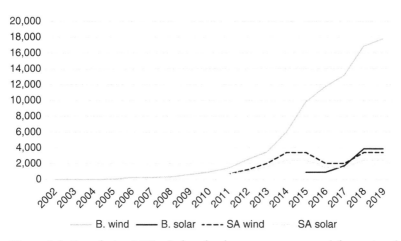

Figure 1.1 Cumulative MW wind and solar power contracted for national grids in Brazil and South Africa, 2002–2019
Sources: www.aneel.gov.br/resultados-de-leiloes; www.eskom.co.za/Whatwe redoing/Pages/RE_IPP_Procurement_Programme.aspx.

expansive. It was about 9 percent of total electricity supply in 2019. Solar power generation there was the latest of any of the forms of generation to start, beginning twelve years after wind power in Brazil. Yet it has now caught up in quantity to wind and solar power in South Africa, where both kinds of electricity share a pattern of advances and retreats and have never quite taken off. They are together less than 5 percent of the built electricity supply in South Africa.

In different ways, the two countries also show the usefulness of considering how multiple political economies of energy transition intersect. For example, most of the articles cited earlier in the chapter see climate change policy as a crucial motivator for adopting wind and solar power. One could understand Brazil's development of wind power as part of its climate action strategy and find evidence in government statements and industry commitments to support that. But no climate action strategy easily justifies producing a great deal of wind power while ignoring the low-carbon potential of solar power in a sunny, tropical country. A climate-based explanation of energy transition in Brazil would be misleading. The contrasting outcomes must come from other dynamics, and I conclude that industrial policy and cost considerations are the political economies that best account for the different fates of wind and solar power in Brazil, undercutting the climate rationale for solar power.

South Africa shows a pattern that appears to be much more consistent with the political economy of climate change. The Electricity Supply Commission (Eskom), the public utility that has historically powered South Africa with cheap coal, is at the center of a state–society coalition that defends that incumbent fossil fuel. Meanwhile, the renewable energy sector – wind and solar power alike – has found other state and civil society allies to help it push for that change which is critical to reducing GHG emissions there. The starts and stops visible in Figure 1.1 reflect their power struggle. Yet the struggle is especially intense because several of the other political economies aggravate the divisions. Will public sector jobs be created in Eskom's coal plants or will jobs be found in the private companies chosen to build wind and solar plants? That industrial policy question moved much of the labor movement from an early alliance with environmentalists in favor of climate action to the coalition resisting energy transition. Arguments about comparative production costs see the same actors in place in their countervailing coalitions. In South

Africa, a climate-based political economy story is incomplete but not wholly misleading.

These brief observations begin to illustrate how energy transition simultaneously engages multiple political economy transitions in potentially different ways in different places. While sharing many common features, the two countries studied here differ on a key element of energy transition (Moe 2015). South African electricity is dominated by a fossil fuel, coal, while Brazil's hydro-based electricity system is not. An important fact in itself, it is also the linchpin of this comparison of two national political economies of energy transition.

1.1 Political Economies of Energy Transition

What sources of energy do states prioritize? This is the basic dependent variable of this book. Will electricity come from fossil fuels or from new renewables like wind and solar power? When and how do states intervene to support a low-carbon transition? Drawing on existing studies of energy transition and comparative political economy, I argue that the answers to these questions engage three stages of analysis. I begin with the generic interests of state and societal actors in four policy arenas related to the electricity sector, the four political economies. However, those interests do not generate outcomes on their own; interests must be actively defended by what I characterize here as pro-reform and status quo coalitions operating inside existing institutions and socioeconomic structures.

The final step in the analytical framework analyzes the interconnections among the policy arenas. These may go well beyond policy coordination issues, as actors and dynamics may spill across the policy arenas to reinforce each other either for interlocking positive ("green spiral") or for oppositional outcomes. I argue that the presence of a strong status quo coalition in the electricity sector that is committed to fossil fuels will generate such politicized and contentious spillovers, while national settings without such an actor may have more technical and bureaucracy-dominant energy transition processes with fewer direct connections among the actors and the debates in the four policy arenas. Sections 1.1.1–1.1.3 and 1.2 develop this analytical and theoretical framework before Sections 1.3 and 1.4 introduce the cases.

1.1.1 Political Economies of Wind and Solar Power: Interests, Coalitions, and Institutions

A standard starting point for analysis of a policy change is to consider the nature and structure of the private and public interests involved (Oye and Maxwell 1994: 594). In environmental policy more generally, certain relationships are expected to hold (Lyon and Yin 2010; Oye and Maxwell 1994): potential beneficiaries are assumed to support a policy change, while those who would be harmed by it will resist. Policy-makers in democracies are assumed to be at least somewhat responsive to how a policy change will affect the interests of their political base. Benefits or harms that are large, concentrated in specific populations, and/or certain are more likely to drive policy processes – not least because those characteristics support collective action – while those that are small, diffused, and/or uncertain are less likely to do so.

Yet interests play a complex role in explaining previous political economy transitions like market reform (Kingstone 1999: 4; Schneider 2004: 458–459). While participants in those transitions often had a basic preference for market- or state-based economic decision-making, those preferences could vary depending on whether, say, trade or financial liberalization was at stake (Schneider 2004: 461). Groups could also accept reforms against their interests if they were offered compensation elsewhere (Kingstone 1999: xxi; Murillo 2001), an idea with parallels in the demands that labor and other actors make for a just energy transition (Stevis and Felli 2015). I expect that interests alone cannot account for a low-carbon energy transition, either.

Wind and solar power also exhibit substantially different structures of interest depending on the vantage point from which they are considered (Hughes and Lipscy 2013: 451–452). The topic of each of the four main chapters of this book departs from a different version of the interests involved in expanding wind and solar power. Each policy arena triggers the active engagement of potentially different sets of actors in both state and society to defend those interests, creating multiple potential alignments of supporters and opponents. Environmental ministries play lead roles in some, for example, while economic agencies and banks dominate in others. As a corollary, each policy arena also offers a unique insight into the drivers of and obstacles to a just low-carbon transition.

Interests cannot generate outcomes on their own. Key participants in the state, economy, and civil society must embody and promote them through concrete actions in order to result in policy change. Coalitional analysis is a very common strategy for explaining political economy outcomes (Hess 2014: 279; Schneider 2004: 456; Shadlen 2017); changes in those state–society coalitions then account for changes in outcomes or maintenance of the status quo. A number of authors have already made related arguments about energy transition, showing that a country's decisions about whether to take climate and energy action are the product of active coalition-building and struggle among three key sets of actors defending their interests: state actors, business associations and firms, and civil society groups (e.g., Breetz, Mildenberger, and Stokes 2018; Downie 2018; Hadden 2015; Hess 2018; Hochstetler and Viola 2012; Meckling 2011; Newell and Paterson 2010; Roberts et al. 2018; Stokes 2013; Vasi 2011; Zysman and Huberty 2014). This book goes on to show that there are multiple coalitions simultaneously being built, grounded in the multiple policy framings of wind and solar power.

Beyond the coalitions themselves, important institutional and socioeconomic legacies affect which actors are present to form coalitions in the first place, and endow them with differentiated power resources. Renewable energy does not emerge in a vacuum. Its fate inevitably reflects path dependencies from existing contexts that may have little to do even with electricity. Better understanding of such historical institutional dimensions is a major component of the emerging research agenda on energy transitions (Lockwood, Kuzemko, Mitchell, and Hoggett 2016; Roberts et al. 2018; Roberts and Geels 2019). Some of these elements are widely shared, if varying, like the contrasting experiences of democracies – which will almost always have more actors actively engaged and potentially powerful in a policy sector, whatever it is – and autocracies of various kinds. This characteristic makes Brazil and South Africa different from the emerging power case most commonly studied, China. Some of the other elements will be more specific, however, like the particular industrial history in Brazil that allows it to make an existing airplane industry one of the building blocks of a wind turbine industry, which South Africa lacks. As this is an emerging research agenda, this book helps to identify relevant dimensions through its case studies.

Finally, principled advocates who lack direct self-interest in the outcomes have helped to promote the global development of the wind and solar industries (Vasi 2011). Principled actors – or those with both self-interested and principled motivations – may appear in any type of coalition, active themselves and magnifying the efforts of other actors (Hadden 2015: 5; Prakash and Gugerty 2010: 1). In energy transitions, an especially important set of principled actors focuses on just transition issues, looking especially for the impacts on marginalized and vulnerable populations (Newell and Mulvaney 2013: 133; Sovacool, Burke, Baker, Katikalapudi, and Wlokas 2017: 677). These relate to substantive outcomes as well as to procedural questions about who is included in policy-making and who is actually influential. If participants view the overall distribution of costs and benefits as unjust, that will affect the fate of wind and solar power and their accompanying low-carbon transition (Roberts et al. 2018: 305).

1.1.2 Interests and State–Society Coalitions in Four Political Economies

Moving beyond abstract discussions of interests and state–society coalitions, I introduce four major political economies of renewable energy in this section. These have been four of the most common potential drivers behind energy transition, either accelerating or blocking energy transition. For each, I draw on existing studies to sketch the nature of the interests involved and the actors who typically make up coalitions in this arena (summarized in Table 1.1). I also identify relevant theoretical frameworks that analysts use to explain outcomes in this policy arena, which identify more specific themes for study. These are then developed further in the chapters themselves, which each focus on one driver.

The focus on climate change and low-carbon transitions in Chapter 2 emphasizes the potentially large but dispersed and uncertain benefits of decarbonization. These are accompanied by concentrated costs for the high-carbon electricity sector, which must be limited to reduce GHG emissions (Levin, Cashore, Bernstein, and Auld 2012; Pearson and Foxon 2012). As a result, the climate frame powerfully mobilizes opponents from incumbent fossil fuel sectors and their allies in government, including energy ministries and utilities (Aklin and Urpelainen 2018; Geels 2014; Huberty 2014: 34–35; Ting and Byrne 2020). The

Table 1.1 *Policy arenas governing renewable electricity production and use*

Policy Arena	Basic structure of interests	Primary state actors expected	Primary societal actors expected
Chapter 2 Climate Change Policy	Broad and diffuse future benefits from climate action; concentrated costs for fossil fuel actors in electricity sector	Environment, energy, and foreign ministries, Legislature, Executive	Organized societal groups, differentiated by attitudes toward low-carbon transition; fossil fuel industries
Chapter 3 Industrial Policy	Broad interests in economic outcomes like innovation, employment, and growth (cobenefits) that are also concentrated benefits for firms in wind and solar sectors; possible costs from rent-seeking	Development and energy ministries, public finance institutions	Firms and industry associations, labor, private finance institutions
Chapter 4 Social Policy/ Service Provision	Diffuse costs for consumers and concentrated costs for electricity-intensive industries; concentrated benefits for those without electricity access	State roles in service provision: utilities, regulators, politicians in electoral democracies	Industrial and household consumers – individual and collective
Chapter 5 Siting Policy	Concentrated costs and/or benefits for hosting communities	Environmental and planning ministries, licensing agencies	Local communities, environmental activists

diffuse and future-oriented nature of the climate benefits of wind and solar power draws in principled proponents who value outcomes beyond short-term interests, such as environmental activists and ministries (Hochstetler and Viola 2012; Hughes and Urpelainen 2015: 52; Levin et al. 2012).

In the climate policy arena, the most important theoretical questions are about state capacity in its classic and broadest sense (Evans, Rueschemeyer, and Skocpol 1985). That is, do states have the capacity to formulate and implement policies that achieve broad public goods, even when powerful societal actors are harmed by those policies (Meckling and Nahm 2017: 741)? This is both the positive capacity to plan and execute policy that provides public goods and the negative capacity to take on powerful societal interests that benefit from existing energy systems. The state's own policy-making and bureaucratic capacities are central to this chapter.

Viewing wind and solar power through the lens of green industrial policy (GIP), as Chapter 3 does, highlights a very different interest calculus: certain, concentrated benefits through rents accrue to a small set of firms in the promoted sector while costs are more widely dispersed (Hughes and Urpelainen 2015: 53; Kelsey and Zysman 2014: 79–81; Pegels 2014a: 1). Since firm assets are specific to different electricity sources, mobilization on industry lines is likely with wind and solar firms and their industry associations being dominant actors along with state economic agencies (Hughes and Lipscy 2013: 459). While the benefits are most direct for the sector itself, national governments also conceive outcomes like jobs and new industry creation as economic benefits or "cobenefits" of energy transition for the country as a whole (Aggarwal and Evenett 2012). In this chapter, just transition concerns emerge in one of their earliest formulations, by labor unions, who wonder whether a low-carbon transition will actually replace current high-carbon energy and industry sector jobs with decent work accessible to those same workers (Stevis and Felli 2015).

Theoretically, this chapter develops debates about how state–business relations can contribute to development. This begins with basic preferences for state or market control over the electricity sector before passing to the specific policies that might promote wind and solar industries. These also involve state capacity but with a narrower focus on how well states can manage positive rents. Classic formulations are concerned with the ability of economic bureaucracies to avoid "capture" by the private sector actors they regulate and to use economic tools to discipline them to avoid excessive rent-seeking (Amsden 2001; Johnson, Alterburg, and Schmitz 2014), while others stress that states need close ties to business for success (Evans 1995: 12). Scholars studying GIP – sector-promoting industrial policies with environmental aims – have argued that the process of developing renewable energy can take advantage of these tensions. The countries that have developed substantial wind and solar power typically experienced a "green spiral" where initial steps towards new kinds of electricity were locked in politically as industry coalitions began to lobby to continue to expand their industry with the support of associated labor, parts suppliers, and so on (Kelsey and Zysman 2014: 79; see also Aklin and Urpelainen 2018; Meckling, Kelsey, Biber, and Zysman 2015).

Chapter 4, on electricity service provision, finds diffuse costs of wind and solar power typically spread across industrial and household consumers, along with some potential concentrated benefits for consumers who currently lack access to electricity (Márquez and Rufín 2011; Monyei, Adewumi, and Jenkins 2018). The diffuse costs come from the historically (much) higher costs of wind and especially solar power, as well as the problems their intermittency raises for the security of electricity supply (Trainer 2007). A small number of consumers in electricity-intensive industries may also face concentrated costs and benefits from any policies chosen for tariffs and distribution in the sector. In this book on two middle-income countries, the question of access to electricity is much more important than in the countries usually studied.

This chapter's theoretical theme invokes all the considerations related to government service provision, including debates about levels and distribution of government provision, tariff-setting and possible cross-subsidization of costs by some consumers or taxpayers, and the political and economic implications of access to electrical services (Golden and Min 2013; Henisz and Zelner 2006; Márquez and Rúfin 2011). Modern standards of competent governance assume that states will oversee and often provide universal access to electricity for household and economic consumption, as it is a critical input into a number of socially and economically desirable outcomes (Brown and Mobarak 2009: 194). The ambition for universality makes the societal actors correspondingly broad, including household consumers, industrial consumers, and those without access to the grid. Each of these may or may not be represented by collective actors promoting their interests.

Finally, Chapter 5 focuses on the impact of renewable energy infrastructure on the local communities and environments where wind and solar plants are sited (Avila 2018; McAdam and Boudet 2012; Stokes 2016). It acknowledges considerable theoretical debate over the nature of the interests at stake. Scholars in economics and energy disciplines tend to assume that there will be net economic benefits for host communities, with much of their debate focused on how to measure and compare the gains (e.g., Brown, Pender, Wiser, Lantz, and Hoen 2012). Geographers and anthropologists, in contrast, are much more likely to see sociocultural and environmental harms, expecting local resistance to defend the human rights of host communities, with vulnerable populations under systemic threat (e.g., Avila 2018; Zhouri and Valencio 2014). This chapter considers both possible logics.

However communities assess their interests, they must be able to organize to affect outcomes. Drawing on theories of the emergence and success of social movements, in this chapter, I assess state actors and institutions for the constraints and opportunities they present for social groups to organize collective action and influence outcomes (McAdam, McCarthy, and Zald 1996; Tarrow 2011). Environmental impact assessment (EIA) and land-use policies, including those developed for historically excluded groups, are particularly important here (Hochstetler and Tranjan 2016; McEwan 2017). Another strand of research examines the ability of social movements and other collective actors to take advantage of structural opportunities that might exist: can they overcome the disincentives to collective action, mobilize resources, and coordinate coalitions that are coherent enough to bring pressure on the state; and *how* will they do so (Hadden 2015; Prakash and Gugerty 2010)?

In this book, I propose that to understand the renewable energy choices of Brazil and South Africa, we need to analyze the multiple status quo and reformist coalitions that form around wind and solar power, depending on the policy sector. Those coalitions are grounded in a generalizable underlying foundation in interests and institutions, and the energy transitions literature is helpful for identifying the effects of those. Actual outcomes, however, are crafted in path-dependent ways out of the distinct political economies of energy in national economies (Edomah 2020; Hughes and Lipscy 2013: 452; MacNeil and Paterson 2012; Nahm 2017). The final shape of the four political economies and the ways in which their elements intertwine – sometimes reinforcing, sometimes counteracting – are likely to be somewhat different for every country. Section 1.1.3 elaborates how that happens.

1.1.3 Interlocking Logics: Four Political Economies Form One National Energy Outcome

National energy transition outcomes derive from the intersection of four quite different policy arenas. At its simplest, the intersection of the four resulting political economies is a policy coordination problem. When issues cross policy arenas, it is easy for the initiatives in one arena to mesh poorly with those in another (Bouckaert, Peters, and Verhoest 2010). Ministries of environment, energy, and economy do not necessarily consult with each other as they follow their bureaucratic mandates. They could work at cross-purposes – as when climate initiatives to reduce GHG emissions are countered by industrial policies supporting fossil fuels – or they could simply omit a potentially important supporting policy or be mistimed and so on. The policy arenas are most likely to drive a consistent outcome if one policy arena dominates or if there are other forms of coordination across arenas. Examining the arenas together, as done in this book, shows a fuller picture and helps account for why the dynamics of single arenas may be difficult to relate to the overall outcomes for wind and solar power. In policy terms, the observation of problematic intersections calls for institutional solutions like a transministerial coordinating committee that can overcome these sorts of coordination gap and problem.

The intersection may go well beyond policies and ministries, however, because energy transition touches so many sectors of society. As producers, workers, consumers, and host communities, ordinary citizens may – or may not – play important roles that are difficult for the state to coordinate. One of the puzzles about renewable energy is that it can present itself as a highly technical area of marginal interest to nonspecialists or form a political flashpoint of contention and dispute. In the first case, there are the policy coordination issues already noted. These are gaps and overlaps that arise when multiple bureaucracies follow institutional procedures and mandates to make choices about what kind of electricity to build and promote, limited by their capacity and resources. But in the second, there is the potential for a much stronger magnifying effect across the arenas, especially when supporters or opponents reach across them and across the state–society divide. GIP scholars have introduced the idea of the green spiral, where there is a positive reinforcing loop between climate policy and industrial interests that leads to energy transition (Kelsey and Zysman 2014). This idea could be expanded theoretically and empirically to acknowledge that consumer and community interests may also reinforce the choice for energy transition. Policy proposals like the emerging Green New Deal are, in effect, aiming to build such a broad-based green spiral by introducing many cognate issues that may also motivate energy transition (Aronoff, Battistoni, Cohen, and Riofrancos 2019; Pettifor 2019; Stokes 2020).[3] There can, of course, be negative spirals too, with opposition to wind and solar power spilling across arenas and blocking energy transition.

Even as all national cases show their own national variations, there may be dynamics that create subvarieties of energy transitions in the same way that others have identified major patterns of social policy provision (Esping-Anderson 1990; Wood and Gough 2006). Returning to the logics of the policy arenas, the climate policy arena is unique in that it is the only rationale for building wind and solar power where a rise in renewable electricity is directly linked to a decline in fossil fuel electricity sources. As Chapter 2 discusses, this policy arena presents wind and solar power as an existential threat to existing fossil fuel sectors and their allies in ways that the other policy arenas do not (see also Moe 2015; Ting and Byrne 2020). Because of the heightened stakes, I propose that the climate policy arena effectively sets the terms for the others. If there are in fact existing and strong fossil fuel sectors that must be limited or eliminated to reduce GHG emissions, their survival depends on their polarizing and politicizing the policy space around wind and solar power. A technocratic approach will not be likely, while the actual balance of power determines whether the outcome is a green or negative spiral.

The two cases of this book, one that has such an electricity sector and one that does not, offer an opportunity to see how these logical possibilities can play out in practice. South Africa has had a powerful and dominant utility, Eskom, that has been committed to the coal-based

---

[3] https://ocasio-cortez.house.gov/sites/ocasio-cortez.house.gov/files/Resolution%20on%20a%20Green%20New%20Deal.pdf.

generation on which its economic survival has depended. As it was a state-owned, vertically integrated monopoly as wind and solar power were proposed, it offers an exceptionally powerful version of this type. In fact, every policy arena but the siting one in South Africa features a sharply contentious and politicized battle between opposing and supporting coalitions centered on Eskom, with many actors reappearing in the different chapters as the political economies interlock and reinforce each other. Figure 1.1 shows how they have fought to a near standstill, not yet a green or a negative spiral.

That form of politicized and contentious energy transition contrasts with the bureaucratic mode of Brazil's transition. With its hydro-based incumbent electricity type and no galvanizing actor like Eskom in the sector, the relevant decisions on wind and solar power are made in routine, mostly technical agencies following standard operating procedures. This style of decision-making is likely to produce uncoordinated results unless there is purposeful coordination. For example, Brazilian bureaucrats determined that since existing local content rules and industry legacies made it more difficult to support an industrial policy for solar power and costs were higher for solar, wind power would grow while solar power waited, even though climate logics and policies called for solar power. The South African variant of energy transition shows all the disruption expected when there is a powerful, high-carbon electricity sector, while the Brazilian one demonstrates that even big transitions can sometimes come in small bureaucratic steps when there is not. Whether these patterns hold beyond these cases can be answered only with further research, especially in other middle-income and developing countries.

1.2 Middle-Income and Developing Countries: Why Would They Be Different?

The analytical framework just outlined draws on and further develops existing analyses of ongoing energy transitions. As already noted, most of the studies cited reflect the experiences of advanced industrialized democracies with some attention to those of China. This book shifts the empirical focus to two emerging economies. It is thus beginning the task of evaluating whether existing accounts of energy transition can help understand a wider set of cases in the developing world. These are crucial cases for global energy and climate futures. It is clear that most future expansion in energy consumption and GHG emissions will come from middle-income and developing countries. However, even the best predictions are limited to presenting an array of future scenarios rather than point predictions: global outcomes will depend on whether these countries choose ambitious and transformative energy strategies or repeat the industrialized countries' reliance on fossil fuels to develop (Intergovernmental Panel on Climate Change 2014, 2018; International Energy Agency 2018).

Much of the writing on energy transitions presumes that there are common patterns of political economy causation that will appear in all countries that are considering increasing their production and use of wind and solar power. In contrast, I argue that it is likely that middle-income and developing countries will show different patterns for two sets of reasons. One is related to the very different characteristics of the wind and solar industries for these later adopters, while the second considers their own economic and political development stages.

To begin with the first point, early adopters of wind and solar power helped create the industries almost from scratch. In countries like Germany and Denmark in the 1970s and 1980s, these were highly experimental, fringe technologies. Operating at the margins of the energy system, they were taken up by local communities, antinuclear ideologues, and small companies (Morris and Jungjohann 2016). Influential theories stressed the innovative edge of the social–technical transition in Europe, which expanded from niches to transform broader societies (Geels 2002). Notwithstanding the scale of eventual transformations, the process itself was evolutionary, moving in small steps over decades.

Renewable energy presents itself very differently for the late adopting middle-income and developing countries, for whom the high cost of early wind and solar power was almost wholly prohibitive. The wind and solar industries are now well-developed global industries, with complex and well-integrated global supply chains (Meckling and Hughes 2017, 2018). Established actors are defending their positions at the World Trade Organization (WTO) (Lewis 2014) and reaching out for larger shares of global markets (Bayer, Schäuble, and Ferrari 2018). The same innovations and efficiencies that brought prices to affordable levels create high entry barriers for new participants (Schmidt and Huenteler 2016). Similarly, utilities that generated electricity from fossil fuels might have thought into the 2000s that renewable energy would never challenge them on scale and cost, but few would make that mistake today.

While these developments are largely negative for middle-income and developing countries, later adopters have new advantages on the financial side of developing wind and solar power. The industries themselves no longer look as risky, even if national banks and investors still face a steep learning curve as they enter particular countries. "Green finance," meant specifically to support environmental goods like renewable energy, is increasingly available from multiple sources (Sachs, Woo, Yoshino, and Taghizadeh-Hesary 2019), while financial actors are pulling away from the risk of "stranding assets" in politically unpalatable fossil fuels (Caldecott 2017). Thus, even if Table 1.1 still captures the basic framework of interests around renewable energy, many of the specific costs and benefits have been nudged up or down. These dynamics hold for all later adopters, disproportionately developing countries, although they also confronted the early adopters after about 2010.

Turning to the second point, the framework here also contends that the quite-different national institutions and economic trajectories of middle-income and developing countries will shape how coalitions can be built around the more abstract interests of Table 1.1. Many of these factors could be effectively ignored in past studies because the advanced industrialized countries shared so many characteristics: they were politically stable democracies, they had effective national bureaucracies, they had achieved economic levels that allowed them a very large scope when making energy choices. None of these characteristics can be assumed to be true for middle-income and developing countries as a group, but nor can they be assumed to be absent. Some are quite strong democracies, while many are not; some have competent bureaucracies in some areas, while others do not; and they have notably fewer economic options. Because middle-income and developing countries vary more, studying them can give us a fuller view of the drivers of energy transition since fewer characteristics can be taken as givens.

Finally, one characteristic that middle-income and developing countries do share is that they have fewer economic resources than developed countries. As a consequence, economic motivations for energy transition are even more likely to outweigh long-term and abstract considerations like climate change than they are for developed countries (Moore 2018). In the global climate change negotiations, for example, middle-income and developing countries often insist on looking for "cobenefits" or "no regrets" policies that would achieve climate and development goals together (Conrad 2012; Delina 2017; Dubash 2013). Middle-income and developing countries in Asia, Africa, and Latin America have already been driving the global growth in energy-related GHG emissions for several decades (Intergovernmental Panel on Climate Change 2000: 106), so identifying and developing such economic drivers for energy transition is critical for limiting future global climate change.

The economic status of middle-income and developing countries also affects energy transition on a smaller scale. Most importantly, many of these countries are still building out national electricity infrastructures. Only 43 percent of Sub-Saharan Africans had access to electricity in 2019, half the global rate of 87 percent, and the rural access rate was only one-quarter of the population (Blimpo and Cosgrove-Davies 2019: 1). This creates bigger challenges for distribution and consumption issues but potentially leaves less of a legacy of powerful actors committed to fossil fuels. This means that many more of them may fall into the pattern of a more technocratic transition, where state capacity and resources, rather than open political opposition, set the limits for energy transition.

1.3 Overview of Methodology and Evidence

The overarching approach of this book is a structured, focused comparison of the national policies around renewable energy in two large developing countries, Brazil and South Africa (George and Bennett 2005). The two countries differ most importantly on the central question of whether or not they have had an electricity sector dominated by fossil fuels (Moe 2015). South Africa has been heavily reliant on coal as its incumbent electricity source, while Brazil has historically drawn on its hydropower resources. This gives wind and solar power fundamentally different positions in the political economy of climate change in the two countries, which I have suggested should set a different, more openly conflictual starting point for energy transition in South Africa than in Brazil.

In the less-systematic features of national political economies, the two countries share major similarities. These include histories of authoritarianism and recent democratic transitions (in 1985 and

1994, respectively), the distinction of being the most industrialized and largest economic powers of their regions, similar development strategies through the twentieth century, ethnically mixed societies with severe income inequality still highly correlated with race, related histories of European colonization and slavery, and significant regional differentiation (Lieberman 2003: 2–3). United Nations data for the last two decades shows remarkably similar upward trajectories in income per capita, although Brazil has managed significantly higher levels of employment and its overall economy is about four times the size of South Africa's. In both, there is a recent history of labor and civil society contestation, with strong links to the parties that governed during all or most of the period of expansion of wind and solar power (Heller 2019; Hochstetler 2008; Seidman 1994). Since the late 1990s, both have been debating whether and how to add wind and solar power to their national electricity grids, so they are on a similar timeline even though Brazil began wind generation first. While there are also many large and small differences between the two, these many similarities mean that a comparison between them should illuminate the importance of the systematic distinction that divides them.

For extending arguments and hypotheses beyond them, emerging economies like Brazil and South Africa are especially interesting political economy cases because they tend to have characteristics of both developed and developing countries. For example, Kelsey and Zysman (2014: 81) say that developed countries have large existing electricity infrastructures that must be revamped for a green economy, while developing countries are still rapidly expanding their electricity networks; both of those statements are true about Brazil and South Africa. Similarly, they tend to be second movers on new technologies and industries, compared to Europe and North America, but first movers in their respective regions. Their duality makes them especially useful cases for beginning to try to apply ostensibly general arguments made on the basis of developed countries' experiences to developing countries.

During fieldwork in Brazil and South Africa, I interviewed key participants in the energy sector and collected relevant documents and data from the public and private sectors.[4] I also observed two

---

[4] While I conducted most of the interviews myself, J. Ricardo Tranjan carried out an important set of interviews in São Paulo and Northeastern Brazil in 2013–2014 for this project. Manjana Milkoreit also participated in an early set of climate interviews.

rounds of global climate negotiations, in Copenhagen in 2009 and in Durban in 2011. Elite interviews with ninety-one individuals involved in the energy sectors in Brazil and South Africa from 2009 to 2018 form an important data source for the book. In elite interviews, specific respondents are chosen for their specialized knowledge and the political importance of their understandings of issues and events. They are interviewed to "help the investigator fill in pieces of a puzzle or confirm the proper alignment of pieces already in place" (Aberbach and Rockman 2002: 673; see also Beckmann and Hall 2013). In this study, I selected such individuals from government ministries, regulatory agencies, public banks, industry associations and firms, energy nongovernmental organizations (NGOs), and social movements and community organizations. I identified major actors primarily through news stories and government documents and websites; a few were indicated by other interviewees. Sixty-seven individuals from the two countries agreed to be identified in this study and their knowledge and points of view appear with full citations in the book. Most of the remaining individuals, almost all technical staff of public entities and representatives of individual firms, are identified by the names of their organizations while a few asked not to be identified at all. No individual from the Department of Energy in South Africa agreed to be interviewed despite numerous requests, but the respondents otherwise cover the relevant organizations.

I used the interviews primarily to reconstruct important policy developments in the two countries. The information in them was supplemented and, where possible, triangulated with other kinds of data, including government reports, quantitative data, and secondary sources. For example, Chapter 4 uses descriptive statistics from national household surveys and Chapter 5 includes new data on community mobilizations against renewable energy projects that was constructed for this project. The chapters contain more detailed discussions of their theoretical expectations and any specific data and methodologies used to assess them.

1.4 Previewing the Evidence for Brazil and South Africa

It should already be obvious that both the analytical framework and the empirical domain of this book are complex. Therefore, the rest of this chapter previews the empirical findings in two ways, as a roadmap to the four chapters that follow. The first route briefly summarizes the conclusions by chapter, so it is organized by the four policy arenas already identified. This is followed by a more general introduction to the actors who appear across the chapters. The chapters provide documentation for the claims here.

1.4.1 Four Political Economies of Energy Transition

The political economy of climate change (Chapter 2) is the heart of the book. Where wind and solar power are central to climate change mitigation strategies, this policy arena sets the stage for sustained conflict with fossil fuel producers and their allies. In South Africa's coal-dominated electricity system, policy debates on climate involve very active contestation between pro-renewables and pro-carbon coalitions, with the latter shifting its preferences to nuclear power if climate must be considered. Both coalitions have state, business, and civil society partners. State institutions there have struggled to develop the capacity to lead an energy transition on climate grounds, with significant evidence of corruption in the sector. Electricity planning has even moved backwards on its renewable energy commitment, as Figure 1.1 reflects. There is an active just transition debate about the impacts of shutting down coal for coal communities. A very different story emerges in Brazil, where GHG emissions come mostly from deforestation. There, increasingly heated climate action debates pay comparatively little attention to wind and solar power. Electricity planning remains a technical domain with cross-partisan support from five presidents. Brazil presents a puzzle for the climate logic in that planners have steadily increased wind power allocations while solar power was significantly delayed and has only begun to expand.

Many countries hope that a shift to renewable energy will also provide a significant economic boost through industrial policy (Chapter 3), as a new industry creates jobs and possibly even new manufacturing roles. This is the chapter that best accounts for Brazil's surprising result of so much more wind than solar power. There is strong interest in developing a manufacturing industry around renewable energy, and it is easier in the Brazilian economic context to create a domestic wind industry earlier. The wind industry now shows an emerging green spiral, although the desire to manufacture components in Brazil also delayed the introduction of wind power through the first decade of the 2000s and largely blocked solar altogether until 2014. In South Africa, essentially the same climate coalitions fight industrial policy debates, with labor activists increasingly taking the side of the pro-carbon coalition in the absence of what they see as adequate plans for a just labor transition. Both countries have generally strong rent management strategies for the emerging sectors, not least because they both use an auction system where prospective generators face extensive price-based competition to secure contracts to supply the national grid.

Chapter 4 focuses on the cost and distribution concerns that are especially important for middle-income and developing countries, including the two studied here. Comparative prices are another domain for argument by the same South African coalitions that appeared in earlier chapters. As costs shifted over time to favor wind and solar power over new coal and nuclear plants, the particularly important consumers in the Energy Intensive Users Group (EIUG) shifted to be more open to renewable energy. Twenty percent of South African citizens still lack electricity services, but distributed solar power has not proved to meet their needs. Instead, wealthy consumers opting out of the unreliable public service are abandoning the grid for private provision. Wind and solar power have not addressed many of the distortions of a profoundly inequitable electricity distribution system. In Brazil, the dropping costs of wind and solar power were another important technical determinant of when each began to be added in quantity to the national grid, although both state and private sector actors are now challenging the use of distribution subsidies to support them. Distributed solar power is beginning a late rise in cities after regulatory changes in 2012 and 2016. The *Luz para Todos* (Light for All) policy has also brought it to remote Amazonian communities, so it has enhanced the equity outcomes of its electricity sector.

Does renewable energy infrastructure bring net benefits or costs for host communities (Chapter 5)? Interestingly, this is the one chapter where Brazil shows considerably more contention over renewable energy than does South Africa. New data constructed for the book shows that a quarter of the communities that host wind projects contest them over their local costs, although solar installations go largely unmarked. This contestation has not changed final outcomes – wind power is still much more prevalent than solar – but the livelihood and land-rights challenges to wind power in Brazil add important new information about how communities in the developing world may react to the many smaller installations required for wind and solar power. In contrast, there is almost no community-based activism around renewable energy in South Africa, although the NGO Birdlife South Africa is very active in siting decisions, seeking to protect birds.

As this brief summary indicates, South Africa, with its incumbent fossil fuel represented by a powerful monopoly utility in the electricity sector and threatened by climate action debates, does show the heightened conflict and open polarization over wind and solar power that is expected. The crossover of actors between policy sectors is especially notable as broad coalitions in favor of transition and the status quo use all arguments and policy arenas (except for siting) to continue their struggle. In contrast, the policy arenas are much more segregated in Brazil, with smaller and largely discrete groups of actors engaging in more routine activities that rarely make headlines. Section 1.4.2 adds names and descriptors to this overview.

1.4.2 *Actors and Agencies: The Raw Material of Policy Coalitions*

A low-carbon energy transition will require the participation of both state and societal actors in whichever coalitions are formed. The state's roles as planner, procurer, and regulator for the electricity sector make it central. Energy issues are often viewed as matters for technical experts, who are very important in this policy area, but this book shows that wider participation may be either granted by the state or seized by nonstate actors themselves. Both the Brazilian and the South African governments increasingly rely on private producers of electricity and need citizens to accept the transition as consumers and neighbors of wind and solar plants. This section introduces the most important players in renewable energy debates in Brazil and South Africa, noting where they are typical or unusual compared to each other and similar actors elsewhere. They do not necessarily appear where Table 1.1 asserts that they should be expected.

Brazil's Ministry of Mines and Energy and South Africa's Department of Energy are the energy-specific government actors that are also present in many other countries. They have overarching responsibility for the sector, including planning and regulating it. Such ministries often have strong interests in maintaining the status quo, which they created, although their responsibilities for the cost and well-functioning of the whole system can create counter-interests. In these countries, the role of the central ministries is somewhat offset by the presence of historically strong national electricity utilities, Eletrobras in Brazil and Escom/Eskom in South Africa. The partial dismantling and privatization of Eletrobras in the 1990s reduced its roles and power resources along with those of the Ministry of Mines and Energy, largely before the rise of wind and solar power. In contrast, Eskom fought off similar changes, so it held a state-controlled, vertically integrated monopoly over the electricity sector until 2010. (Early adopters often had multiple, even hundreds of, utilities.) That year the Department of Energy decided to have private firms build wind and solar power instead of Eskom. Eskom is the only major builder and operator of coal power plants, so the choice of electricity type intersects with the contested balance of public and private roles in renewable energy. That makes these issues key to the South African story as they may not be elsewhere, including in Brazil. Eskom consequently shows up as a prominent actor in many policy arenas where an electricity utility would not be expected, including in climate change and industrial policy debates.

Both countries use competitive auctions to select the private firms that have built essentially all of South Africa's wind and solar power and much of Brazil's. These firms and their industry associations are the only actors who play large roles in every chapter. They are always promoters of more wind and solar power in national electricity systems, using all rationales from climate to cost. They gain influence from the investments and jobs they can mobilize and are the proximate conveyers of many of the benefits and costs of wind and solar power. While the industry firms share many pro-transition interests, the chapters on industrial policy and costs raise issues that often divide the interests of firms that install power plants from those that are part of the supply chain for them. The firms also compete against each other to win elections and finance. Public utilities could also build wind and solar power, as Eletrobras and some state-level utilities do in Brazil (competing in the auctions), so this actor is present only because political actors have decided that it is. The firms that build other kinds of electricity plants in Brazil have not openly taken on wind and solar power, perhaps because an expanding system made room for all of them.

Organized civil society actors are also present in all of the chapters, but they take very different forms. Principled environmental and human rights organizations are advocates for more wind and solar power in both countries. Because they also typically pay attention to environmental and just transition costs, they may raise questions about how renewable energy is deployed, however. They draw on both moral and expertise resources to write policy documents, draw media attention, bring court cases, and support local communities. Local communities and grassroots consumers also weigh in; while they are not notably antagonistic to wind and solar power in the abstract, they tend to mobilize against concrete costs of building and using plants in particular locations. Labor unions, especially in South Africa, show up in multiple chapters, sharing a similar package of support and concerns about wind and solar power. They are powerful enough in numbers and disruptive resources to prompt national consideration of their demands rather than just local responses.

Consumers are especially important in Chapter 4, where their specific situations give them quite varied opinions about how wind and solar power affect their access to and the cost of electricity. South Africa has an especially important consumer group, the EIUG, whose 28 firms use 40 percent of the country's entire electricity supply, 24 hours per day, 365 days per year.[5] The EIUG's electricity dependence makes it an actor with significant interests in any topic that affects the whole sector, and so it also debates climate change and industrial policy. It is increasingly in favor of wind and solar power as their prices drop. Brazil's electricity system has no real equivalent, as its large consumers group is much less dominant.

Brazil's Ministry of Environment and South Africa's Department of Environmental Affairs have mandates for addressing climate change and carrying out EIAs that intersect with wind and solar power development (Chapters 2 and 5). Such ministries favor wind and solar power for the GHG reductions that they bring, although they sometimes challenge the siting of particular projects. Environmental ministries could strike different balances in this "green vs. green" set of dilemmas, but in both of the countries considered here, they lean to promotion of wind and solar power. Both are comparatively weak ministries in their

[5] Interview with Piet van Staden, Past Chairman of EIUG, Johannesburg, 2018.

national contexts, which is especially important in the discussion of climate change and especially for South Africa.

Partisan actors and politicians are most likely to be engaged in issues and debates that affect larger groups, like climate change and electricity service provision. While this is broadly true across the two countries, political actors still play very different roles in Brazil and South Africa – whatever the policy arena – and may do the same elsewhere.

President Fernando Henrique Cardoso's center-right Brazilian Social Democratic Party (PSDB) administration initiated the first wind power policy in Brazil in 2002. President Lula da Silva and his leftist Workers' Party (PT) which followed in 2003 then implemented and greatly expanded the program. The post-PT governments gained office through a controversial impeachment of PT president Dilma Rousseff in 2016. Her vice president Michel Temer (2016–2018) and outsider President Jair Bolsonaro (2019–2023) took the country in a market-oriented direction that changed some of the supporting policies around wind and solar power. Both remained supportive of renewable energy itself, however. Thus, wind and solar power have operated largely outside partisan politics in Brazil. Smaller, technical agencies following their normal activities often have had larger impacts on the sectors. The Brazilian National Economic and Social Development Bank (BNDES), for example, played a very important role in financing wind power installations that is not matched in South Africa – or for Brazilian solar power.

In South Africa, the African National Congress (ANC) has won every post-apartheid election since 1994, winning national parliamentary and most subnational majorities (Booysen 2011). While that might suggest a coherent position on wind and solar power, former president Jacob Zuma (2009–2018) exercised a large personal influence on the renewable energy sector for much of its existence that sometimes advanced and sometimes crippled it. Ongoing corruption investigations suggest that he had personal interests at stake, especially in supporting nuclear power over other alternatives. The party itself is very divided on key debates about which kind of electricity should be produced by whom. Since 2018, when President Cyril Ramaphosa replaced Zuma in a closely contested leadership change, Ramaphosa's substantial executive authority has been thrown behind the coalition supporting wind and solar power. As a result, it is difficult to say whether the overall effect of partisan politics is to support or delay wind and solar power in South Africa, although partisan engagement is often high and its influence is strong.

For the most part, the stories told in these chapters are domestic ones. At the same time, the firms and civil society organizations include some international actors among them and/or draw resources or ideas from international actors. The unions in both countries have been active in international just transition debates. The state actors are all domestic, of course, but they participate in international negotiations and sometimes receive international resources. Those on climate change have been especially influential. The domestic versus international cleavage has not generally been a large part of the debate around wind and solar power in either country, although the chapters do note a few exceptions. In other countries, it could become a major factor (e.g., Marquart 2017).

2 | Wind and Solar Power in the Transition to a Low-Carbon Economy

Electricity generation using fossil fuels contributed 31 percent of global GHG emissions in 2014.[1] Those emissions are on the verge of irrevocably damaging the global climate system, with serious economic and environmental effects already appearing. The scientists on the Intergovernmental Panel on Climate Change (IPCC) have concluded that switching to low-carbon sources of electricity, including both wind and solar power, is one of the fastest and most cost-efficient ways to reduce future carbon in the atmosphere (Intergovernmental Panel on Climate Change 2014: 20).[2] The global climate system ultimately needs a low-carbon transition that not only increases wind and solar power but also decreases existing GHG-dense sources of electricity like coal and forgoes adding future capacity for those sectors. This is a more zero-sum view of electricity choices than appears in the other chapters of this book because it focuses as much on sunsetting the old as on promoting new kinds of electricity (Hess 2018: 178; Princen, Manno, and Martin 2015). The problem also has the longest time frame, as climate change builds and must be addressed over decades.

These observations establish the structure of interests in the climate policy arena that was already laid out in Chapter 1. First, there is a general, but diffuse, interest in establishing institutions and policies that reduce GHG emissions to avoid future climate change. Building wind and solar power can advance this aim. Interests like this generate supporting coalitions – if they exist at all – that form wide and shallow

[1] Climate Watch, "Global Historical Emissions," www.climatewatchdata.org/ghg-emissions?breakBy=sector&chartType=percentage.
[2] Following common usage, I refer to this as decarbonization and a low-carbon transition, although the aim is to reduce all greenhouse gases, not only carbon.

Wind and solar powered electricity are not free of greenhouse gas emissions, but they are among the lowest-carbon options. A lifecycle analysis of the emissions associated with wind ($34 \text{ g } CO_2\text{e/kWh}$) and solar PV ($50 \text{ g } CO_2\text{e/kWh}$) is much lower than that of coal ($960 \text{ g } CO_2\text{e/kWh}$ with scrubbing; 1050 without) (Nugent and Sovacool 2014: 241).

networks, often targeting the elections and legislatures where broad policies are set (Schneider 2004: 475). They will go well beyond the electricity sector itself. It is not unusual for coalitions in favor of climate action to also include both principled activists and those with concrete self-interests in climate action, including those committed to a just transition (Hochstetler and Viola 2012; Kelsey and Zysman 2014: 85–86; Newell and Mulvaney 2017).

At the same time, there is a potential second set of interests in the climate policy arena: when the existing electricity supply is based on fossil fuels, the fossil fuel sector has an intense interest in resisting these developments (Downie 2018; Moe 2015). Such fossil fuel sectors typically have substantial structural and mobilizational power that is "locked in" by being embedded in physical infrastructures, social institutions, political power relations, and prevailing norms (Geels 2004; Jacobsson and Lauber 2006; Meadowcroft 2009; Mitchell 2011; Unruh 2000). Facing an existential threat, the sector would be expected to form close networks to lobby and pursue its interests in maintaining the status quo (Schneider 2004: 468). Accelerating energy transition may depend on the weakening of this sector (Roberts and Geels 2019: 225).

While all countries share the diffuse interest in climate action, only some will have an electricity sector that is grounded in fossil fuels. Those countries will face considerably more contention over renewable energy if the interest structure of the climate change arena drives wind and solar power outcomes. The status quo coalition could either challenge the formulation of general climate plans or resist the implementation of those plans by trying to block growth of wind and solar power in the electricity matrix in particular. Final renewable energy outcomes will depend on the balance of power between the coalitions supporting energy transition and those defending the status quo. For countries without such a fossil fuel sector, pursuing climate action should translate more straightforwardly into more wind and solar power.

Given the structure of interests just outlined, climate policy formulation and its implementation in the electricity sector require a strong state that is oriented toward seeing long-term strategic needs to address climate change. It must be able to promote solutions even when they mean imposing costs on powerful actors with vested interests in the status quo (Meckling and Nahm 2017: 741; Pearson and Foxon 2012: 121).

Consequently, this chapter has a theoretical focus on state capacity, both in the positive sense of the ability to plan and execute policy that provides public goods – here, mitigating climate emissions – and in the negative sense of the ability to confront powerful societal interests (Cingolani, Thomsson, and Crombrugghe 2015; Evans 1995; Evans, Rueschemeyer, and Skocpol 1985; Power et al. 2016). This will be especially critical for countries with a well-developed electricity sector based on fossil fuels, such as South Africa. As a result, Brazil and South Africa represent strikingly different variations on the challenge of a low-carbon transition and, correspondingly, they position wind and solar power very differently in their climate politics and policy.

In South Africa, which depended on coal for 95 percent of its electricity supply until 2013, high carbon intensity in a historically privileged coal-based electricity sector has in fact led to a pitched battle between the coalitions for and against energy transition. As I trace in more detail in Section 2.2, this battle over climate change policy was not fought openly. Both sides accepted the need for climate action but differed on what that might require. The two decades up to 2009 saw a steady increase in state capacity to formulate first environmental and then more specifically climate policy, although environmental agencies continued to depend on civil society and the electricity parastatal Eskom for some tasks. Public debate on climate action was muted, with ongoing indecision about the level of South Africa's climate ambitions, until former president Jacob Zuma suddenly announced an international climate action commitment at the Copenhagen negotiations in 2009. After that, the debate spilled into the open. The Department of Environmental Affairs (DEA) continued to build climate capacity with a burst of activity after 2010 but could not manage what became increasingly heated debate over just how any climate commitment would be implemented in the electricity build plan. Eskom led a status quo coalition that fought increasingly hard to keep wind and solar power out of the build plan, arguing for nuclear power instead. Large nuclear installations built by Eskom would have retained more of its historical position in the sector. Subsequent developments have shown that the status quo coalition's theoretically expected opposition to energy transition was reinforced by the Zuma administration's corruption of Eskom and the electricity sector that also led to the preference for nuclear power. The renewable energy outcomes of these battles were repeated fits and starts (see Figure 1.1 in Chapter 1).

In Brazil, the hydro-based electricity sector is already comparatively low carbon, and GHG emissions have been concentrated in deforestation and the nonelectricity energy sector. The country also built environmental capacity over decades that culminated in striking decreases in deforestation and its associated emissions after 2005. Wide, if shallow, political consensus and electoral considerations also set out new climate policies and institutions after that, although agribusiness interests pushed back hard as they regained political power after 2011 and especially under President Jair Bolsonaro (2019–2023). These debates largely operated without reference to wind and solar power, however. A more technocratic style of decision-making continued in the electricity sector itself, as expected given the lack of strong actors linked to fossil fuel sources of electricity. Yet those technocrats were clearly not following a climate logic as they expanded wind power after 2001 while leaving solar power out of their electricity plans until 2014. Since climate motivations would favor both kinds of renewable energy, the sources of the differences between wind and solar outcomes must be found in other chapters.

I begin this chapter, in Section 2.1, with a discussion of state capacity applied to climate change politics. In Section 2.2, I then show the national debates in South Africa around making climate action commitments at the national and international levels. Section 2.3 then showcases the South African plans for building new electricity generation capacity – and wind and solar power in particular – which visualize the prevailing balance of power for implementing any climate commitments over time. Sections 2.4 and 2.5 do the same for Brazil. The conclusion, in Section 2.6, returns to the question of how well state capacity for climate action accounts for the outcomes of wind and solar power production in the two countries. Overall, the logic of the climate political economy is a significant driver of wind and solar outcomes in South Africa, but less so in Brazil.

2.1 Understanding Climate Action as a Question of State Capacity

Scholars of comparative political economy have a long-standing interest in understanding state capacity (Cingolani et al. 2015; Evans et al. 1985; Kohli 2004; Kurtz 2013; Weiss 1998). Little of this literature considers climate change or even environmental challenges more generally. Even so, a central focus of this literature – whether the state is willing and able to formulate and implement public goals even when they might be opposed by powerful social groups (Cingolani et al. 2015: 193; Meckling and Nahm 2017; Skocpol 1985: 9) – is clearly relevant for climate action. Because the climate political economy potentially activates environmental and economic as well as energy sectors, it requires a wider theoretical framing than the common formulation of regulatory capture that focuses more narrowly on the relationship between only, say, electricity utilities and their regulators (Berry 1984; Mitnick 2011).

A theoretical focus on state capacity requires first justifying a focus on the state. There are few defenders of states among scholars of climate change: they have been slow to make international agreements to address this global problem and slow to fulfill the promises they do make. Many have turned instead to look for action from nonstate or transnational actors from nongovernmental organizations (NGOs) to businesses to cities (Bäckstrand and Kronsell 2015: 1; Bulkeley et al. 2014). States really cannot be ignored, however. They have significant legitimate authority and resources to effectively address climate change, if they choose to do so, a claim institutionalized in the Nationally Determined Contributions that make up the 2015 Paris Agreement on Climate Change. So, three decades after the state was brought back into comparative political economy (Evans et al. 1985), it has to be brought into the comparative political economy of climate change.

Global climate negotiations have also been built around a related preoccupation with state capacity (Willems and Baumert 2003). The negotiations have historically divided national obligations for climate action according to what UN documents routinely refer to as a formula of "common but differentiated responsibilities and respective capabilities" (Bortscheller 2009–2010; Stone 2004). The last clause once exonerated middle-income and developing countries from mandatory climate action under the 1997 Kyoto Protocol except for reporting on voluntary action. Negotiations since then have led to open international disputes over when large and comparatively wealthy and capable developing countries like Brazil and South Africa should commit to undertake action to reduce their climate change emissions (Hochstetler 2012). Both, in fact, made voluntary commitments in Copenhagen in 2009 and joined the Paris Agreement in 2015. Those international debates play a comparatively large role in this chapter.

Scholars focused on Africa have argued persuasively that environmental stewardship is also critical in middle-income and developing states more generally. In this context, however, any environmental imperative must be balanced with an economic one (Chandrashekeran, Morgan, Coetzee, and Christoff 2017: 4; Death 2016; Swilling and Annecke 2012). This difficult double task is taken on by states that are generally less capable in conventional terms. Nonetheless, bureaucracies that do not look like the Weberian ideal may also govern with some effectiveness, especially embedded in networks that blur state and society and national and international divides (Death 2016: 52; Evans 1995; Hochstetler and Keck 2007: 16–20). If we are to consider the roles of states in addressing environmental imperatives beyond the wealthy, industrialized world, state capacity must be researched rather than just assumed, as it varies significantly. Basic descriptive analysis of the kind provided in this chapter is key to this task (Duit 2016: 70).

Climate researchers have begun to explore the importance of state capacity for explaining climate action. They often focus on the choice of specific instruments for reducing greenhouse gases, mostly in developed countries (e.g., Hughes and Urpelainen 2015; Meckling and Nahm 2017; Willems and Baumert 2003). The analytical choices made do not always make the translation to lower capacity settings, however. For example, in an otherwise exemplary article, Jonas Meckling and Jonas Nahm take bureaucratic capacity for implementation for granted (Meckling and Nahm 2017: 743). Similarly, state capacity is often operationalized as the existence of a relevant agency (e.g., Hughes and Urpelainen 2015: 58). In lower capacity contexts, this is not a safe assumption: the Brazilian Special Secretariat of the Environment would count, although it was created in 1973 with three employees in two rooms and had little real capacity for well over a decade (Hochstetler and Keck 2007: 27). The eventual Ministry of Environment did not even have a professional civil service track until 2003 (Abers and de Oliveira 2015), but it achieved some significant, if precarious, environmental governance with civil society (Hochstetler and Keck 2007: 223–225).

State capacity to formulate and implement policy in advanced developing countries like Brazil and South Africa is especially difficult to gauge in general terms. Both had ambitious authoritarian states that were able to implement demanding visions from apartheid to classic developmentalism (Evans 1979; Fine and Rustomjee 1996; Seidman 1994). Even so, they are equally characterized by very uneven levels of capacity. "Islands of excellence" like South Africa's National Treasury (Pearson, Pillay, and Chipkin 2016) coexist with institutions like Eskom, now featuring in reports of "state capture" by narrow interests allied with Zuma (Chipkin and Swilling 2017; Public Protector 2016). Brazil's state agencies also display considerable variation in their levels of capacity and independence (Bersch, Praça, and Taylor 2017). State capacity and independence in the environmental area in both countries is thus less a given than it is struggled over in particular instances (Hochstetler and Keck 2007: 223–225). Contingent coalitions will reflect the distinct political economies of GHG emissions in their national economies and create distinct climate action logics (MacNeil and Paterson 2012; Nahm 2017; Pegels 2014b).

2.2 South African Climate Capacity and Initiatives

The basic pattern of GHG emissions in South Africa implies very serious barriers to climate action through building wind and solar power because the electricity sector and the economy are so oriented toward coal, while the Brazilian route should be easier. As Figure 2.1 shows, about 80 percent of the GHG emissions in South Africa are linked to the energy sector, so South Africa simply cannot reduce its GHG emissions in any significant way without replacing its coal generation with renewable energy (Winkler 2009). This means that South African climate politics displays the full array of interests just outlined: as the government began to articulate a diffuse and general interest in climate action, opposition rose from a highly concentrated set of interests that defend ongoing coal mining and coal-based electricity generation.

It is straightforward to identify the actors positioned on either side of energy transition in South Africa. The side of the traditional coal-based mining economy had strong support in the governing ANC party, the parastatal Eskom, and the powerful industry groups and state agencies of the "Minerals-Energy Complex" (Fine and Rustomjee 1996; McDonald 2011). On the other side, an incipient counter-economy has wind and solar power at its center (Baker 2015a; Baker, Newell, and Phillips 2014; Power et al. 2016). The state institutions most closely related to the counter-economy are the DEA and sometimes the National

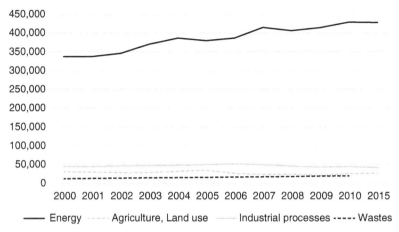

Figure 2.1 South African GHG emissions (Gg CO$_2$eq) by sector, 2000–2010, 2015
Source: Department of Environmental Affairs 2014: Appendix A, online at ht tp://unfccc.int/resource/docs/natc/zafnir1.pdf. One Gg is a metric kiloton. Updated for 2015 by Republic of South Africa (2018: 67–68).

Treasury and the Department of Energy, which is divided on renewable energy and climate change. These have struggled to develop the capacity needed to both formulate and implement climate policies. Global climate negotiations also enter the story, pushing South Africa to consider climate action when it might not have done so otherwise.

2.2.1 Early Developments and Actors

The early phases of global negotiations on climate change coincided with South Africa's transition away from an apartheid system in 1994. South Africa opted out of mandatory action in the Kyoto Protocol phase so that it could address its post-apartheid priorities: "the alleviation of poverty; the provision of basic services for all South Africans; equity; employment creation; and economic growth" (Government of South Africa 2000: viii). The post-apartheid government had little capacity to take environmental action of any kind. A new national Department of Environmental Affairs and Tourism (DEAT), created in 1994, spent its early years writing basic environmental legislation. The National Environmental Management Act of 1998 does not mention climate change or GHG emissions.[3] Instead, the DEAT created a nonstate National Committee on Climate Change in 1996 to provide it with expertise it lacked on the subject (Chandrashekeran et al. 2017: 5–6).

External deadlines pushed the next developments in climate policy. South Africa wrote its first communication to the United Nations Framework Convention on Climate Change (UNFCCC) in 2004, as well as a National Climate Change Response Strategy (Vorster, Winkler, and Jooste 2011: 243–244). While ambitious in its aims, the Response Strategy included few implementing or monitoring instruments (Chandrashekeran et al. 2017: 6). The DEAT next prepared for new international demands for action by again drawing on external expertise, this time from the University of Cape Town's Energy Research Centre for a study of possible long-term mitigation scenarios (LTMSs) (Borland, Morrell, and Watson 2018: 58–59).[4] The LTMS proposal to have GHG emissions peak by 2020, plateau for a decade, and subsequently decline was adopted as a governmental planning document in 2008 along with proposals for a new Carbon Disclosure project, a carbon tax, and an Energy Efficiency Accord (Upadhyaya 2016: 470; Vorster et al. 2011: 243–244; Winkler 2010). Despite this activity, there was considerably more planning than implementation. Achieving the scheduled peak, plateau, and decline of GHG emissions could be done only with cooperation from the electricity sector, which was proceeding on a very different track.

From 1922, Eskom had gradually concentrated control over electricity generation and distribution (Eberhard 2007: 215; Morris and Martin 2015). Eskom's near-monopoly of information and expertise in the electricity sector made it a formidable power, able to resist other agencies' planning directives. Another nonstate expert group had written an Energy White Paper in 1998, for example, that called for beginning the energy transition. The 2003 Renewable Energy White Paper told Eskom to have independent power producers (IPPs) build renewable energy plants, directives that it ignored until it was forced to adhere to them in 2011 (Eberhard 2007; Rennkamp et al. 2017:

---

[3] www.gov.za/sites/default/files/a107-98.pdf.
[4] Interview with Robert Scholes, Systems Ecologist with the Council for Scientific and Industrial Research (CSIR), Durban, 2011; interview with Harald Winkler, Energy Research Centre, University of Cape Town, Cape Town, 2011. Both participated in the LTMS studies.

216).[5] Even after a new Department of Energy moved to take planning functions from Eskom in 2009, the government had to return to Eskom to produce its Integrated Resource Plan (IRP) for 2010 since the modeling expertise simply was not available elsewhere.[6] Eskom continued to play a major role in South Africa's delegations to the UN climate meetings, with an "undersourced" government asking for it to supply the technical side on anything related to electricity.[7]

Eskom's capacity, in a literal sense, brought a turning point in this standoff. After fifteen years with minimal new electricity construction, it began building two large new coal power plants, Medupi in 2007 and Kusile in 2008. But Eskom was only breaking ground when electricity supply shortfalls started forcing scheduled electricity blackouts (load-shedding). Costs for both plants have nearly tripled while the time frames have already grown years beyond the original schedule.[8] Repeated load-shedding, construction problems, and maintenance failures undermined Eskom's reputation as an actor that could manage the electricity sector and its perceived capacity. As an observer summarized, Eskom's leaders were no longer seen as "gods" (cited in Baker et al. 2014: 809).[9]

2.2.2   *The Years 2009 to 2011: A "Boom Cycle of Documents"*

Jacob Zuma challenged Thabo Mbeki for the presidency of the ANC and thus the country in 2009. When Zuma won, he changed the political landscape. Institutionally, he created a freestanding Department of Energy with new powers (2009) and paired environmental issues with water rather than tourism, briefly creating a Department of Water and Environmental Affairs (2010). By 2011, it was simply the Department of Environmental Affairs (DEA).[10] He

---

[5] Interview with Anton Eberhard, Professor at the Graduate School of Business, University of Cape Town, Cape Town, 2013. Eberhard participated in the expert committee that wrote the 1998 White Paper, as well as other activities.
[6] Interview with Callie Fabricius, General Manager, Energy Planning and Market Development, Eskom, Germiston, 2014.
[7] Interview with official at Eskom, Johannesburg, 2014.
[8] www.fin24.com/Economy/Eskom/why-medupi-and-kusile-are-eskoms-achilles -heel-20160706.
[9] Interviews with Eberhard 2013; Scholes, CSIR, 2011.
[10] In 2019, the Department of Environmental Affairs became the Department of Environment, Forestry and Fisheries. For simplicity, this book refers to all these

secured World Bank funding to complete Medupi and Kusile, even as his government initiated broader climate action discussions.

A multiday consultative Climate Change Summit brought many stakeholders together to debate future directions in March 2009. The Summit exposed significant divergence over what South Africans should do to address climate change, if anything. The main agreement was for more debate and consultation on key issues like electricity planning, the role of nuclear power, and a carbon tax.[11] Given those disagreements, there was broad surprise when Zuma went to the UNFCCC's annual negotiation in Copenhagen at the end of 2009 and made an international promise for significant climate action.[12] Although observers speculate that Zuma's decision was driven by his realization that South Africa's fellow large emerging powers – Brazil, China, and India – would be making commitments, he has never explained his sudden motivation for a significant pledge, which was not based on a national consensus in favor of climate action.[13]

These changes led to a set of developments in 2009–2011 that reset South Africa's climate agenda from stasis to action, creating what one activist called "a boom cycle of documents."[14] The Cabinet promptly endorsed Zuma's international commitment. It set up a National Committee on Climate Change, although key agencies like the Presidency, the Treasury, and the Department of Public Enterprises (DPE), which oversees Eskom, participated only sporadically, weakening it (Giordano et al. 2011: 32). The DEA led in drafting a Green Paper and then the National Climate Change Response White Paper of 2011, which translated the Copenhagen promises into sectoral strategies and

varying forms as the Department of Environmental Affairs (DEA), as this was its core function, although the book uses the full names for cited documents and interviews.

[11] Foreword by Peter Lukey, Acting Deputy Director General: Climate Change of the Department of Environmental Affairs (Giordano, Hall, Gilder, and Parramon 2011). See also the parliamentary hearings on the eventual National Climate Change Response Green Paper at https://pmg.org.za/committee-meeting/12587/.

[12] https://unfccc.int/files/meetings/cop_15/copenhagen_accord/application/pdf/southafricacphaccord_app2.pdf.

[13] Interview with Eberhard 2013; interview with Mike Levington, Vice Chairperson South African Photovoltaic Industry Association (SAPVIA), Johannesburg, 2018; and other confidential interviews.

[14] Skype interview with Melita Steele, Lead Climate and Energy Campaigner, Greenpeace Africa, 2014.

programs for action for both adaptation and mitigation (Department of Environmental Affairs 2011).

2.2.3 Efforts to Implement: The Department of Environmental Affairs as a Weak Center

The Green and White Climate Papers proposed an implementation structure that put the DEA at the convening center of climate action. The DEA is a weak center, however, as it cannot do many of the actions required to reduce GHG emissions and address climate change impacts (Chandrashekeran et al. 2017: 7; Upadhyaya 2016). The DEA has had to manage its capacity gaps by mobilizing stronger links across the government and with civil society.[15] Progress was slow and uneven after 2011 and often invisible beyond a small group of committed actors.

Even so, from 2014 to 2018, the DEA developed a Mitigation Potential Analysis (2014), National Atmospheric Emission Reporting Regulations (2015), an Air Quality Offsets Guideline (2016), a National Pollution Prevention Plan Regulation (second draft 2016), National GHG Emission Reporting Regulations (2017), a Declaration of GHG as Priority Air Pollutants (2017), and Climate Change Mitigation Policies and Measures (2017) before producing the first draft of a full Climate Change Bill in 2018. The DEA also wrote its first and second Annual Climate Change Reports for 2016 and 2017. Several of these use a "carbon budgets" approach that asks the minister of environmental affairs to set an overall national GHG emissions threshold and then parcel it out as a carbon budget to specified "persons" (including juridical persons, i.e., corporations) (Department of Environmental Affairs 2018). Sasol, a major industry emitter, has challenged the justification of this legislation in air pollution terms in the courts, leading the DEA to seek approval of the 2018 Climate Bill to strengthen the legal foundation of its work (Rennkamp 2019: 762).

The DEA produced two drafts of nearly all of these bills and regulations, seeking – and receiving – written comments from civil society groups, businesses, and other ministerial departments and other levels of government, as well as presenting the work orally to these groups and responding to comments and questions. This consultation was a huge and time-consuming task, but it was the only way to move

[15] Interview, DEA official, Pretoria, 2014.

beyond the limits on what the DEA itself could do.[16] Many of these initiatives address the crippling lack of credible data on GHG emissions in South Africa. Even with the new regulations, data is being reported only on a voluntary and experimental basis until 2020 and requires developing reporting and analysis capacity for all participants (Trollip and Boulle 2017: 10–14).

2.2.4 Civil Society: Principled and Self-Interested Actors Press for Life Beyond Coal

The national climate debate has never been a mass discussion in South Africa. In fact, just 45 percent of South Africans agreed in 2015 that climate change is a very serious problem.[17] Even so, there is a strong mobilized contingent among that minority of concerned South Africans. For them, the DEA has not moved nearly fast enough. Civil society actors began pushing for climate action when the new coal construction after 2007 brought an old economic model back to life. For several years, activists found climate action to be a unifying aim (Cock 2012: 25), drawing on "a relatively small group of dedicated individuals and organisations" to mobilize larger networks (Death 2014: 1225). Eighty organizations formed a coordinating committee for the 2011 climate negotiation session in Durban, organizing an alternative space for global NGOs and social movements, and convening a mass march of 12,000 people (Cock 2012: 25–26). This temporarily papered over some enduring divisions of both purposes and strategies, broadly characterizable as a fault line between a reformist green and an anti-capitalist red-green grouping of activists (Cock 2012: 26; Death 2014).

The more reformist green group is led by organizations like WWF South Africa, committed to serious climate action and interested in influencing and supporting state climate initiatives (Cock 2012: 28). While they are often critical of specific initiatives, this group also seeks opportunities to support governmental capacity in the sector where it can. Under various names, energy/electricity caucus groups have

---

[16] Interview, DEA official, 2014. Comments from stakeholders that led into the 2018 Climate Bill draft are summarized in Department of Planning, Monitoring and Evaluation 2017.
[17] www.pewglobal.org/2015/11/05/1-concern-about-climate-change-and-its-consequences/.

presented joint civil society positions in parliamentary hearings, commented on legislative projects and governmental energy plans, and held public discussions about South Africa's energy and climate options.[18] Members of the caucus produce and commission technical analyses of climate and energy questions that they introduce into governmental and public debates (e.g., Fakir 2017; Teske and Lins 2011).

The red-green group is led by the EarthLife Africa and groundWork organizations that sometimes participate in energy caucus activities but also have ties to other organizations that are more critical of market solutions. Their social base has included not just labor organizations like the Congress of South African Trade Unions (COSATU) but also the "precariat," building on a strong environmental justice frame (Cock 2012: 25). This group has embraced strategies that are more challenging to the South African state's solutions to its energy and climate problems. EarthLife Africa and groundWork were instrumental in putting together a request for a World Bank Inspection Panel that found that the Bank had violated its own policies in approving the loan for Medupi in 2010 (World Bank Inspection Panel 2011).[19] With the Centre for Environmental Rights (CER), they have followed a legal strategy to try to stop the government's coal-based energy agenda outright in their "Life After Coal" campaign.[20] While the organizations in the Life After Coal campaign are active and have won some important legal cases that are discussed in Section 2.3, the broader red-green coalition has disintegrated as the labor movement itself has fractured in the aftermath of the Durban negotiation in 2011 (Cock 2012: 26; see Chapter 3).

The Life After Coal campaign is a strong voice for just transitions for local communities that have historically hosted coal mines and electricity plants. Their analyses focus on the human costs of South Africa's energy choices, producing urgent studies like groundWork's blunt "Coal Kills" report (groundWork 2018; Centre for Environmental

---

[18] See, for example, their comments on the process and substance of the draft 2018 Integrated Resource Plan hearings, at https://cer.org.za/news/concluding-the-draft-2018-irp-public-hearings-ngos-write-to-energy-committee. Interviews with Brenda Martin, Lead Organizer of the Energy Caucus and Director of Project 90x2030, Cape Town, 2013; Megan Euston-Brown, Sustainable Energy Africa, Cape Town, 2013; and Saliem Fakir, WWF South Africa, Cape Town, 2013.

[19] Interview with Tristan Taylor, EarthLife Africa, Johannesburg, 2013.

[20] Email interview with Nicole Loser, Attorney, CER, 2018.

Rights 2017). Local communities have paid a heavy price in both environmental quality and local health and will now have few economic alternatives if coal leaves (Campbell, Nel, and Mphambukeli 2017; Naidoo 2015: 1050; Thompson 2018). The Life After Coal campaign is insistent that those dynamics must be addressed even as it also insists that coal mining end to address health, climate change, and other environmental impacts (groundWork 2018).[21]

2.2.5 Private Sector: Hesitation without Open Blockage

Not surprisingly, these climate action developments also galvanized the private sector, which became actively engaged in commenting on and trying to influence the developing policies after 2010. Alongside Eskom, South African businesses and industry associations have not openly mobilized against the country setting climate mitigation aims. Even the big producers of GHG emissions in the Energy Intensive Users Group (EIUG) are careful to stress that they recognize the need for South Africa to reduce its emissions. Their Industry Task Force on Climate Change (ITTCC) requires its members to accept the science of climate change.[22] Commenting on a specific climate document, however, the ITTCC cautioned: "Business sees no reason for South Africa to have a legislative framework for climate change which is one of the most stringent in the world."[23]

On the overarching framework, many firms are disturbed by what they see as a triple costing to them of climate action: they do not object per se to the DEA's idea of set carbon budgets, although they are keen to see them reflecting accurate data (Trollip and Boulle 2017). Most firms have gradually accepted wind and solar power, changes initiated through the Department of Energy. But they argue strongly against a carbon tax[24] – the National Treasury also presented drafts of a Carbon Tax Bill in 2015 and 2017 – and they really object to having

---

[21] Email interview with Loser, CER, 2018.

[22] Interviews with Piet van Staden, EIUG, 2018; Jarradine Morris, EIUG spokesperson, Johannesburg, 2018; Kevin Morgan, CEO EIUG and Shaun Nel, spokesman EIUG, Johannesburg, 2014; and Eskom official, 2014.

[23] Climate Change Legal Framework, http://ittcc.org.za/projects/. This page lists the joint industry response of some large industrial emitters to a number of proposed climate actions and informs this paragraph along with the interviews cited in Footnote 21.

[24] Interviews with Morris, EIUG, 2018; Morgan and Nel, EIUG, 2014.

all three of these mechanisms together, especially since they are being developed with only partial coordination by two departments and the Treasury (Rennkamp 2019).

Other ministries provided more positive incentives for climate action around the same time as the White and Green Papers, further muddling the business response. The Economic Development Department designed a New Growth Path in 2010 intended to help move the economy to a new greener economy. The accompanying National Infrastructure Plan and Green Economy Accord promised 300,000 new jobs related to clean infrastructure (Cock 2012: 22). The Department of Trade and Industry (DTI) and the DPE also wrote multiple Industrial Policy Action Plans and developed a renewable energy plan called the South African Renewables Initiative. The National Policy Commission added a broader National Development Plan that was released in 2012. It has a major chapter on sustainable development that calls for a just transition to a low-carbon economy, although the chapter fits awkwardly with other chapters that see a continued reliance on South Africa's traditional economy (National Planning Commission 2012). Finally, the program for contracting IPPs to build wind and solar power began in 2011 and won substantial praise (Eberhard, Kolker, and Leigland 2014). It is discussed in Section 2.3.

All of these initiatives together set a bewildering array of both positive economic incentives and new regulatory controls after 2009, all designed for some kind of climate emissions outcomes. The DEA has limited power to force coordination and policy integration is incomplete: the plans set different incentives and targets for different "green" outcomes, including wind and solar power generation, and the programs also include incentives for projects that are not green. Thus, the total result is less a specific climate mandate than it is indicative of the widening of the climate debate after Zuma's Copenhagen commitment and the inability of any single actor to lead the effort.

In summary, South Africa's coal-dominated status quo proponents have not tried to block national climate policies and institutions altogether. Especially between 2009 and 2011, numerous initiatives laid the foundations for climate action, with their acquiescence. The DEA proved a weak center for developing those foundations, despite pressure and inputs from civil society sectors seeking a just energy transition with different strategies. Eskom and its state and industry allies made limited responses to a confusing array of both state regulations and incentives for climate action. Yet while the theoretically expected status quo coalition did not fight against general climate policy, it used its power to take on the more specific question of whether climate plans would be translated into producing more wind and solar power, arguing increasingly strongly against.

2.3 South Africa: Translating Climate Plans into Energy Choices

South Africa can meet its climate goals only if it moves away from its coal-based energy system. That means building non-fossil fuel sources of electricity like wind and solar power and shutting down existing coal facilities at the end of their life cycle or even before, an existential threat to the existing sector. Historically, Eskom would have written any roadmap for energy transition, but the new Department of Energy took the electricity planning responsibility for itself in 2010. In particular, it was to produce an Integrated Resource Plan (IRP) with a binding build plan for electricity, to be updated biannually using new demand and cost data. The Department of Energy has only slowly accumulated the capacity to do so, leaving it highly vulnerable to pressures against renewable energy.

In this section, I trace the politics behind South Africa's IRPs: the officially adopted first plan for 2010–2030 (Department of Energy 2011) and the unadopted updates (Department of Energy 2013, 2016, 2017, 2018, 2019). As Figure 2.2 shows, the plans projected quite different levels of procurement of different fuel sources between 2010 and 2030. A dramatic planning story even at face value, it has turned out to connect to darker state capture dynamics (Chipkin and Swilling 2017).

The Department of Energy began working on the first IRP in 2010, but it had large gaps in both information and modeling capacity. The EIUG, which uses more than 40 percent of the national electricity supply, was very influential in the first IRP, especially on the quantity and nature of future electricity demand.[25] The Department of Energy also had to return to Eskom for modeling and analysis skills.[26] The 2010 IRP does lead off in new directions, following the Department of

[25]   Interview with van Staden, EIUG, 2018.
[26]   Interview with Fabricius, Eskom, 2014.

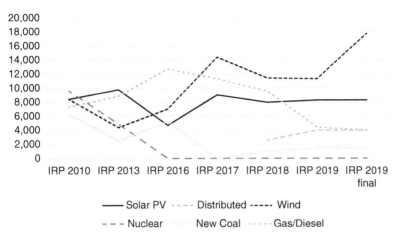

Figure 2.2 Projected total electricity procurement to 2030 by fuel type in drafts of the South African Integrated Resource Plan for Electricity
Sources: Department of Energy 2011, 2013, 2016, 2017, 2018, 2019a, 2019b.

Energy's directives to honor South Africa's new climate commitments while maintaining energy security and developing local industrial clusters. Since it assumes a GHG emissions constraint will come after 2024, it includes then-costly wind and solar power and proposes introducing them immediately in order to develop related industries and skills (Department of Energy 2011: 6–8). Industry and civil society made 5,090 comments on the IRP in 479 submissions, many on the cost of the various options and on whether nuclear power or renewables was the preferred noncarbon option. An early draft did not contain wind and solar in current build plans, but NGOs claim credit for having helped to put them in the final version.[27] The final adopted IRP proposed 9.6 GW of new nuclear power by 2030, but it also included a 17.8 GW build of the wind and solar power that the planners saw as experimental. Coal had just 6.3 GW of new build, although it was the fuel that both Eskom and the EIUG then trusted most as a source of baseload electricity.[28]

At the time of the first IRP in 2010, the question of how wind and solar power would be procured was still unsettled. The IRP itself assumed that it would be procured through a feed-in tariff and so discussed how the tariff might be set to avoid excessively high costs.

[27] Interview with Robert Fischer, Project 90x2030, Cape Town, 2013.
[28] Interviews with Fabricius, Eskom, 2014; Morris and Nel, EIUG, 2014.

After load-shedding began in 2008, the National Energy Regulator (NERSA) had decided to use one of the tools in its portfolio to push renewable energy forward over Eskom's stalling. NERSA controls rates/tariffs, and it set up the Renewable Energy Feed-In Tariff (REFIT) in 2009 to promote renewable energy production in the private sector (Pegels 2014c: 130–131). The process served the purpose of drawing private investors to South Africa to put together proposed projects, but it was stymied by Eskom, which continued to refuse to sign agreements that would give the facilities access to the national grid. It was not clear that NERSA had the constitutional authority to create such a plan and neither the Department of Energy nor the Treasury supported it (Bode 2013: 73–74),[29] but it was the existing framework at the time of the first IRP.

Given the legal impasse, competitors offered other procurement models. The South African Renewables Initiative (SARI) brought together a coalition of people who were interested in trying to attract new international climate funds to South Africa with individuals in the DPE and the DTI. SARI was launched during the 2011 Durban climate negotiations with European representatives who promised new climate finance for wind and solar power procurement; it was presented as one of South Africa's "Nationally Appropriate Mitigation Actions" (Upadhyaya 2016: 472). However, while internationally attractive, the coalition had not built ties early enough with the new Department of Energy, which developed its own program instead.[30]

The Department of Energy turned to the Treasury to help develop its plan, eventually named the Renewable Energy Independent Power Producers Procurement Programme (REIPPPP) (Eberhard et al. 2014). This program uses auctions to contract IPPs rather than the parastatal Eskom to produce electricity for the first time. Placing the semiautonomous program under the shield of the Treasury – necessary because the National Treasury had to guarantee the loans (Bode 2013: 73–74) – left room for a highly competent program officer to develop an island of efficiency that was beyond the Department of Energy's own capacity (Pegels 2014c: 139). The REIPPPP is often singled out as the one piece of South Africa's climate policy that has been effectively implemented (Rennkamp and Marquand 2018; Trollip and Boulle

[29] Interview with Eberhard, Cape Town, 2013.
[30] Interview with Fakir, WWF South Africa, 2013.

2017). South Africa's submission to the Paris Agreement on Climate Change showcases it.

With the REIPPPP and a parallel program for coal IPPs in place, the second IRP had to be refined to reflect initial commitments of capacity to be built through these programs. The Cabinet had also agreed to produce nuclear power in some unspecified amount (Department of Energy 2013: 19). These promises vied with a clear slowing of demand as South Africa's economic growth stagnated and electricity prices rose, suggesting that less of all kinds of electricity would be built than originally contemplated. The original IRP had managed to appease competing constituencies in part through its plans to build electricity using all fuel sources. With less electricity needed, wind and solar power began to be more explicitly competitive with nuclear power as alternative ways to meet South Africa's climate obligations. In addition, Eskom had originally thought that it might build any renewable energy procured,[31] but the new plans made it clear that IPPs would build them, threatening Eskom's monopoly on generation – which a nuclear build would retain.

The DEA's peak-plateau-decline scenario was officially integrated into this second IRP draft (Department of Energy 2013: 26). The new version of the IRP pleased no one as it placed artificial annual limits on wind and solar power and declared that the original plan's 9.6 GW of nuclear power might not be needed (Department of Energy 2013: 12). This set off a firestorm, with key ANC figures up to Zuma insisting on keeping nuclear in the mix. The new wind and solar industry associations joined civil society activists in pushing for wind and solar power without artificial limits instead. "Nuclear energy is the big zombie," said one.[32] Long-standing community antinuclear activists joined the groups mobilized in response to the energy plans.[33] Activists were also alarmed by the continuing coal build plans. Amid all the cross-currents, this IRP draft was never finished or approved. Even so, the Department of Energy announced that South Africa and Russia had signed an initial

[31] Interview with Eskom official, 2014.
[32] Interview with Taylor, EarthLife Africa, 2013; also, interviews with Johan van den Berg, CEO of South Africa Wind Energy Association (SAWEA), Johannesburg, 2014; Mike Levington, Vice Chairperson of South African Photovoltaic Industry Association (SAPVIA), Johannesburg, 2014; Euston-Brown, Sustainable Energy Africa, 2013; Martin, Project 90 x 2030, 2013; Steele, Greenpeace, 2014.
[33] Interview with Peter Becker, Koeberg Alert Alliance, Cape Town, 2013.

framework agreement for nuclear procurement in September 2014.[34] This agreement rested legally on the original IRP.

In 2016, another attempt to update the original IRP could not be finished in the context of a dramatically escalating debate over what kinds of electricity should be built. The first 2016 draft was just a sketch, showing cost curves for wind and solar power shifting down quickly, as bid prices dropped with South Africa's successive auction rounds (see Chapter 4). Nuclear prices and capital costs, meanwhile, were rising steadily, but the very first version had 25 GW of nuclear.[35] The subsequent public draft showed a least-cost scenario, instead, which called for larger quantities of wind and solar power while keeping annual build limits and new nuclear build only in 2037 and after (Department of Energy 2016: 26).

Activists and the renewable energy industries continued to push for a more serious climate response and more wind and solar power.[36] The EIUG, by this time, had lost some of its skepticism of wind and power and become increasingly critical of nuclear power because it was so costly.[37] A revised version of this plan, issued in November 2017, addressed some of these concerns. It showed that lower demand and changing comparative prices meant that no new coal beyond that already coming online or nuclear power should be built before 2030. More detailed modeling of GHG emissions levels and climate policies also kept both coal and nuclear out until 2050 unless artificial annual limits on wind and solar power were imposed (Department of Energy 2017: 34).

Eskom and the Minister of Energy responded to the 2016 and 2017 drafts by strongly defending the nuclear program, arguing in parliamentary hearings that nuclear power should be built instead of renewable energy because it equally met South Africa's climate commitments while being no more expensive.[38] Starting at the end of July 2016,

---

[34] www.dailymaverick.co.za/article/2018-10-03-zuma-mahlobo-joemat-petterssson-nkoana-mashabane-strong-armed-nene-into-signing-secret-russian-nuclear-deal/#gsc.tab=0.

[35] Interview with Levington, SAPVIA, 2018.

[36] For an example of their comments, see the WWF comment on this 2016 draft: http://dtnac4dfluyw8.cloudfront.net/downloads/WWF_South_Africa_inputs_on_the_draft_Energy_and_Resource_Plans_Final.pdf.

[37] Interview with van Staden, EIUG, 2018.

[38] Hearing on 25 October 2016, at http://linkis.com/pmg.org.za/committee/W9PMt.

Eskom refused to sign final contracts for the twenty-seven wind and solar power projects selected in recent auction rounds (3.5 and 4.0) through the REIPPPP, arguing that the electricity was unneeded and too expensive. While the Department of Energy, the Treasury and even the Zuma administration expressed support for the REIPPPP, the contracts went unsigned until March 2018, after Zuma was pushed from office.

By 2016, the shadow story of state capture for nuclear power was becoming increasingly visible (Chipkin and Swilling 2017: 53–54, 64–66). The first pieces of the story actually date back to 2010, when Zuma's son Duduzane bought an unprofitable uranium mine with members of the Gupta family of businessmen. The expectation was that the mine would become profitable with the large nuclear build put into the first IRP and defended strongly by Zuma afterwards. Former finance minister Nhlanhla Nene testified to a parliamentary hearing in 2018 that, in July 2015, he refused to cosign a guarantee letter to the Russian government that South Africa would contract a nuclear program with it if the Russian government would fund it. Extensive Treasury modeling exercises had shown that the nuclear build was completely infeasible financially.[39] Nene was fired in December 2015, hours after telling the Cabinet that nuclear energy was too expensive for South Africa to build (ibid.: 54). In a short period of time, South Africa had three finance ministers and five ministers of energy as the Zuma government struggled to keep its nuclear ambitions on track.

The nuclear part of the story was halted by some of the civil society actors already introduced. Once EarthLife Africa learned about a secret intergovernmental agreement on nuclear procurement with Russia in 2014, it joined with the Southern Africa Faith Communities' Environmental Institute to pursue a more activist strategy.[40] Led by a group of mostly women, they held a weekly vigil outside parliament. While the organizations continued to oppose nuclear power on environmental and cost grounds, they also filed a court case on procedural

---

[39] www.dailymaverick.co.za/article/2018-10-03-zuma-mahlobo-joemat-pettersson-nkoana-mashabane-strong-armed-nene-into-signing-secret-russian-nuclear-deal/#gsc.tab=0. Nene's complete testimony is available at www.scribd.com/document/390031857/Minister-of-Finance-s-Statement-at-the-State-Capture-Inquiry#download.

[40] Their activities are described here: http://m.news24.com/news24/Opinions/IN-FOCUS/in-focus-i-meet-the-women-who-stopped-the-nuclear-deal-20170508.

grounds of nonconsultation. Transparency groups like Right to Know and Open Democracy joined in the antinuclear activities along with unions, some twenty organizations in all. The court found on May 1, 2017 that the government's action was illegal and the procurement could not go forward without public consultation and parliamentary debate that would include fuller discussion of likely costs.[41] That decision did not rule out nuclear power altogether, but it stalled what had been the Zuma administration's effort to pursue nuclear power quietly and quickly.

Another fight over coal broke out as the nuclear plans were being stopped. Successive IRPs continued to rely on coal, especially as supplied by new IPPs, and initial auctions even identified early winning bidders. At the same time, Eskom was scheduled to close five older coal plants as they reached the end of their normal lifespan. Most of the civil society groups already discussed strongly supported closing those plants and even accelerating other shutdowns, while arguing against new coal procurement whether from Eskom or the IPPs. They did so in comments on the IRPs as well as on the environmental impact assessments (EIAs) for specific plants, which also allow comments and challenges. A grassroots women's group called Women Building Power Campaign held its first energy and climate justice camp near the new Kusile coal plant in September 2018, in opposition both to the mines and the plants and to their exclusion from governmental decision-making.[42]

The Life After Coal campaign joined in these activities, but it also took the new coal projects to court. In the Thabametsi case, the court found that climate change needed to be assessed in the coal project EIAs, setting a precedent for further litigation and instigating another court challenge when the Thabametsi project was approved even after a subsequent EIA. Attorney Nicole Loser sees the court cases as successful in sending "a clear message of public opposition to unnecessary and dirty new coal plants."[43] The Campaign has also argued that the IRPs should be presented for stakeholder consultation in the communities where

---

[41] http://earthlife.org.za/2017/04/nuclear-deal-blocked-judgement-made-on-the-south-african-governments-secret-trillion-rand-nuclear-court-case/.

[42] https://womin.org.za/images/WoMin_Newsletter_IssueSeptember_2018_English.pdf.

[43] Interview with Loser, CER, 2018. The Thabametsi court documents are at https://cer.org.za/wp-content/uploads/2017/03/Judgment-Earthlife-Thabametsi-Final-06-03-2017.pdf.

electricity production actually takes place, locations where the Campaign plans to work for a just transition away from coal.[44]

Eskom began to fight increasingly hard to defend its own generation, beginning with the REIPPPP contract refusals in 2016. While Eskom has genuine corporate concerns about the shift in generation plans as generation is 60 percent of its revenues (Morris and Martin 2015: 35), its opposition was also related to state capture dynamics. The Public Protector wrote a complaint about efforts by then-CEO of Eskom Brian Molefe to use Eskom's procurement power to shift coal contracts to the same Gupta family and other cronies of the Zumas (Public Protector 2016; see also Chipkin and Swilling 2017). Parliamentary hearings have confirmed these and other accusations of corruption in Eskom's top politically linked management.[45]

To justify shifting the coal contracts, Eskom failed to make critical investments in its existing mines which then could not supply their contracted amounts. This led to the much more expensive trucking in of coal from new mines – and a new Coal Transporters Forum that added urgency to the labor demands with road-blocking strikes and a court case in 2017, asking that the REIPPPP contracts not be signed.[46] Ironically, Eskom's mismanagement for these political purposes and the consequent added costs may have finally and most decisively squandered its capacity advantage in the energy sector, leaving it essentially bankrupt by 2018. Eskom's Chief Financial Officer has warned: "If we go down, we bring down the sovereign and the economy" since South Africa's national government has guaranteed Eskom's increasingly unpayable debt.[47]

In these debates, the position of unions has been especially complex. South Africa's unions repeatedly stress their commitment to significant climate action: "We were, and remain, absolutely clear that renewable energy is essential to mitigate climate change and that the RE [renewable energy] sector is not developing as fast as it needs to and that a socially owned and controlled sector can push its development far

---

[44] Interview with Loser, CER, 2018.
[45] www.parliament.gov.za/storage/app/media/Links/2018/November%202018/2 8-11-2018/Final%20Report%20-%20Eskom%20Inquiry%2028%20NOV .pdf.
[46] www.iol.co.za/business-report/energy/opinion-south-africas-energy-sector-needs-a-transition-plan-10783292.
[47] Eskom CFO Calib Cassim, at www.moneyweb.co.za/news/south-africa/wide-ranging-post-sona-interview-with-eskom-cfo/.

faster than it is currently doing" (Cloete 2018: 4–5).[48] The South
African Federation on Trade Unions (SAFTU, a new trade union confederation created in 2017 by breakaway unions) agreed in a July 2018
conference that fossil fuels must be phased out while addressing working-class and workers' interests (Morgan and Domingo 2018: 13–14).
Given the mix actually on offer in South African government policy –
wind and solar power, produced by private firms, with inadequate
protection for coal workers and communities – the labor movement
did not join the Life After Coal campaign in its court case, however.
Instead, it joined an obscure group, Transform RSA, in legally challenging REIPPPP's wind and solar contracts and protested against the
closing of coal plants (Cloete 2018).[49] The labor movement's actions
have picked the side of fossil fuels, notwithstanding its insistence that it
stands with the other side in favor of climate action.

When Cyril Ramaphosa took the presidency and named new ministers in 2018, one of his first major policy decisions was to force Eskom
to sign the REIPPPP contracts it had avoided. Another draft version of
the IRP came a few months later, also showing that the balance of
forces had returned to supporting wind and solar power. New Minister
of Energy Jeff Radebe stated clearly that the "basic rationale" for
building renewable energy was South Africa's international climate
commitment, although he also drew a longer domestic time frame
back to the 1998 White Paper on Energy Policy (Department of
Minerals and Energy 1998).[50] The first post-Zuma IRP was written
without the participation of the EIUG and distributed in
August 2018.[51] The IRP had no new nuclear power in the period
ending 2030 (Department of Energy 2018: 41). Its longer time coverage
to 2050 even showed decommissioning of the small existing nuclear
generation (ibid.: 49), although an amended version of this IRP in 2019
planned instead to extend the lifespan of the existing Koeberg station
by twenty years (Department of Energy 2019a: 15). The 2018 IRP draft
estimated that 200 MW of distributed generation will be added

[48] Karl Cloete is the National Union of Metalworkers of South Africa's (NUMSA) deputy general secretary and he is writing here in the *SA Labour Bulletin*.
[49] http://saftu.org.za/renewable-energy-is-necessary-but-not-at-expense-of-jobs-says-saftu/.
[50] Media speech on February 24, 2019. Online at www.ee.co.za/article/the-status-of-electricity-generation-in-south-africa.html.
[51] Interview with van Staden, EIUG, 2018.

annually, and the next year's revision raised that to an estimated 500 MW/year, acknowledging that consumers had moved ahead of policy regulating this (ibid.: 16).

The 2018 IRP draft noted yet another fall in demand and prioritized private electricity developers as generators over Eskom. It included the new coal contracted from IPPs, creating an excess supply of electricity and some gap years in solar and wind procurement (Department of Energy 2018: 41). Significant coal plant decommissioning – 12 GW by 2030, 28 GW by 2040, 35 GW by 2050 – would eventually bring down the share of coal in the electricity matrix, helping to meet climate goals and further sidelining Eskom's generation share. Coal's share would have dropped more quickly with no annual build limits for wind and solar power in the modeling (Department of Energy 2018: 11–12).

The 2018 and 2019 IRP drafts were not finalized on their original schedules and energy analyst Chris Yelland attributed the delay to the ongoing opposition of labor movements, who prefer more coal and nuclear production through Eskom than the draft contemplated.[52] The 2019 amendment of this draft, responding to almost 6,000 comments including from labor unions, explicitly backed away from the question of whether Eskom or IPPs would build new electricity plants. Instead, it asserted a clear conclusion that least-cost considerations supported only solar, wind, and gas plants, whoever would build them (Department of Energy 2019a: 64, 82). Despite this, when yet another revised IRP was finally adopted in October 2019, small nuclear power and various kinds of "clean coal" had slipped back into the adopted version (Department of Energy 2019b: 11–12), while another 6,400 MW of wind power were also added (ibid.: 42). A strategy was to be developed that would allow Eskom to participate in building new capacity (ibid.: 17). These were the compromises that emerged in final discussions.

In its comments on the 2018 draft, Eskom corrected some factual information but largely agreed with the draft, a radical shift in position.[53] Not surprisingly, the renewable energy industry sectors were again arguing for more and more regular wind and solar procurement, as the industries were already set back significantly by the two

---

[52] www.ee.co.za/article/analysis-paralysis-over-south-africas-irp-for-electricity-presents-massive-economic-risk.html#.XEAhtKTLeEc.

[53] www.ee.co.za/wp-content/uploads/2018/12/Eskom-comments-to-DoE-on-Draft-IRP-2018.pdf.

years (2016–2018) when Eskom would not sign contracts.[54] The energy and environmental NGOs sent a letter together in October 2018 demanding an urgent shift from fossil fuels to renewable energy, with no nuclear energy, and asking for a Just Transition plan that addresses the concerns of workers. They also asked for fuller consultation.[55]

The same paragraph (in all the post-2018 versions) mentions concerns for coal communities and workers after decommissioning but notes that there is no quantification of the full costs or socioeconomic impacts on them (Department of Energy 2019b: 44). The final version references the International Labour Organization's 2015 principles for a just transition and says that the multiple existing just transition initiatives should be brought together in one.[56] The final version also makes an explicit choice to prioritize economic impacts and energy security over shutting down electricity plants that are not in compliance with environmental regulations (ibid.: 44); this leaves host communities of coal plants in poor environmental conditions and limits their prospects of a just transition. Researchers at Stellenbosch University, led by Michelle Cruywagen, have used national data to make a first estimation of just transition costs for sunsetting coal in South Africa, putting them at US$360 million.[57] Two-thirds of these costs are for rehabilitating the coal communities, while one-third are labor-related costs.[58]

In summary, electricity build plans proved to be the major site of contention targeted by the status quo coalition. The Department of Energy was now the central state actor (versus the DEA in broader climate policy), but it also lacked the capacity to both develop and push through its own preferred electricity build plans, even with support from the renewable energy industry and much of civil society. The powerful, if declining, state-controlled utility Eskom was able to wield many tools to block an energy transition through wind and solar

---

[54] Interview with Levington, SAPVIA, 2018. See also the IRP itself, which summarizes comments received in Appendix D.

[55] www.egsa.org.za/resources/climate-change/response-to-irp-public-hearings-and-expectations-for-the-irp-itself/.

[56] www.ilo.org/wcmsp5/groups/public/—ed_emp/—emp_ent/documents/publication/wcms_432859.pdf.

[57] Unless otherwise indicated, all currency numbers have been translated into approximate US dollar equivalents using historic currency conversion rates.

[58] www.dailymaverick.co.za/article/2019-12-10-r6-billion-first-estimate-of-just-transition-in-south-africa/.

power. This outcome fits with the theoretical expectation of the climate political economy that incumbent fossil fuel sectors will strongly resist their own obsolescence. That outcome was also reinforced by a less systematic factor, namely the Zuma administration's deep and corrupt commitment to building nuclear power instead. Together, they have strongly undermined the development of wind and solar power in South Africa, notwithstanding the country's climate action commitments.

2.4 Brazilian Climate Capacity and Commitments

In contrast to South Africa, Brazilian GHG emissions have come disproportionately from deforestation and land-use change. Annual rates of deforestation dropped substantially after 2005 before recently rising again (Figure 2.3).[59] Most electricity has been generated through hydropower, usually lower in GHG emissions than fossil fuel plants (Barros et al. 2011).[60] In the energy sector itself, however, GHG emissions have increased in Brazil almost every measured year. A major driver of these increases is the production and consumption of the petroleum fields discovered offshore in 2007 (Observatório do Clima 2018: 20), so Brazil also has an incumbent fossil fuel with powerful supporters, although it is mostly used in transport applications.[61] These features have meant that much of the public debate about climate policy and implementation in Brazil has not been about electricity at all. The comparative success in controlling the major source of GHG emissions (deforestation) while economic growth continued also lowered the temperature of the debate and widened the coalition of supporters for a time before conflict flared again as agricultural interests pushed back after 2011 (Hochstetler and Viola 2012; Viola and Franchini 2018).

---

[59] This discussion uses SEEG data compiled by Brazilian climate and energy NGOs from public sources. The SEEG data is reliable and more regularly updated, so used here.

[60] Hydropower has historically been considered free of GHG emissions and the Brazilian government and many in the sector continue to agree (e.g., Tolmasquim 2016: 9). Empirical studies have found varying levels of emissions, particularly methane, in large tropical reservoirs, so many environmentalists question hydroelectric power on climate change grounds (e.g., Fearnside 2002).

[61] Interview with André Ferreira, Instituto de Energia e Meio Ambiente (IEMA), São Paulo, 2018. Ferreira leads the energy analysis of SEEG.

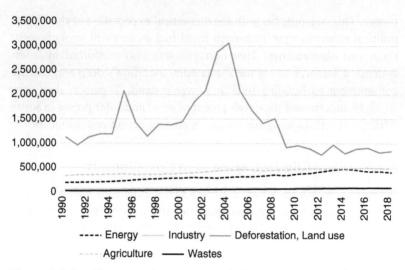

Figure 2.3 Brazilian greenhouse gas emissions (Gg CO_2eq) by sector, 1990–2018
Source: http://plataforma.seeg.eco.br/total_emission.

It is also straightforward to identify the actors on either side of a low-carbon transition in Brazil, but they have much less to do with the electricity sector than in South Africa. One of the most active cleavages has been between the coalition of both principled and self-interested actors trying to stop deforestation and the agribusiness group that has concrete economic interests in turning forests into fields and grazing areas (Aamodt 2018). Much of the fight over Brazil's climate positions has been between them. In addition, Brazil discovered new deep-sea oil fields in 2007, creating another set of actors to resist turning away from fossil fuels. Without a strong fossil fuel presence in the electricity sector, it has remained largely outside the lines of contention. In fact, wind and solar power enjoy broad bipartisan support, even from President Bolsonaro who is committed to promoting economic growth over environmental protection in the Amazon and elsewhere. This section outlines how Brazil's climate action capacity has developed in this quite different context.

2.4.1 Early Developments and Actors

Brazilian state capacity in the environmental area began earlier and has reached farther than that in South Africa. Brazil's first national environmental agency was created in 1973 and grew rapidly. Environmental framework legislation was written in 1981 and an environmental ministry followed in 1985 (Hochstetler and Keck 2007). State-level environmental agencies made big gains in controlling pollution in the 1980s, even as deforestation rose steadily after the 1970s, gaining ever more national and international attention with minimal effects. Brazil chose to host the UN Conference on Environment and Development (UNCED) in 1992 despite being a climate and biodiversity villain due to its inability and unwillingness to gain control over its Amazon region (Hochstetler and Keck 2007; Viola and Franchini 2018).

The Ministry of Science and Technology (MCT) was the first agency to take on climate change for Brazil, gaining the responsibility in 1994. Much of its agenda was internationally focused, helping the Foreign Ministry Itamaraty to develop its climate positions in the negotiations for the UNFCCC, launched at the 1992 conference. The MCT was instrumental in developing global agreements that exempted Brazil from immediate international obligations for climate action, like the idea of Common but Differentiated Responsibilities and the Kyoto Protocol that reserved climate action for developed countries (Lisboa 2002). With the Foreign Ministry, the MCT continues to advocate for the claim that the historical responsibility of developed countries for GHG emissions should make them the first and still primary actors to take on responsibility for reducing emissions (Carvalho 2012; Viola and Franchini 2018: 78–79, 152). Even so, the MCT oversaw the first Brazilian reports on its climate actions and developed systems for collecting and reporting data on its GHG emissions.[62] It presided over early widening of climate policy discussions to include other ministries in the Inter-ministerial Commission on Climate Change of 1999 and the Brazilian Forum on Climate Change, created in 2000 to bring the private sector and civil society into the debate.

2.4.2 *Conquering Deforestation and Building Climate Capacity and Commitments*

The profile of the Ministry of Environment in climate politics began to rise in 2003, when Marina Silva became president Lula da Silva's (no

---

[62] Sirene.mcti.gov.br, to become sirene.mctic.gov.br.

relation) first minister of environment in the Workers' Party's (PT's) first national administration. As a former PT Senate leader with personal origins in an Amazonian rubber-tapper family, she had both partisan and activist credibility that allowed her to play a larger role than previous ministers had in this comparatively weak ministry (Hochstetler 2017). Silva's profile rose with her administration's unprecedented ability to bring deforestation – the country's largest source of GHG emissions – under control (see Figure 2.3).

The story of how Brazil's deforestation was controlled, especially in the Amazon region, is complex and beyond the scope of this book. Scholars have identified a number of simultaneous developments. These include new command and control programs of the Ministry of Environment itself like the Plan for Action to Prevent and Control Deforestation in the Legal Amazon (PPCDAm), stronger satellite monitoring, and demarcation of new protected areas (Carvalho 2012: 157; Schwartzman, Moutinho, and Hamburg 2012; Viola and Franchini 2018). They also include private governance initiatives for the soy and beef farming that spurred deforestation (Viola and Franchini 2018: 108–109; Waroux et al. 2019).[63] For Silva's executive secretary, João Paulo Capobianco, the most important result of all these individual developments was to create a sense among potential deforesters that the state was present in the region and observing their behaviors for the first time, a sense that has declined since revisions to the Forest Code in 2012.[64]

Silva drew on the expertise of Brazilian civil society both to populate her ministry and as additional, sometimes critical, supports from outside the government (Aamodt 2018; Nasser de Oliveira 2015; Observatório do Clima 2008; Oliveira 2016). Environmental and human rights activists, including Capobianco himself, held 38 percent of her leadership positions (Abers and Oliveira 2015: 10). These activists, insiders and outsiders, were especially important in helping to redefine deforestation as a climate change issue.

As the global climate negotiations began to demand more efforts from large developing countries like Brazil after 2007, the issue moved

[63] Additional studies question the results of some of these programs, especially as deforestation rates have crept up since 2012 (e.g., Gibbs et al. 2016; Gibbs et al. 2015; Richards, Arima, VanWey, Cohn, and Bhattarai 2017).
[64] Interview with João Paulo Capobianco, former executive secretary of the Ministry of Environment, São Paulo, 2018.

up the domestic political agenda. The presidency began a more active role in Lula's second term, overseeing the writing of a National Plan on Climate Change and presiding over a new Inter-ministerial Committee on Climate Change that would oversee it. The Ministry of Environment would now be its executive, with eight other ministries and the Forum, while the MCT continued to coordinate the technical side (Schaeffer et al. 2015: 8–9). Silva had clashed many times with Lula's government in his first term and the two took time to negotiate her participation as minister in his second term. Lula wanted Silva to take on the climate role because of international acclamation for her success in deforestation and she wanted his support for a ministerial reorganization and strengthening (Oliveira 2016).

The two preferences coincided in a new Secretariat of Climate Change and Environmental Quality in the Ministry of Environment in 2007. Its first secretary was Thelma Krug, who had helped develop Brazil's remote sensing systems for monitoring deforestation and later became vice-chair of the IPCC. Silva also oversaw the creation of a professional environmental career path. While no new positions in the Ministry of Environment were advertised from 1995 to 2002, leaving only occupants with short-term contracts, Silva hired 1,474 specialists in her 5 years through public competitions (Abers and Oliveira 2015: 17). These career positions are especially important for maintaining the ministry's activities even when elected politicians are less interested in climate action, as has been the case since 2011.[65] New resources accompanied the changes, including almost US\$1.3 billion donated by Germany, Norway, and Petrobras to an Amazon Fund for deforestation efforts that has been administered by Brazil's National Economic and Social Development Bank (BNDES) (Carvalho 2012: 159).[66] Remarkable capacity improvements thus accompanied the new administrative home for climate change.

There is no question that this new state capacity was an important part of the story of Brazilian climate action, especially the improvements in its deforestation tallies. At the same time, the final push for climate action depended on widening the climate debate beyond just government bureaucracies and environmental movements, a process that both made climate action commitments possible and also set the

---

[65] Interview with Capobianco, MMA, Brasília, 2018.
[66] www.fundoamazonia.gov.br/en/donations/.

stage for subsequent decline. After 2007, a growing number of actors signed on to support climate change. These included those with instrumental commitments to climate action, like the Amazonian governors who saw possible international funds for forest protection and coalitions of industrialists who worried that there might be restrictions on their exports if they failed to push Brazilian climate action forward (Hochstetler and Viola 2012).

When Marina Silva left her position and then decided to run for president in the 2010 election, climate action became a central focus of electoral politics. The Brazilian population is broadly supportive of climate action, with 86 percent agreeing that it is an important issue.[67] All three major presidential candidates went to the 2009 climate negotiation in Copenhagen and competed with each other to support climate action. It was in this atmosphere that Brazil made its first voluntary commitment to international climate action in 2009. It also passed a comprehensive climate law at the beginning of 2010, although Lula did veto the clauses that promised a move away from fossil fuel production under pressure from the Ministry of Mines and Energy (Aamodt 2018: 15). The unprecedented gains in controlling deforestation underpinned both commitments. Important parts of climate action have evident multiparty support in Brazil, like this climate legislation which was supported by all major parties.

2.4.3 Retreats and Gains in Climate Policy Implementation after 2010

The political consensus behind climate action was never complete. A caucus of agriculturalists and others with an interest in deforestation began to gain strength and political power in the National Congress after 2003, trying to roll back EIA, indigenous rights, and the 1996 Forest Code with its strict limits on deforestation on private land. After the 2010 election, they had the power to force through a revised Forest Code in 2012, over the objection of environmentalists, the Senate, and the executive (Viola and Franchini 2018: 140–141). Business leaders slipped from sight as it became clear that the United States would not take climate action (Viola and Franchini 2018: 161). In general, the

---

[67] www.pewglobal.org/2015/11/05/1-concern-about-climate-change-and-its-consequences/.

next years were overwhelmed by larger political phenomena like economic recession, a huge corruption scandal, the controversial impeachment of Lula's copartisan Dilma Rousseff, and the eventual election in 2018 of a new president, Jair Bolsonaro.

Bolsonaro represented a break with not just Brazil's two leading parties but many of the foundations of Brazilian politics, too. His environmental agenda looks very much like that of the agriculturalists (Vialli 2018). His influential sons, also politicians, are even climate change deniers, previously a rarity in Brazil.[68] As they provide active political leadership against climate action for the first time, the thinness of popular commitment to it has become clearer. With a political system that is increasingly divided between supporters and critics of the PT, the anti-PT position is linked to being against climate action.[69] Nonetheless, the only positive promise that the Bolsonaro campaign made for environmental governance was to continue Brazil's renewable energy programs (Vialli 2018), suggesting that this is a rare pocket of policy consensus.

At the same time, smaller-scale changes set up both advances and retreats on climate policy. Under Rousseff and her replacement, her vice president Michel Temer, environmental budgets were already cut drastically after 2013 (Hochstetler 2017; SEEG 2018a: 48; Viola and Franchini 2018: 140). Such budget cuts undermined the capacity improvements that came earlier. Rousseff's Minister of Environment, Izabella Teixeira, was technically respected internationally but had few links to environmentalists and was perceived as following Rousseff's pro-growth strategy without questions. Rousseff favored the petroleum sector and other big development projects central to the corruption scandal (Arruda de Almeida and Zagaris 2015; Hochstetler 2017). The Temer and Bolsonaro governments are more committed to market forces and austerity, but they follow Rousseff in having little positive agenda for environmental protection. Deforestation has climbed back up to a point where Brazil's ability to meet its 2020 commitments is in question.[70]

---

[68] www1.folha.uol.com.br/ambiente/2018/11/hostilidade-de-filhos-de-bolsonaro-a-aquecimento-global-preocupa-ambientalistas.shtml.
[69] Interview with Andre Nahur, Coordinator Climate Change and Energy, WWF, Brasilia, 2018.
[70] Interview with Capobianco, MMA, 2018.

Meanwhile, the Ministry of Environment has overseen steps toward implementing the climate commitments. Decree 7390/2010 wrote the first five action plans for implementation, including energy plans that placed the Ministry of Energy's planning processes at the center (see Section 2.5). Some clauses like the proposed carbon tax proved too difficult to negotiate, but other proposals like adaptation measures moved quickly and became part of Brazil's Nationally Determined Contribution to the Paris Agreement.[71] After a significant lull in 2015–2016 when few parts of Brazil's climate policy infrastructure were operating, a coalition of business and civil society actors came together to reactivate the Brazilian Forum on Climate Change, forming eleven technical bodies that formulated proposals for climate implementation to give to the 2018 presidential candidates (SEEG 2018a: 48), as they had done in 2014. The group did succeed in getting the Paris Agreement ratified in 2017 (Instituto Clima e Sociedade 2018). Brazil's closest equivalent to South Africa's EIUG of big industrial consumers has not prioritized climate and renewable energy, although some of its members do.[72] Yet sixty large businesses, whose revenues equal about 45 percent of the national GDP, have rejoined the Brazilian Business Council for Sustainable Development (CEBDS) and helped develop the set of ten recommendations for the 2018 presidential candidates. Four of their proposals addressed the electricity sector, urging the government to exceed its Paris promises to have 45 percent renewable energy, including wind and solar, in the energy system (CEBDS 2018: 13).

The dominant role of deforestation in Brazil's GHG emissions profile has created a very different politics of climate action there. It has been highly contentious, more so than in South Africa, but the contention has remained largely outside the electricity sector, which has little fossil fuel production. This set the possibility of more technically oriented electricity planning in the sector, which did appear, following the climate political economy logic. As Section 2.5 shows, however, that planning has so far favored wind power but not solar, suggesting that it is influenced by more than just climate motivation, which favors both.

---

[71] Interview with Adriano Santhiago de Oliveira, Departamento de Mudanças Climáticas, MMA, Brasília, 2014.

[72] Interview with Victor Hugo Iocca, Coordinator of Electric Energy, Associação Brasileiro de Grandes Consumidoras Industriais e de Consumidores Livres (ABRACE), Brasília, 2018.

2.5 Brazil: Translating Climate Plans into Energy Choices

In the 1990s, the Cardoso government partially privatized the electricity sector, taking electricity planning from the parastatal Eletrobras in favor of private, market-driven investment (see Chapter 3). Multiple economic and fiscal crises meant that there was essentially no new capacity built in the sector in the 1990s. When a severe drought brought the electricity system into its own crisis in 2001, widespread blackouts set the stage for the first wind procurement in 2002, through the Program of Incentives for Alternative Energy in Electricity (Proinfa). The timing of the introduction of alternative renewables into the electricity grid thus reflected the need to reduce the system's overreliance on large hydro, an energy security concern.[73] Proinfa was a product of the energy bureaucracy, preceding broader public debate.

In the Cardoso version (Law 10,438/2002), the program invited independent power producers to provide 1,100 MW each of wind, small hydro, and biomass-based electricity to the system, responding to a feed-in tariff guaranteed for twenty years. In a second phase, nonhydro renewable energy was to reach 10 percent of national electricity consumption by 2022.[74] The incoming PT government (2003–2010) amended the law the next year (Law 10,762/03), keeping the initial tranche but introducing an auction system for the second stage (Lucas, Ferroukhi, and Hawila 2013; Tolmasquim 2012). In this system, the electricity regulator ANEEL holds periodic auctions where the hundreds of electricity generators in the country can bid to supply electricity under long-term, fixed price contracts. Some reserve auctions are only for particular kinds of electricity while others allow different types to compete against each other with different caps in price for each type. The continuity of Proinfa across the administrative handoff shows again that nonhydro renewables have been largely a nonpartisan issue in Brazil.

Lula did recreate state electricity planning after a hiatus of almost a decade. The Ministry of Mines and Energy gained the Energy

---

[73] Interview with Elbia Melo (now Gannoum), Chief Executive Officer of the Brazilian Wind Energy Association (ABEEólica, *Associação Brasileira de Energia Eólica*), São Paulo, 2014. J. Ricardo Tranjan conducted this interview for the book, along with others that are identified in footnotes by his initials (JRT). Gannoum was then chief economist in the Ministry of Mines and Energy and conducted the analyses showing the feasibility of the Proinfa program.

[74] www.planalto.gov.br/ccivil_03/leis/2002/L10438.htm.

Research Enterprise (EPE) in 2004, which carries out long-term indicative planning for the sector (e.g., Empresa de Pesquisa Energética 2014b). Despite the break in planning, EPE was able to put together a high-capacity and good-sized bureaucracy quickly, with most employees hired following civil service exams. The bureaucracy has strong technical skills, using optimization analyses to generate complex grid expansion plans based on criteria that include site and economic data, forecasts of future demand, a preference for low-carbon options, and other criteria.[75]

These result in annual recommendations of the amounts of different kinds of electricity that should be procured and lists of possible locations and projects. They also recommend price ceiling levels for the auctions based on economic analyses. The reports are dense with justifications and supplemental analyses and can run over 800 pages each.[76] The Ministry of Mines and Energy then plans specific auctions each year, also consulting with the electricity regulator ANEEL, and EPE sets maximum prices (Bradshaw 2018: 94). These processes are all overseen by the National Council on Energy Policy (CNPE), created in 1997 (Law 9478) and presided over by the Minister of Mines and Energy. It can make both overarching and detailed changes in national energy plans, but the vast majority of its interventions are in the oil and gas sector, not electricity.[77]

EPE's ten-year planning documents are produced almost every year, with occasional thirty-year plans. They see little of the drama of the South African IRP even though drafts are also presented for discussion and comment. The one exception is in the area of hydropower, where EPE technocrats were surprised when environmental activists mobilized strongly against their first plan that showed that water resources would allow forty more large hydroelectric dams, mostly in the Amazon region (Empresa de Pesquisa Energética 2006: 281). From EPE's point of view, it was only a technical statement about what physically could be built,[78] but the listing has been taken as a signal

---

[75] Interviews with Ricardo Cavalcante Furtado, Superintendent of Environment, Empresa de Pesquisa Energética, Rio de Janeiro, 2009 and a technical consultant, Empresa de Pesquisa Energética, Rio de Janeiro, 2012.

[76] They are readily available online at www.epe.gov.br/pt/publicacoes-dados-abertos/publicacoes/plano-decenal-de-expansao-de-energia-pde.

[77] See the resolutions listed at www.mme.gov.br/web/guest/conselhos-e-comites/cnpe.

[78] Interview with Furtado, EPE, 2009.

of governmental intentions and helped to mobilize a large coalition of national and international actors against large hydropower in the Amazon (Bratman 2014; Hochstetler and Tranjan 2016; Zhouri and Valencio 2014). In addition to pressuring the government, activists have also targeted the firms, banks, and institutional investors involved (e.g., Greenpeace 2016a). The Movement of those Affected by Dams (MAB) leads a more openly critical group of social movements and labor organizations in the Labor and Peasant Energy Forum (POCE) that wants to end the entire private concession system along with large hydropower (Just Transition Research Collaborative 2018: 17–18).[79] The mobilized opposition to hydropower has been mentioned in numerous planning documents as a limit on Brazil's electricity choices (e.g., Tolmasquim 2016: 123–126).

Beyond hydropower, there has been much less attention to the plans, which remain largely technical documents for bureaucratic audiences. While comments are invited on drafts, they do not typically change the documents although industry lobbies and political actors may influence outcomes.[80] Even so, a cluster of NGOs in the Climate Observatory (*Observatório do Clima*), a Working Group on Infrastructure and Energy (*GT Infraestructura e Energia*), and a Front for a New Energy Policy (*Frente por Uma Nova Política Energética*) individually and collectively comment on EPE's plans and have positioned themselves as strong supporters of more wind and solar power as well as pressuring from outside governmental processes.[81] Some NGOs, like the Institute of Energy and Environment (IEMA) and WWF-Brasil have contributed numerous studies that aim to provide a technical basis for environmentally sound energy choices (e.g., WWF-Brasil 2015a, 2015b).[82] Unlike the anti-hydro activists, these are more accepting of the basic framework of the energy system, even as they work to improve its choices. Some organizations like Greenpeace Brasil span the two types. Civil society engaged EPE more directly starting in 2016, when the Climate and Society Institute (*Instituto Clima e Sociedade*)

---

[79] Interview with Gilberto Cervinski, Member of the National Coordination of the MAB (JRT), São Paulo, 2013.
[80] Interviews with energy analyst, EPE, Rio de Janeiro, 2014 and EPE technical consultant, 2012.
[81] Interviews with Marcelo Lima, Energy Campaigner, Greenpeace-Brasil, São Paulo, 2018; Ferreira, IEMA, 2018; Nahur, WWF-Brasil, 2018.
[82] http://energiaeambiente.org.br/produto_tipo/publicacoes.

organized a series of events that brought EPE's analysts together with civil society and business to discuss the climate–energy nexus (Instituto Clima e Sociedade 2017).[83]

Businesses themselves are not united on what kind of electricity to build and the importance of climate change in the choices. The Brazilian Association of Large Industrial Energy Consumers and Free Consumers (ABRACE) focuses strongly on price issues, clearly placing them above climate concerns, which it does not mention in public statements on energy policy.[84] As already discussed, sixty of the largest Brazilian businesses in the Leaders Council of the Brazilian Business Council for Sustainable Development (CEBDS) are quite a bit more in favor of climate action and increasing renewable energy, including wind and solar power (CEBDS 2018). The wind and solar power industry associations also frequently cite the climate benefits of their industries.

EPE's plans have sometimes been outweighed by economic crisis responses from the rest of the government, as when the National Council on Energy Policy canceled an expected auction for wind and solar power in 2016 when demand lagged, without any consultation or warning (Bradshaw 2018: 112). While responding to the 2008 global financial crisis, the Lula government also allowed municipalities and states to propose their own shovel-ready energy projects for inclusion in the Program for Growth Acceleration (PAC) (Burrier 2016), to the dismay of EPE's analysts.[85]

Looking at the planning documents themselves to see how they reflect climate concerns, the very first one makes only a single general reference to international climate agreements (Ministério de Minas e Energia 2006: 241). Subsequent plans spend increasing amounts of time discussing the greenhouse effect and climate policies. The IPCC's Fourth Assessment Report inspired EPE to begin including GHG emissions in its optimization models in 2007 (Ministério de Minas e Energia 2007: 55) and to begin using IPCC methodology in 2010 (Ministério de Minas e Energia 2010: 318). Starting in 2011, EPE, through meetings of the Brazilian Forum on Climate Change, acknowledged that its ten-

[83]   www.icv.org.br/2017/05/organizacoes-socioambientais-abrem-espaco-de-dialogo-com-epe-para-discutir-planejamento-da-matriz-eletrica.

[84]   For example, abrace.org.br/2018/01.26/corajosas-arrojadas-e-desafiantes. Interview with Iocca.

[85]   Interview with EPE consultant 2012; interview with Celso Knijnik, Director of the Energy Program of the PAC, Ministério de Planejamento, Brasília, 2014.

year plans need to help Brazil meet the specific commitments the country made in Copenhagen (Ministério de Minas e Energia 2011: 283) and later in Paris.

At the same time, the organization uniformly insists that Brazil's dependence on hydropower means that it does not need to decarbonize its electricity sector; it is already one of the cleanest in the world (Tolmasquim 2016).[86] Thus, EPE's primary arguments for wind and solar power recognize them as low-carbon sources and increasingly a substitute for hydropower with its nonclimate social and environmental problems, but that was not the primary motivator for bringing either into the grid. In fact, there is no good climate change rationale for procuring lots of wind power and very little solar power, as Brazil did until 2017. A climate rationale would seek both.

Wind power originally found a place in the grid plans as a comparatively cheap and quick way to diversify the matrix and provide energy security (Ministério de Minas e Energia 2006: 77). As Figure 2.4 shows, EPE's models were originally quite conservative on wind power, projecting nearly flat procurement totals over the next decade with just Proinfa's low levels. But the modeled procurement levels, which always begin with the real current-year totals, began to rise quickly in every year in the plans produced from 2009 to 2018. The turning point was in the 2010 plan, after the winning bids to build wind power in the first auction in 2009 were very competitive versus other fuel sources, "against all market predictions" (Ministério de Minas e Energia 2010: 57). From then on, EPE considered wind to be a climate-friendly substitute for hydropower.

EPE noted in 2010 that it did not plan to contract more fossil fuel plants beyond those already auctioned and being constructed, now that wind and other renewables had shown themselves to be "adequate and appropriate," including on price (Ministério de Minas e Energia 2010: 77). This decision showed up in subsequent planning for fossil fuels in the electricity sector, as seen in the leveling off in Figure 2.5. The rise of

---

[86] EPE does not accept the contention by some activists and scholars that Brazilian hydropower has high GHG emissions in the form of gases leaking from reservoirs. Instead, EPE draws on its own and other studies that concluded that only the Balbina dam had GHG emissions higher than those of fossil fuel plants and that better design can lower the emissions (Ministério de Minas e Energia 2007: 437–438). That is not the same as saying that they have no emissions, but it has satisfied EPE (Tolmasquim 2016: 112).

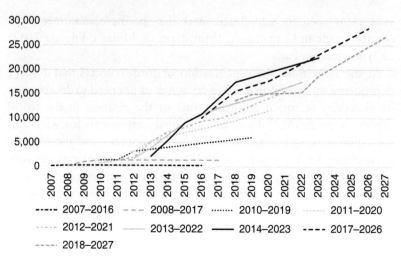

Figure 2.4 Wind power total procurement projections in successive 10-year plans in Brazil, 2007–2018
Source: Calculated from data in Ministério de Minas e Energia, 2007–2018.
Note : Starting points for each series are actual contracted/built quantities for that year.

fossil fuel sources in the electricity matrix after the 2001 electricity crisis had alarmed activists and is one of the pieces of evidence often cited to illustrate Brazil's backward movement on climate implementation (e.g., Viola and Franchini 2018: 89–91).

However, the most significant increases in planned fossil fuel plants came in the 2018 draft, for the decade to 2027. This year's plan reflected a major change in electricity planning as the penetration of wind power was scheduled to reach 12 percent of the grid by 2027 with solar half that. Given the intermittency of these forms of electricity, EPE now planned a massive build-out of natural gas plants to complement the more variable new forms of electricity at peak times (Ministério de Minas e Energia 2018: 56) (Figure 2.5). The plan also indicated that Brazil would retire some dirtier oil and diesel plants, but the addition of so much natural gas – effectively replacing hydropower as a system stabilizer – will push GHG emissions up and risks other environmental impacts (Instituto de Energia e Meio Ambiente 2018a). The proposal has led energy and climate NGOs to prioritize finding an alternative to natural

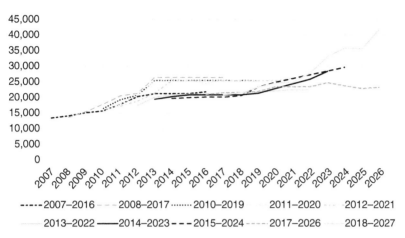

Figure 2.5 Fossil fuel projections in successive 10-year plans in Brazil, 2007–2018
Sources: Calculated from data in Ministério de Minas e Energia, 2007–2018.

gas and to resist the new gas, but a strong international and domestic oil and gas lobby favors the greater use of gas in its own right.

Solar power had been mostly omitted from the annual plans, without comment, except for some use in solar water heaters. This major tool for combating climate change was not attractive to planners, although the ten-year plan of 2012 noted that it would become desirable if global prices continued to drop (Ministério de Minas e Energia 2012: 90). Two years later, solar went into the build plan, with an auction scheduled in 2014 for delivery in 2017 and more growth afterwards (Ministério de Minas e Energia 2014: 90). Although nothing had changed about solar power except its price, it now was lauded for all of the good qualities of wind power, including its use as a substitute for fossil fuels. The delayed start showed that other logics – those covered in Chapters 3 and 4 of this book – had outweighed solar power's climate change virtues. Subsequent plans put solar power's rate of increase on the fast track that wind had followed (see Figure 2.6).

EPE manages the centralized part of the grid. It calculates expected aggregate demand and devises build plans to meet it. Meanwhile, however, the electricity regulator ANEEL wrote new distributed solar regulations in 2012 and more permissive ones in 2015, largely for nonclimate-related reasons. As these took hold, EPE's 2017 plan

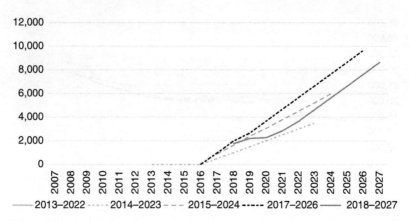

Figure 2.6 Grid-scale solar projections in successive 10-year plans in Brazil, 2007–2018
Sources: Calculated from data in Ministério de Minas e Energia, 2007–2018.

suddenly recognized the possibility of 770,000 distributed connections by 2026, mostly solar power (Ministério de Minas e Energia 2017: 221). This was a vertiginous increase after the 670 small generators counted in the previous plan (Ministério de Minas e Energia 2015: 373). After even faster take-up next year, the 2018 plan anticipated 1.35 million adopters by 2027, or 11.9 GW, or up to 21 GW depending on the regulations chosen (Ministério de Minas e Energia 2018: 209). For EPE, this entered into its plans mostly as lower centralized demand. Almost all of these new distributed systems will be in urban areas, but, in remote regions, they may replace the diesel-based systems that currently mean that just 0.8 percent of the electricity supply generates 10 percent of its GHG emissions (Bezerra et al. 2017: 5). Since the rationale for distributed power in Brazil has been mostly price-based, all these points are discussed further in Chapter 4.

While decentralized solar power expanded on a largely nonclimate track, the increase in centralized solar power was especially quick after Brazil sent its Nationally Determined Contribution (NDC) document to the Paris Agreement. Solar power had to be forced into the procurement model as a policy choice in order to keep Brazil on track for its Paris pledge of keeping its GHG emissions 37 percent below the 2005 levels by 2025. EPE warned that emissions from electricity would then be at only 3 percent of Brazil's total emissions and the sector really could not do more to help Brazil meet its Paris pledge (Ministério de Minas e Energia 2018: 245).

As the final point suggests, Brazil continued to see high and growing GHG emissions in the energy sector, even as they were increasingly limited in the electricity sector itself. There is a kind of schizophrenia between EPE's careful parsing of the GHG implications of the electricity grid and the ways it fails to discuss and propose containing the freely growing emissions from oil production and use, grown to 57 percent of all energy and industrial process emissions in 2018 (SEEG 2018b: 2). The electricity and petroleum halves of the annual ten-year plans are strikingly distinct. While the press and activists have noted the GHG emissions from oil production, refining, and use, Petrobras itself has an optimistic discourse on carbon capture and storage and expresses certainty that environmental risks can be managed in the environmental licensing process – arguments readily accepted by its regulators and apparently EPE (Braathen 2015; Viglio, Di Giulio, and da Costa Ferreira 2017).

The most open debate on the petroleum has been about how oil and gas royalties would be distributed. A small portion originally went to a Social Fund that supported climate action among other things but was later mostly moved to health and education. Coastal producing communities depend heavily on royalty payouts even as the payments appear to have contributed to local resource curses and weaker development outcomes (Lima-de-Oliveira and Libby 2017). Brazil's major trade union, the Unified Workers' Confederation (CUT), attends the global climate negotiations and has participated in discussions of just transition internationally.[87] Activists have brought little of the debate to Brazilian electricity except around hydropower (Just Transition Research Collaborative 2018: 17–18). Moving away from petroleum would present just transition challenges for oil workers and communities, but the debate is not far advanced in Brazil and has not been linked to wind and solar power at all.

Like coal in South Africa, oil production in Brazil is deeply embedded in the national political economy. Domestic oil production is about 12 percent of Brazilian GDP (Lima-de-Oliveira and Libby 2017: 577).

---

[87] See, for example, www.cut.org.br/artigos/cop-22-movimento-sindical-avanca-no-debate-sobre-transicao-justa-apesar-de-conju-d2b6.

The state-controlled oil company Petrobras received the single largest loans ever made by BNDES, over $13 billion in just a few large loans and credit facilities in 2009 (Hochstetler and Montero 2012: 1492). A new suite of tax and regulatory incentives for fossil fuels was developed between 2013 and 2017, notwithstanding Brazil's climate commitments (INESC 2018).

In 2014, a giant corruption scandal was uncovered based on state contracting and construction with Petrobras and large hydro and nuclear power at its heart (Arruda de Almeida and Zagaris 2015; Jucá, Renno, and Melo 2016). Called the *Lava Jato* (car wash) scandal, it has been corrosive for Brazilian politics, involving numerous high-ranking politicians, and economically very costly for the firms involved and the economy as a whole. It is harder to see more specific impacts on wind and solar power than in the South African case, however. The electricity projects most clearly involved – the Belo Monte hydroelectric dam and the Angra 3 nuclear plant – dated back to the 1970s in conception and were both included in EPE's first ten-year plan (Ministério de Minas e Energia 2007).[88] They were never directly counterpoised to the new kinds of electricity, and the wind and solar deployments of Figures 2.4 and 2.6 happened after they were already underway.

In short, if this were a book about oil production, Brazil would have issues of just transition and state capture that would parallel South Africa's. In the South African case, those problems spilled over into the planning and procurement of wind and solar power while they did not in Brazil. State capacity may explain that in part, with the Brazilian EPE mastering a technical planning process that used climate rationales, among others, to steadily add wind power to the national grid. The near absence of solar power until after 2014 is less readily comprehensible through the lens of either state capacity or climate policy.

2.6 Conclusion

This chapter uses the lens of the climate policy arena to investigate the development of wind and solar power in Brazil and South Africa. Major sections of the chapter examine whether and how coalitions of

---

[88] Interview with Celso Knijnik, Director of Energy of the Program of Growth Acceleration (PAC), Brasília, 2018.

state, civil society, and business actors in each country joined to write climate action commitments and then instantiate them in concrete electricity planning processes. The logic of the climate political economy includes two sides: the widespread but diffuse interest in action that will reduce future climate change by reducing GHG emissions and the concentrated interests that fossil fuel sectors have in resisting the existential threat of such action. Following the arguments of climate scholars, this requires a focus on the state's capacity to recognize that diffuse interest and then to formulate and implement policies even when powerful opponents resist. The two countries have fundamentally different starting positions in the climate political economy in that South Africa has a historically powerful coal-based electricity sector with many political and economic allies, while Brazil does not. In Chapter 1, I proposed that that difference should create inherently more conflictual and blocking dynamics around wind and solar power in the climate policy arena in South Africa, which might spill over to other domains. This chapter supports that proposal.

South Africa's state capacity to formulate and implement climate action was historically weak, especially compared to the powerful coal-based Minerals-Energy Complex. The DEA did slowly build the capacity to formulate climate institutions and policies after 2004, with some civil society and industry support. The larger story in South Africa, though, is of a country that has not quite been able to commit to either climate action or renewable energy. Even initial steps to break the monopoly of coal depended on more circumstantial developments, including an electricity supply crisis and Zuma's unexpected international climate action commitment at the 2009 negotiations in Copenhagen. Court cases brought by principled activists were most decisive in blocking the options of new nuclear or coal-fired power plants in the short term, skipping over limited state capacity to force climate action.

The state-controlled electricity parastatal Eskom has been the natural center of the anticipated opposition from the fossil fuel sector, as it is literally dependent on an economic model of generating electricity from coal. Eskom did not overtly block the development of climate policy altogether, although it and its allies raised many questions about specific instruments and time frames. The theoretically expected open resistance came to the building of wind and solar power itself. From the start, Eskom refused to follow a 2003 directive to include them and complied with early procurement of wind and solar power only as it struggled to

generate enough electricity to meet national demand. But Eskom outright refused to sign contracts for wind and solar power from 2016 to
2018 until a change of national president brought it back into compliance. From 2011 to 2019, the Department of Energy's repeated efforts
to update the electricity build planning documents showed widely fluc-
tuating proposals about how much coal, nuclear, wind, and solar power
should be built. All but the last, in late 2019, were blocked by a coalition
of Eskom, labor unions, and sectors of the governing ANC with close
ties to Zuma. They insisted that any climate action commitments must
be met with nuclear power, not wind and solar plants. Subsequent
chapters will show that this mobilized opposition spilled over into
other policy arenas and generally raised the levels of politicization and
conflict around wind and solar power in South Africa.

The fundamental logic of the climate policy arena, where actors who
are dependent on fossil fuel generation will strongly mobilize to protect
their own interests against climate action, is clearly relevant. For most of
these years, Eskom and its allies managed to outweigh the more limited
capacity of state agencies like the DEA and the Department of Energy,
which have favored wind and solar power installation. Over time, it has
become increasingly clear that the fossil fuel coalition's systematic interest
in protecting itself was also supported by the personal, corrupt interest of
Zuma and a small group around him in building nuclear power. Thus,
a state capture logic reinforced the more systematic climate logic in
restricting wind and solar power development. By contributing to
a broader weakening of Eskom's financial position and management
capacity, however, those corrupt interests may have inadvertently helped
lay a foundation for future climate action (Roberts and Geels 2019: 225).

In his first major international statement on climate change in
September 2019, President Ramaphosa struck very different notes, stressing South Africa's self-interest and global responsibility to take on serious
climate change commitments. He promised $11 billion for a Just
Transition Transaction Fund that was meant to recover Eskom's financial
strength and protect coal workers while transitioning away from coal –
only to have his government post a new version without that promise two
days later.[89] Those would have been critical promises that set South Africa

---

[89]   www.dirco.gov.za/docs/speeches/2019/cram0923.htm; www
      .dailymaverick.co.za/article/2019-10-02-ramaphosas-11bn-climate-fund-or-
      how-the-smart-money-could-turn-mpumalanga-into-the-envy-of-the-world/.

on a very different track, using just transition strategies to overcome the opposition from the fossil fuel sector. Their quick removal shows that South Africa continues to be deeply divided on how fully to take on a climate action agenda.

In contrast, Brazil does not have an incumbent fossil fuel sector in electricity generation, as it has relied mostly on hydropower. As a result, climate action debates – while contentious in themselves – rarely focus on electricity. Almost all of Brazil's GHG emissions have historically come from deforestation. Brazil's Ministry of Environment and its allies did, after 2004, build some remarkable capacity to reduce deforestation, which set the stage for more ambitious climate policy in 2009–2010. Climate action commitments drew on support from many sectors of Brazilian society in the first decade of the 2000s before opposition from agribusiness rolled back some of the gains in the second decade. Proponents of the diffuse and future interests associated with climate action have had a difficult time countering the rural sector's more immediate economic interests. In his speech to the United Nations in September 2019, President Bolsonaro struck a defiant and aggressive tone, calling media reports on fires and deforestation in the Amazon falsehoods with a colonialist spirit and asserting Brazilian sovereignty over an abstract "global interest." On climate, he quoted the biblical verse John 8:32: "Know the truth and the truth will set you free."[90] Throughout these ups and downs in climate policy and action, wind and solar power themselves retained cross-partisan support in Brazil. Five presidents from four political parties favored them, even President Bolsonaro, who had few other pro-environment positions.

Their insulation from the heat of climate action debates left wind and solar power development in the domain of technical energy planners in Brazil, who unveiled their plans with few of the conflicts of the South Africans. Starting with an initial tranche in 2001 and then much more after 2009, they scheduled ever larger shares of wind power procurement for the national electricity grid. They pointed out that this could both complement and replace hydropower as a climate-friendly source of electricity, helping Brazil to meet its climate action commitments. Although the same could be said of solar power, this was largely left out

[90] www.itamaraty.gov.br/pt-BR/discursos-artigos-e-entrevistas-categoria/presi dente-da-republica-federativa-do-brasil-discursos/20890-discurso-do-presidente-jair-bolsonaro-na-abertura-da-74-assembleia-geral-das-nacoes-unidas-nova-york-24-de-setembro-de-2019.

of the plans until 2014, despite Brazil's abundant solar resources. It is difficult to justify these different fates on climate grounds, suggesting that the difference between the two kinds of renewable energy must reflect the logic of one or more of the other chapters. However, the low-conflict approach to wind and solar power in Brazil is consistent with the larger political economy of climate change, as it derives from the absence of an equivalent actor to Eskom with its dependence on fossil fuels in the electricity sector.

The theoretical framing of this chapter posits that there is a widespread diffuse interest in reducing the emissions that result in climate change and asks to what extent the Brazilian and South African governments acknowledge that general interest. States do not only respond to the general interest, of course, but may also reflect the particular interests of politicians or institutions. In both countries, there were serious corruption scandals in the energy sector during the same years that wind and solar power were considered. Zuma and a small group of cronies targeted Eskom as one of the two state-controlled enterprises with the largest state procurement budgets. They pursued nuclear and coal projects from which they could personally benefit directly instead of wind and solar power, stunting the growth of the latter. There was also a widespread government procurement scandal in Brazil, which targeted the state-controlled oil company Petrobras and several large electricity projects, among many others. In the Brazilian case, the direct impact on wind and solar power acquisition was small. The influence of corrupt motivations in electricity procurement is not inevitable (it is different even in these two countries) and does not stem directly from the climate political economy. However, the clear possibility that public and private actors in the energy sector might seek private gains in large infrastructure projects should probably be recognized as an additional potential barrier to states' willingness and capacity to take effective decisions in favor of the public interest in a low-carbon energy transition. Ironically, the fact that it seems much more complicated to arrange corrupt schemes around the many small projects of wind and solar power, otherwise a virtue, may be an argument against them for actors looking for private gains.

3 States, Markets, and Energy Transition: Good Industrial Policy?

Market forces alone did not generate the dynamic wind and solar power sectors that exist around the world today. Electricity from fossil fuels and large hydropower has been dominant, not least because market failures allowed those industries to externalize environmental and other costs (Schlömer et al. 2014: 1332–1333; Stern 2007) and they are deeply embedded in existing physical and social infrastructures (Geels 2014). Much of the existing wind and solar electricity has therefore depended on specific governmental policies to encourage it, including both demand- and supply-side industrial policies (Aklin and Urpelainen 2013: 643; Chen and Lees 2016; Hochstetler and Kostka 2015; Meckling 2017; Nahm 2017; Pegels 2014a: 3–4; Zysman and Huberty 2014). In this chapter, I focus on the economic interests that states might have in promoting renewable energy, including broad public interests like economic growth, security of electricity supply, and increasing employment. States might also have public industry-specific interests, such as promoting a new national industry in what is often seen as a major growth and innovation sector. The industrial policy logic is one that evaluates the importance and role of such economic initiatives and their outcomes in the wind and solar power industries.

The renewable energy industries themselves could be state-owned enterprises (SOEs) or could promote private firms. That means that a first distinction in this political economy is the larger decision about the appropriate roles of the public and private sectors in the electricity sector. Both Brazil and South Africa chose to introduce independent power producers (IPPs) in electricity for the first time with their wind and solar programs. Wind and solar power installations in both countries are largely built and operated by private developers that supply electricity for the public grid under long-term contracts from governmental purchasers (Bayer, Schäuble, and Ferrari 2018). This is in contrast to their historical systems where vertically integrated state-owned monopolies – Brazil's Eletrobras and South Africa's Eskom – built and operated plants that generated electricity that they then distributed to end-consumers. Industrial policies for the sector also potentially provide incentives for private manufacturing firms to set up operation, grow, and innovate in order to supply components (Zysman and Huberty 2014).

Such renewable energy firms are assumed in this chapter to hold basic self-interested profit motivations, with the possibility that their self-interested activities might also help achieve public interests if guided by effective regulation. Well-managed renewable energy deployment or manufacturing industries could generate new constituencies for wind and solar power on economic grounds that would also lay a solid economic foundation for future industry expansion, a particular concern of middle-income and developing countries. Conversely, undisciplined firms in any part of the sector could capture such large profits that wind and solar power would be economically infeasible. In addition, if manufacturing capacity is sought where the economic bases for it are very weak, deployment could be not just economically unviable but also possibly significantly delayed or available only at a quality that is too low to be usable.

Introducing wind and solar power has thus meant significant new roles for both the public *and* the private sectors in Brazil and South Africa. These new roles create a distinct political economy for wind and solar power, one that stresses the concentrated benefits, or rents, that state policies can create for a comparatively small number of sectoral firms (Pegels 2014b; Schmitz, Johnson, and Altenburg 2015). Managing these rents invokes a specific and narrower kind of state capacity than that of climate change, one where state actors need to avoid "capture" by the private interests they are regulating in order to assure that public interests are met as well as private profit (Berry 1984; Mitnick 2011). The framing is narrower because it typically involves primarily energy and industry ministries and private firms, rather than the broader set of actors engaged in the climate policy arena. Labor unions and workers also see concentrated benefits and losses in the jobs outcomes that are one of the major promises of industrial policy, a classic formulation of the just transition debate (Stevis and Felli 2015).

This chapter examines specific policies to promote wind and solar power industries in the context of two fundamental issues of state–business relations. The first contextualizes decisions about renewable energy in broader discussions of public sector reform. I show how both countries developed hybrid models for the electricity sector using private as well as state actors (Eberhard 2007; Oliveira 2007; Victor and Heller 2007b). Such broader framework debates about the public–private balance in the electricity sector often spill over into wider, even partisan domains (Murillo 2009). The second pays attention to how the policies address questions of rent management that emerge any time governments create investment opportunities for private profit (Amsden 2001; Pegels 2014b; Schmitz et al. 2015; Zysman and Huberty 2014). These typically take the form of technical discussions that usually remain out of public sight. The most likely political coalitions involve wind and solar firms – and their workforces – interacting closely with national industry and economy ministries along with public and private sources of finance. The fine details of incentive policies may have large impacts on the costs and profits that are major concerns of all participants.

As Chapter 1 has already stressed, late adopters of wind and solar power like Brazil and South Africa are already facing industry structures that are very different from those of the early adopters in Europe and North America and even China. Established actors now dominate almost every part of global supply chains and are prepared to defend their positions (Lewis 2014; Meckling and Hughes 2017, 2018). Where national industrial conditions and capacities permit (Schmidt and Huenteler 2016), the international actors can accelerate the process of localization of some elements of wind and solar industries by opening local subsidiaries, but these may crowd out local competitors and will be responsive to global as well as local market dynamics. The innovation frontier has moved far ahead of new adopters as well. Conversely, some actors like the financial sector may be more ready to support what were once seen as very risky investments and may even be attuned to the risk of "stranded assets" as fossil fuels become politically obsolete (Caldecott 2017). This chapter will help to understand how such larger changes are made manifest in these specific locations, but the general point is that industrial policy considerations for countries like Brazil and South Africa will differ from those of earlier adopters.

Previewing the cases, Brazil partially privatized its electricity sector in the 1990s, creating a mixed system under governmental control where both state-owned and private enterprises could compete to build renewable energy and other forms of electricity. An electricity supply crisis in 2001 opened the economic case for alternative sources of electricity. Thus, privatization preceded the consideration of wind and solar power, and was not a major theme for their development. The specific economic motivations and policies that are the focus of this chapter then immediately differentiated between wind and solar power in Brazil.

Policy-makers in the Ministry of Mines and Energy calculated that Brazil could readily create a national manufacturing sector for wind power that could provide industry development benefits that would counter its high costs. Two ideologically different governments required localization in the first procurement initiative, a limited feed-in tariff called Proinfa. Similar economic calculations led Brazil to choose auctions as a procurement mechanism a few years later and to open them to wind power. While the auctions had no industrial policy component, winners often secured cheaper funding from the National Economic and Social Development Bank (BNDES), which did. The various localization requirements slowed the actual introduction of wind power until after 2009, but eventually the localization requirements contributed to a substantial national industry, with rents effectively managed by the auction system. All of these developments also helped generate the expected additional political constituency for wind power.

Solar power in Brazil, in contrast, was slowed by cost calculations and the difficulty of developing a national manufacturing industry given the existing industrial structure. Similar dynamics to those of wind power emerged only much later, in 2014. Even then, a different role for BNDES finance and more limited governmental incentives continued to slow the growth of grid-scale solar power and associated manufacturing, especially in a context of economic crisis and limited demand. In short, the economic potential for wind and solar power in Brazil has clearly shaped how much of each is produced, from the soaring levels of wind power generation to the slow rise of solar. It is a straightforward and largely bureaucratic story of the interactions between government policies and business responses. Rent management has been active there and has resulted in some localization of the wind value chain, with solar possibly eventually following.

In South Africa, discussions of the economic dimensions of renewable energy have struggled to move beyond the initial question of the balance between state (Eskom) and private firms in the electricity sector, going on at the same time as consideration of energy transition. Eskom, labor unions, and parts of the African National Congress (ANC) have argued hard for continuing state control, while other parts of the ANC and the energy and economic agencies have argued against. The fact that private firms produce nearly all South Africa's renewable electricity while Eskom produces its coal- and nuclear-powered electricity creates a reinforcing cleavage that has strongly hindered energy transition. As a result, procurement demand for wind and solar power has been both low and uncertain in the face of the status quo coalition's opposition, providing limited incentives for private industry development. So far, there are comparatively few rents to be managed. As a corollary, positive outcomes like jobs are much lower than promised, hardening the opposition of labor unions in a negative spiral.

As this summary suggests, industrial policy is one of many fronts in a politicized confrontation between wind and solar power versus traditional sources of electricity in South Africa. Although the topic of this chapter is economic incentives rather than climate action ambitions, the coalitions are very similar and reinforce the limited outcomes for renewable energy development. Benefits from South Africa's green industrial policy (GIP) have not proven robust enough to overcome opposition by important state and labor actors, contributing to the gridlock already described in Chapter 2 over whether and how wind and solar power will be expanded.

Turning to the organization of the chapter itself, I begin, in Section 3.1, with a brief survey of the larger debates about states and markets in the electricity sector, summarizing typical demand and supply sides of GIPs and sketching the rent management dilemmas that emerge. I also present arguments that GIP can actually transform the political economy in ways that make renewable energy production self-reinforcing and push the energy transition forward more forcefully in a positive green spiral (Kelsey and Zysman 2014: 79). The bulk of the chapter examines the specific packages of GIP for wind and solar powered electricity that were adopted in Brazil (Section 3.2) and South Africa (Section 3.3) and the political coalitions that have in fact formed around them. The conclusion (Section 3.4) summarizes the outcomes and shows how they reflect and reinforce some of the patterns already observed in the climate political economy.

3.1 Green Industrial Policy: A Political Economy of States and Markets

The right balance between state and market actors is a central theme in both academic and policy discussions of the electricity sector. As electricity became widely commercialized in the twentieth century, SOEs were dominant players in what was generally considered a natural monopoly. Like other SOEs, they often drew on subsidized state resources and served social functions besides simply providing electricity (Victor and Heller 2007c: 23–24). The SOE model was praised for taking advantage of economies of scale and for guarding the public interest, but it was blamed for expensive and inefficient electricity provision. The neoliberal "standard market reform model" of the 1980s and 1990s recommended unbundling and privatizing the sector, with private actors under the oversight of independent regulatory agencies and meant to attract new private investments in infrastructure (Gratwick and Eberhard 2008; Hochstetler and Kostka 2015; Naqvi 2016; Victor and Heller 2007c: 6–7). Brazil and South Africa join many other countries in having hybrid electricity models even after undergoing privatization initiatives (Eberhard 2007; Oliveira 2007).

Within those hybrid models, there is plenty of scope for introducing industrial policies: "sector- and industry-specific policies that aim to direct industrialization in line with some definition of the national interest" (Khan and Blankenburg 2009: 336). The GIP variant uses the tools of traditional state-led industrial direction to promote economic activities that are less harmful for the environment while also achieving economic aims (Schwarzer 2013: 2; Swilling and Annecke 2012). In GIP, state policies encourage "the development of industries that produce 'green goods', … [d]irectly address environmental problems," or produce goods in an environmentally better way (Cosbey 2013: 3). GIP strategies to promote the production and use of wind and solar power rather than fossil fuels may achieve all those goals. The 2008 global financial crisis made GIP mainstream, as the crisis legitimated more active state intervention even in countries with strong pro-market orientations. Governments worldwide saw renewable energy production and industry development as a particularly promising growth sector (Aggarwal and Evenett 2012).

The dual nature of GIP indicates two, possibly contradictory, measures of the success of this kind of policy for wind and solar powered electricity. On the one hand, success can be measured by the quantity of clean energy that is produced, both through the policy directly and through the longer-term potential for clean energy production that it promotes. On the other hand, the success of GIP can also be measured by traditional industrial policy metrics like the numbers and kinds of job created, the strength and international competitiveness of the new industries it supports, and so on. The hope for GIP is that both of those versions of success can be simultaneously achieved (e.g., Hess 2012; Kelsey and Zysman 2014; Rubini 2012).

GIP does have an apparently inherent contradiction, however: the fastest way to bring large quantities of renewable electricity into national grids is to simply import and install the cheapest global components (Matsuo and Schmidt 2019). Using the state to promote new national industries that support wind and solar generation can slow or even block deployment. Like any sectoral or targeted industrial policy, GIP also creates concentrated benefits for the firms and labor in the sector, creating policy rents (Pegels 2014a: 5). This leads to the need for effective rent management, where governments ideally offer the right amounts and kinds of rent at the right time. Successful uses of industrial policy depend on mechanisms of control, including eventually withdrawing supports from infant industries (Amsden 2001). The aim is to maintain rents long enough to motivate firm innovation and learning, without keeping them so long that they block competition in favor of nonperforming recipients. A second issue for management is how governments might influence the distribution of the rents among actors and purposes (Khan and Blankenburg 2009: 349; Schmitz, et al. 2015: 813–814). GIP scholars argue that a close alliance of state, business, and civil actors is optimal for achieving the right bundles of policies in this sector (Schmitz et al. 2015: 825). At worst, there is the danger that entrepreneurs will "capture" the state and have their interests prioritized over the public good, with costs higher than necessary and inappropriate policies chosen (Evans 1995; Schmitz et al. 2015: 815).

Despite the possible problems, some scholars have argued that the GIP dynamic is still the most beneficial for renewable energy production in the long term. The countries that have gone furthest in expanding their use of wind and solar power experienced a "green spiral – a process of policy feedback in which initial incremental steps to jointly address economic and environmental issues might over time build up industrial coalitions with material interests in favor of sustaining and expanding efforts at climate change mitigation" (Kelsey and Zysman 2014: 79). In this view, the possible delays and short-term economic distortions pale against the political and economic value of creating additional industry and labor actors with a stake in more renewable energy. The economic support coalition is especially critical when powerful electricity sector incumbents – themselves typically long-time recipients of rents and subsidies – push back (Meckling, Kelsey, Biber, and Zysman 2015; Schmitz et al. 2015: 817).

Turning to the rationales for GIP, countries at all levels of development share some motivations for promoting wind and solar power. All, of course, are part of the same climate system that is causing increased weather volatility and dislocations around the globe as it warms (Chapter 2). Economic theory offers many rationales for when state intervention might be needed because market forces will under-provide a collective environmental good like increased renewable energy production (Cosbey 2013: 4–5; Pegels and Becker 2014; Schwarzer 2013: 29–31). Adding renewable energy to national electricity grids raises formidable coordination and infrastructure needs that are hard for market actors to overcome (Cosbey 2013: 5). The large scale of energy finance and the high levels of uncertainty and unfamiliarity associated with emerging technologies together make private sources of finance reluctant to fund renewable energy projects (Cosbey 2013: 4; Schwarzer 2013: 37–38). Knowledge externalities mean that private firms may hesitate to develop new technologies that others will quickly copy (Cosbey 2013: 4). All of these market failures call for direct state provision, for example, of finance or planning, or for states to provide extra incentives for private participation.

GIP to promote renewable electricity is also especially attractive to middle-income and developing countries. Many of them are still expanding electricity production and use, so they may be able to diversify their electricity sources without directly confronting sunk costs in fossil fuel-based infrastructure and associated political coalitions (Goldemberg 1998: 730). The renewable energy industry is also commonly presented as a comparatively new and open industry, with lots of associated jobs, although wind and solar power actually require significant design and manufacturing capabilities, respectively

(Schmidt and Huenteler 2016: 14). While it will be difficult for developing countries to become leaders in this rapidly developing sector, the rewards are expected to be particularly high. China is an aspirational model here, as it has gone from essentially no wind industry to being a global leader in both production and genuine innovation in less than a decade (Lewis 2013).

There are many tools that countries might use to promote renewable electricity through GIP, each associated with particular rent management dilemmas. Rather than cataloging all of them (see Lewis and Wiser 2007; Lewis 2013; Pegels and Becker 2014), I focus here on presenting the demand- and supply-side mechanisms that have been used in Brazil and South Africa.

Governments have extensive control over the demand for wind and solar power because state agencies are nearly always involved in electricity procurement for national grids. States have used two primary strategies for drawing private firms to produce wind and solar power. Feed-in tariffs (FiTs) that offer attractive long-term purchasing contracts for renewable electricity give generating firms the confidence to begin production (Lewis and Wiser 2007). Procurement auctions, where governments ask for generators to bid to be the low-cost supplier of a given amount of renewable electricity in exchange for long-term purchasing contracts, do the same (Lucas, Ferroukhi, and Hawila 2013). Both FiTs and auctions typically set prices to provide subsidies, offering a financial reward or rent per unit produced. The efficiency of FiTs depends on how well the tariffs are set to reflect actual costs. The competitive bidding of auctions itself limits costs if there is lots of competition and states typically set ceilings. They have a different risk, of underbidding that leads to failed projects and higher administrative costs (Pegels and Becker 2014: 54–56). Auctions reward lean, market-competitive firms proposing large installations, while FiTs have drawn in a wider variety of participants, including community-owned projects (Grashof 2019), so the choice may affect distributive outcomes.

Demand itself can spur a renewable electricity industry, with construction and installation firms coming first. Localization of the manufacturing value chain also depends in part on demand. In 2014, interviewees in Brazil and South Africa thought annual demand would have to be above 400 MW/year for localization of production

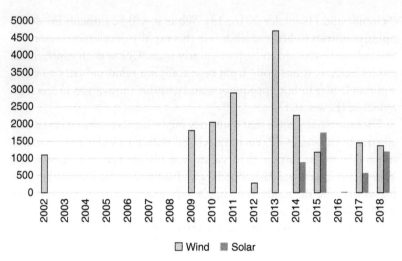

Figure 3.1 Annual wind and solar power procurement in Brazil, 2002–2018
Source: calculated from data at www.aneel.gov.br/resultados-de-leiloes.

there.[1] As the wind industry grew in Brazil, manufacturers there wanted annual demand of 2–3 GW (Ferreira 2017: 150), showing the accelerating expectations of the green spiral.[2] Figures 3.1 and 3.2 show that actual annual procurement in both countries has deviated quite a bit from a model of stable procurement. There was a long gap in new wind procurement in Brazil and solar demand began only in 2014. South Africa actually saw steps backwards, when Eskom refused to sign purchasing contracts for auction winners between 2016 and 2018.

To fully localize renewable energy production in a country, especially a middle-income or developing country, requires supply-side GIP. What localization means varies: it can mean everything from being an assembly base for imported components to national manufacturing of some or all components to wholly local innovation and research and development (R&D) of new technologies (Lewis and Wiser 2007: 1845; Schmidt and Huenteler 2016). The traditional tools of industrial policy continue to be relevant for GIP.[3] International trade policies can protect infant

---

[1] Interviews with Mike Levington, SAPVIA, Johannesburg, 2014; Eduardo Tosta, Agência Brasileira de Desenvolvimento Indústrial (ABDI), Brasília, 2014.
[2] Interview with Jorge Boeira, ABDI, Brasília, 2018.
[3] Many of these tools fit poorly with the World Trade Organization's (WTO's) rules (Rubini 2012; Wu and Salzman 2014), but disputes and challenges at the

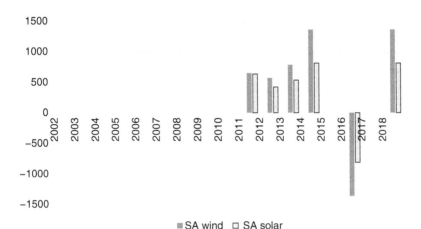

Figure 3.2 Annual wind and solar power procurement in South Africa,
2011–2018
Source: calculated from data at www.eskom.co.za/Whatweredoing/Pages/R
E_IPP_Procurement_Programme.aspx.

industries or support exports (Schwarzer 2013). Local content requirements set a minimum percentage of locally manufactured inputs, often
enforced as a condition for connection to the grid, receiving higher
payments for electricity or accessing subsidized credit (Lewis and Wiser
2007: 1851–1852). Other financial and tax incentives, like long-term
loans at favorable rates or tax breaks, may motivate local production or
innovation (Gallagher, Anadon, Kempener, and Wilson 2011: 374;
Schwarzer 2013: 13–14). The rents for all these are the classic ones of
industrial policy. They also depend on rent management strategies like
monitoring performance and withdrawing the rents for nonperformance
or when they are no longer needed to spur the industry. If incentives are
designed to create an economic role for domestic actors, they need to be
controlled for efficiency (Khan and Blankenburg 2009: 340).

All of these tools have been used in some combination by the countries that first developed renewable energy technologies and by the
emerging powers now hoping to join them (Gallagher 2013;
Gallagher et al. 2011; Lewis and Wiser 2007; Naqvi, Henow, and

WTO have been mostly limited to reciprocal challenges between major producers
(Lewis 2014). Interviewed policy-makers in both Brazil and South Africa saw few
external limits to their GIP choices for renewables.

Chang forthcoming). Which tools are selected from this extensive tool set both depends on the national political economy of electricity and also reshapes it (Lachapelle, MacNeil, and Paterson 2017: 320). The political coalitions built around economic interests pursue those interests in existing national institutions and industrial structures. Sections 3.2 and 3.3 now examine those processes in Brazil and then South Africa, looking at how policies were selected and put into place.

3.2 State and Market in the Brazilian Electricity Sector

New sources of electricity like wind and solar power enter into existing sectors that already have substantial physical and socioeconomic structures. This survey of Brazilian electricity begins with a review of that existing electricity sector, with particular attention to the changing roles of state and market actors within it. It then turns to the introduction of wind and solar power, showing that active industrial policies were central to the introduction of wind power in 2002 and the subsequent management of the sector over time. Conversely, difficulties with creating a manufacturing sector around solar power were a source of significant delays in taking advantage of Brazil's extensive solar resources, although an industrial policy dynamic finally began in that sector in 2014.

Large-scale electricity generation in Brazil began with private hydroelectric power at the end of the nineteenth century, but it really took off with the rise of developmentalism and industrialization after 1930. Judith Tendler's pathbreaking study called the Brazilian electricity model "entrepreneurship in the public sector" in its title because of how the state used electricity SOEs to support broader industrial policy (Tendler 1968). Four regional SOEs were brought together in 1962 under one powerful holding company, Eletrobras. Eletrobras also controlled other electricity assets and planned and coordinated the sector, mostly oriented around large hydroelectric plants (Leite 2009; Oliveira 2007: 36–37). It held most national expertise on electricity at all stages of production and use.

The center-right government of Fernando Henrique Cardoso began to unbundle and privatize the sector in 1995, following the standard reform model. This was just one piece of broader national administrative reforms. The government privatized 70 percent of electricity distribution capacity and 30 percent of generation capacity (Bradshaw

2018: 71–72; Tolmasquim 2012: 6–14). The policies were also responsive to private firms, who were impatient with the slow pace of privatization under Cardoso and focused their criticisms on the "antiquated energy utility sector" (Montero 2014: 38). The opposition Workers' Party (PT) and its close labor associate, the Unified Workers' Confederation (CUT), strongly contested efforts to privatize the sector, and especially marquee parastatal Petrobras (Hunter 2010: 64–65). They managed to forestall many of the plans for Petrobras but were less successful for electricity. The Ministry of Mines and Energy gained responsibility for many of Eletrobras's planning and oversight functions, but it lacked in-house expertise and those functions languished (Tolmasquim 2012).

The reforms made other changes in markets and distribution networks but retained a central dispatch system where both state and private generators provide most of their electricity to a central pool that is then sold out to as many as sixty-four distribution agents. The latter are required to contract enough electricity for their expected demand over the next five years (Esposito 2010: 242–243). This hourglass-like constriction continued to allow for significant state control, even in a system where many of the generators and distributors are private. A regulatory agency, ANEEL, was created to oversee the sector along with other operational agencies (Bradshaw 2018). Following the government's general orientation, there were no industrial policy initiatives for the sector.

When the PT took the national presidency in 2003, then-president Lula da Silva directed new reforms in the sector to address energy security, cheap electricity rates, and universal access – all topics discussed in Chapter 4. A Working Group within the Ministry of Mines and Energy then debated whether those aims could be best achieved by recreating state control over the industry in Eletrobras, a choice many favored.[4] The group consulted extensively with producer and user groups and discussions extended into the National Congress. The chosen reforms did not return to the SOE model, but they did add back a number of public institutions that would oversee the working of

---

[4] This is based on the historical account in Mauricio Tolmasquim's presentation of his 2012 book on the reforms (Tolmasquim 2012). Tolmasquim led the Working Group, working closely with Dilma Rousseff who was then minister of mines and energy.

the system as a whole. These included the Energy Research Enterprise (EPE), which does planning for the sector (Chapter 2).

A signature reform that had a major impact on wind and solar power was to introduce auctions where potential generation agents would compete for long-term contracts to supply electricity (Tolmasquim 2012). Some of the auctions allow different types of electricity to compete directly on price, while other auctions contract particular kinds of electricity to ensure a desired balance for energy security. As noted in Section 3.1, auctions are considered to be good forms of rent management when there is ample competition, although they run the danger of bids that are too low for feasibility. Brazilian auctions require technical, financial, and environmental prequalification of potential projects in an effort to make sure that winners can build their bid projects (Bayer, Berthold, and de Freitas 2018; Bradshaw 2018). Eletrobras and state-level public utilities can and do compete successfully for contracts. While Lula's administration was reintroducing industrial policy elsewhere, its directives for electricity reform did not include any direct industrial policy measures. Labor and manufacturing industry associations were not an active part of the Working Group's debates and none of the reforms addressed possible manufacturing in the sector. EPE's many optimization criteria for its planning exercises do not include industrial policy.

The CUT and other influential union confederations spent most of their efforts trying to convince successive PT administrations to overturn Petrobras's partial privatization (Henrique 2012: 67). They remobilized to try to block president Temer's decision to privatize six of Eletrobras's distribution units in 2017–2018, using strikes and court action, but ultimately failed on that too. Thus, private actors continued to flourish in the electricity sector despite the changes in government. The labor movement has been critical of the auctions in principle, calling them another variant of privatization (Henrique 2012: 69). Some civil society actors concurred with the labor movement's critique, with the Movement of those Affected by Dams (MAB) placing the model of private generation for public contracts at the heart of its critique of the electricity sector. In the view of both labor and MAB, the auction format means that generation is done by actors that are too interested in profits and costs rather than by more socially oriented

SOEs.[5] When their traditional PT allies chose this model, the critics had few other political options to push for more redistributive aims for electricity generation.

3.2.1 Brazilian National (Nonhydro) Renewable Electricity Programs

Within this larger electricity framework, Brazil took its first significant steps to introduce wind power into its electricity matrix in 2002. Proinfa followed severe droughts in 2001. These droughts devastated Brazil's traditional hydropower plants and made complementary electricity sources that could be constructed quickly very attractive. The outgoing, market-oriented Cardoso administration made this the first opportunity for new private generation for the national grid. IPPs added 1,100 MW each of wind, small hydro, and biomass-based electricity to the system. Proinfa joined its FiT with a temporary local content requirement to spur the industry, placing the program squarely in the realm of industrial policy.[6] The Lula administration continued Proinfa, but its subsequent auction system – which has no localization policy – was used to actually procure most of the wind and solar power now operational in Brazil.

Both the Cardoso and the Lula administration's version of Proinfa included national content requirements, or localization, as its most significant industrial policy component. This was an unexpected choice for Cardoso's center-right government, which rested on Ministry of Mines and Energy economists' calculations that the then-high additional costs of adding renewable energy to the grid could be offset in the longer run if such requirements successfully localized production and innovation in the sector.[7] Solar was considered too expensive and too challenging for local manufacturers for inclusion in Proinfa even under these terms (Empresa de Pesquisa Energética 2012a: 1). The center-right included a requirement for 50 percent national content

---

[5] Interview with Gilberto Cervinski, MAB, São Paulo, 2013 (JRT).
[6] Proinfa included another incentive directed at distributors and consumers, offering a 50 percent discount for electricity from alternative sources if the plant's installed capacity was 30 MW installed or fewer. This is discussed in Chapter 4.
[7] Interview with Melo, ABEEólica, 2014, São Paulo (JRT). She was a leading economic analyst in the Ministry of Mines and Energy in 2002 when Proinfa was designed.

only in Proinfa's first stage – the sort of rent management often favored
by proponents of disciplined industrial policy (Amsden 2001) – but the
leftist Lula administration asked for 60 percent national content in the
first stage and 90 percent in the second.[8] These choices were made with
little evident influence from a nonexistent industrial sector.

In their rhetoric, Lula and his PT successor Dilma Rousseff gave
a more explicit industrial policy framing to their renewable energy
policies than Cardoso had. The first Brazilian industrial policy under
Lula was the 2003 Industrial, Technology, and Foreign Trade Policy
(PITCE). It favored "renewable energy, biofuels ... and activities
derived from the Kyoto Protocol" as central elements of a modern
economy where the state would support Brazil's innovative capacities
and global competitiveness (Governo do Brasil 2003: 10). The federal
government's 2011 "Bigger Brazil Plan" (*Plano Brasil Maior*), issued
under Rousseff, gave even greater emphasis to the possibility of industrial development through development of the wind and solar
industries.

BNDES repeated these claims that green industries are a promising
future growth direction.[9] The bank became a particularly important
actor in this industrial policy story in the second procurement phase
after 2005, when the Ministry of Mines and Energy began to use its
price-based auctions to select the projects that would be built for the
national grid. Despite the PT's stated industrial policy ambitions for
renewable energy, the Ministry of Mines and Energy has consistently
and explicitly disavowed an industrial policy role for its procurement
(Ferreira 2017: 157). Intense lobbying by the Brazilian Machinery and
Equipment Industry Association (ABIMAQ) and Brazil's Ministry of
Development, Industry, and Foreign Trade (MDIC) has not resulted in
a mandatory local content requirement for auction participation.[10] In
this gap, localization incentives have been introduced through BNDES.

Projects that can gain BNDES financing have an advantage in the
cost-driven auction system since its financing for wind and solar power

[8]   www.planalto.gov.br/ccivil_03/leis/2003/l10.762.htm.
[9]   Interview with five members of the BNDES Infrastructure and Structuration of
      Projects sectors, Rio de Janeiro, 2012; telephone interview with Sérgio
      Weguelin, the then Superintendent of the Environment sector of BNDES, 2011.
[10] Interviews with Tosta, ABDI, Brasília, 2014 and Boeira, ABDI, Brasília, 2018.
      See also www.abimaq.org.br/site.aspx/Abimaq-Informativo-Mensal-Infomaq?
      DetalheClipping=48&CodigoClipping=939.

projects comes at rates well below market levels. For wind, the subsidized rates were about 4 percent below market rates, although they have risen over time (Bayer 2018: 2648; Melo 2013: 131). BNDES, which is mandated to promote employment in Brazil, has historically required 50 to 60 percent domestic content by weight and value for all its loans. Applied to wind and solar power, these became the most effective guarantor of ongoing localized production of electricity components. Among BNDES's sources of these finance lines are US$1 billion in green bonds that it launched in May 2017 on the Luxemburg Green Bonds exchange – which paid for eight wind power installations – and another US$1.5 billion in periodic credit line agreements with international development banks (BNDES 2018: 4, 9).[11]

Brazil's electricity policy instruments require the balancing of multiple economic considerations. IPPs will refuse to bid if the contracts offered have price ceilings that are not lucrative enough, which is what the IPPs did in the first wind-only auction in 2008.[12] The government had to change the trading model, allowing the production of power in a windy year to compensate for less windy years, before enough firms would participate, for example (Tolmasquim 2012: 242–244). So, states must be sensitive to firms' preferences. However, the risks of "political capture, windfall profits and rent-seeking" (Pegels 2014a: 1) require state actors to discipline firms as well. Consequently, Brazilian auctions are also constructed with many mechanisms to promote competition (Lucas et al. 2013: 18–19). The two-stage auctions pit firms against each other, and the resulting tariffs are substantially lower and less profitable for firms than was Proinfa's FiT (Lucas et al. 2013: 22). This outcome supports the Brazilian state's major economic concern of keeping the prices charged to consumers and industry low (Chapter 4). While these considerations so far generally hold for both wind and solar power, the intersection between the policies and the distinct characteristics of their technologies and industries means that the

---

[11] www.bndes.gov.br/SiteBNDES/bndes_en/Institucional/Press/Destaques. Press releases at this site for 2016–2018 show credit lines for US$750 million from the Inter-American Development Bank, US$300 million from the BRICS New Development Bank, US$142 million from Germany's KfW, and US$100 million from the Development Bank of Japan, all for renewable energy, as well as US$206 million from the French Development Agency for energy efficiency and climate change.

[12] Interview with Melo, ABEEólica, São Paulo, 2014.

same overarching aims and policies contributed to the very different outcomes for the two that are observed in Figure 1.1.

3.2.2 *Wind Power Policies and Outcomes in Brazil*

GIP interventions in support of wind power in Brazil have tightly interwoven the demand and supply sides. As already noted, Proinfa's demand for wind power was directly linked to the requirement of 50 or 60 percent local content. Since Proinfa unofficially ended, twenty auctions contracted wind power between 2009 and 2018, presenting a significant demand stimulus to the industry. BNDES provided about R$27.5 billion (very roughly US$9 billion) to finance major parts of 264 wind power installations between 2003 and 2017 (Ferreira 2017: 105). While this is fewer than half the plants, firms bidding for projects greatly preferred the cheaper BNDES finance, and so manufacturing firms had a strong incentive to become preferred BNDES suppliers by meeting its local content requirements even if not all their components went to projects with the BNDES finance. Other incentives have also supported industry development, requiring rent management.

The growth in wind power demand itself is clear: the Brazilian government had contracted to have almost 18.0 GW installed capacity built through the end of 2018 (see Figure 3.1 for annual procurement). The basic "green" requirement of GIP for wind power – that clean renewable electricity be produced – has clearly been met. The demand also helped meet the industrial policy ends of building a local wind power components industry. Both project developers and upstream suppliers look for large and steady levels of procurement.

The years of strong demand attracted many national and international bidders in the auctions. Eletrobras had the largest share of wind plant ownership, with 11 percent in forty-eight plants, while Paraná's state utility owned 5 percent. Foreign and domestic private firms rounded out the top ten in market share (Bayer 2018: 2652). Brazil's market concentration of auction winners was comparatively low, dropping from an initial 60 percent for the top five firms to 31 percent before rising again to 37 percent (Bayer, Schäuble, and Ferrari 2018: 310). Forty-four firms landed contracts to build 397 plants between 2010 and 2014. Smaller firms remained in the mix as twenty-five different owners competed successfully to build five plants or fewer,[13] although there are very few small owners with projects that totaled fewer than 50 MW (Bayer, Schäuble, and Ferrari 2018: 312). Overall, participation and competition in the auctions remained high.

The slowdown in procurement that began in 2016 hit project developers hard. The uneven demand presented even more problems for component suppliers, who must invest in facilities and specialized training in order to establish production lines, giving them significant ongoing costs. Both developers and manufacturers have lobbied hard to have demand return to earlier levels, with support from the Brazilian Association of Wind Energy (ABEEólica).[14] Even as demand rebounded in 2017 and 2018, it was well below what industry actors wanted to supply. In the August 2018 auction, just 48 wind projects were selected from 928 wind projects qualified and registered for the auction.[15]

Developers and suppliers have had less congruent interests with respect to local content requirements. As recently as 2008, there were only two manufacturers of wind components in Brazil. In simulations, the national production requirements were shown to reduce wind capacity below what would otherwise have existed (Dutra and Szklo 2008: 73). It took eight years for Proinfa's first 1,100 MW of wind power to be built, in part from the delays introduced as firms localized production. In those years, China built a globally competitive wind industry (Lewis 2013), but Brazil did not get ahead of the global developments. As continuing auctions for wind power showed ongoing demand after 2009, however, other firms have seen opportunities and their new production facilities in Brazil have been critical to the further expansion of wind generation capacity. They also have been an important political constituency for wind power.

As noted earlier in this section, BNDES's local content rules have been especially important for shaping the growth and development of national manufacturers. BNDES's Finame line finances wind farm

---

[13] Calculated from data in Bayer, Berthold, and de Freitas 2018, table 1. These numbers do not include the twelve additional generators for Proinfa (Bayer, Schäuble, and Ferrari 2018: 312) or those providing 658 MW through "other business models" at the end of 2015 (Bayer 2018: 2646).

[14] Interview with Boeira, ABDI, Brasília, 2018.

[15] www.canalenergia.com.br/noticias/53073680/leilao-a-6-contrata-21gw-de-potencia-e-viabiliza-r-768-bilhoes-em-investimentos.

developers who promise to source components from manufacturers whose products are certified as meeting BNDES's local content requirements. They, in turn, can seek funding from BNDES's Finem line for manufacturers (Ferreira 2017: 104). Until 2012, the rules simply required developers who wanted BNDES finance to source their turbines from a list of those that met the bank's local content requirements: the manufacturers were to install a factory in Brazil and build turbine models with 60 percent national content, measured by a formula that subtracted the price of imported components from the pre-tax sales price of the wind turbine (the Build-Down calculation of local content). The national content could be any product but tended to be heavy and low-tech components like blades and towers (Ferreira 2017: 130). While wind power is complex from a design perspective, much of the manufacturing is labor-intensive and uses readily available industrial skills like welding and casting (Schmidt and Huenteler 2016: 12).

BNDES had initially offered firms a flexible timeline for implementing the domestic content requirement, conditioning new support on moving additional production to Brazil. The bank shocked the industry in 2011, however, informing six of eleven firms that they had fallen behind in nationalization and BNDES would not finance installation contracts that included their products (Melo 2013: 130). It is a rare instance of BNDES disciplining firms for noncompliance with the conditions of its loans and an important example of active rent management (Schneider 2015). That was the beginning of a series of developments meant to increase both the quantity and the quality of local manufacturing for the wind sector while managing the rents accrued.

A new local content policy, laid out in December of 2012, detailed exactly how BNDES would account for domestic content in turbines. It set out a series of six stages for nationalizing production of increasingly more sophisticated components, a classic GIP aim.[16] BNDES developed the schedule internally but in consultation with developers and some suppliers (Ferreira 2017: 140). While deepening national production capacity, these requirements played a significant role in slowing the construction of wind power plants again – second only to delays in building transmission lines (Bayer, Berthold, and de Freitas 2018: 103).

---

[16] www.bndes.gov.br/SiteBNDES/export/sites/default/bndes_pt/Galerias/Arquivos/produtos/download/credenciamento_aerogeradores_metodologia.pdf.

For manufacturers, however, the new schedule was very important as a signal of future markets and provided clear incentives to steadily develop or bring in new capacities.

In October 2017, BNDES announced new criteria for local content that now prioritize high-technology imports, the possibility of innovation, skills building, and international competitiveness.[17] Even as the new criteria were implemented at the end of 2018, BNDES continued to keep its specific regulations for wind and solar power, but these might eventually change too. The new criteria seem fairly well calibrated to the wind sector's industry development stage and will push it further forward, but they appear quite demanding for solar power, which is at an earlier stage of development.

Other tax and tariff policies promoted the sector, important since taxes would normally be 25.7–30.2 percent of the total investment in a wind plant. The 1997 Convenio ICMS No. 101, to cite the most important example, exempts wind and solar components from the 13.6–17 percent ICMS tax (a value-added tax) until at least 2021 (Ferreira 2017: 100). This favors project developers unless they are trying to meet the local content requirements, since it raises the comparative prices of domestic components. A June 2007 law that exempted infrastructure from the PIS and COFINS taxes could discount up to 9.25 percent more of the total cost of components for developers (Ferreira 2017: 102–103), although it applies only to some projects (Tolmasquim 2012: 244). Several short-lived decrees and new laws (e.g., 13,097/2015 and 13,169/2015) after 2014 have left the tax incentive system contradictory, as developers and manufacturers seek different provisions.

Successful rent management depends on contacts between state and industry so that policies can reflect – but not be captured by – industry needs (Evans 1995). Under Rousseff's governments (2011–2016), sectoral councils of business, government, and labor met regularly to talk about sectoral needs. The meetings continued informally into the Temer years (2016–2018) when the government was opposed to industrial policy and demand for new electricity plants stalled in ways

---

[17] www.bndes.gov.br/wps/portal/site/home/financiamento/servicos-online/creden ciamento-de-equipamentos/normas-aplicaveis-credenciamento/novo-regulamento-para-o-credenciamento-de-maquinas-equipamentos-sistemas-industriais-e-componentes.

harmful to the emerging industries.[18] Reports from the meetings show
wide discussion of sectoral developments and the identification of items
for further discussion and comanagement even when new governmental initiatives could not be formally undertaken. The meetings allowed
different subsectors, like project developers and industrial manufacturers, to participate in frank discussions of the sector's overall dynamics
with related government agencies.

More visibly, the Brazil Wind Power conference is the most important space for developers, policy-makers, and manufacturers to meet.
BNDES considers it to be effectively "the forum for debate about the
Local Content Policy of BNDES" (Ferreira 2017: 145). Industry association ABEEólica is an organizer of the conference. Public and private
actors in the states that have wind capacity are enthusiastic supporters
and have planned additional initiatives alongside the national policies.
The most notable is the National Wind Forum (*Fórum Nacional
Eólico*), launched in Natal (in Brazil's poorer Northeast region) in
June 2009 and running annually since.[19] These meetings offer technical
information but are also designed to allow interaction between policy-
makers and private actors in the sector. These are some of the most
visible manifestations of what is now a strong domestic political coalition of public and private actors supporting the wind industry.

Turning to outcomes, the Brazilian Agency of Industrial
Development (ABDI), part of MDIC, conducted an impressive mapping of the whole wind power production chain in Brazil that it
published in 2014 (Agência Brasileira de Desenvolvimento Industrial
2014) and then updated in 2018 (Agência Brasileira de
Desenvolvimento Industrial 2018; see also Sebrae 2017a). The documents were meant to show the state of the industry and help private
firms in Brazil and abroad identify possible niches they might fill.[20] In
all, some forty-three firms were found to be already producing part of
the wind power production chain in 2014 (Agência Brasileira de
Desenvolvimento Industrial 2014: 40–42). A few years later – after
implementation of BNDES's second local content policy and in the
context of significant demand – a new accounting found 235 firms in

---

[18] Interview with Boeira, ABDI, 2018.
[19] www.viex-americas.com/eventos/forum-nacional-eolico/.
[20] Interviews with Tosta, ABDI, 2014 and Boeira, ABDI, 2018.

Brazil that were involved in some part of the wind turbine production chain and another 400 providing related services (Agência Brasileira de Desenvolvimento Industrial 2018).

The BNDES finance was clearly an impetus for both national and international firms. In 2018, six manufacturers made wind turbines, all of them credentialed with BNDES.[21] Only one of those was a Brazilian firm, WEG, which had started to make turbines in 2012, while the rest were large manufacturers from first generation wind countries. Two Brazilian firms were among the four building blades, bringing technology from Brazil's aeronautics industry (Ferreira 2017: 165). The largest concentration of Brazilian firms was among the fifteen building low-tech towers (Ferreira 2017: 164–166). Among the forty-two localized suppliers credentialed by BNDES in 2017, twenty-two were foreign firms and twenty were Brazilian (Ferreira 2017: 170). The BNDES list in 2018 still had thirty-eight firms on it, showing that the weak demand that began in 2016 and higher lending rates had not yet discouraged many manufacturers.

These policies and results essentially involve localization of the wind power manufacturing sector, but they say little about the sector's ongoing ability to innovate and renew itself. Nineteen institutions, including seven universities, have some research and/or training in the wind sector (Sebrae 2017a: 70–71). Research is limited by a lack of resources. A review of R&D and innovation funds for the sector found four different funds, in the electricity regulator ANEEL, the national innovation fund FINEP, and BNDES (Ferreira 2017: 109–120). The funds themselves did not move large amounts of money and distributed little of it to wind sector actors in particular. Wind projects received just 4.7 percent of the total finance from ANEEL's R&D program between 2008 and 2015, for example, some US$57 million (Ferreira 2017: 111). Basic infrastructure for innovation, like a testing facility that could certify that new products meet international quality standards, has not been built, despite strong recommendations from the Ministry of Science and Technology (MCT) in 2015 (Centro de Gestão e Estudos Estratégicos 2015). Thus, Brazil's GIP has been oriented to localization

---

[21] The companies are Acciona, GE, Siemens Gamesa, Vestas, WEG, and Wobben. See www.bndes.gov.br/wps/portal/site/home/financiamento/servicos-online/cre denciamento-de-equipamentos/consulta-fornecedores-produtos-credenciados. Search terms were "eolic" and "aerogerador."

rather than innovation. Localization is, of course, a necessary precursor to innovation.

Another measure of the success of GIP is the jobs created. Strong jobs outcomes can bring labor into the green spiral, but both the information and the outcomes here are less complete. The International Renewable Energy Agency (IRENA) tallied 36,000 jobs in the Brazilian wind sector in 2014 (International Renewable Energy Agency 2015: 16), 41,000 in 2015 (International Renewable Energy Agency 2016b: 8), a 21 percent drop to 32,400 in 2016 (International Renewable Energy Agency 2017: 9), and a few more at 33,700 in 2017 (International Renewable Energy Agency 2018: 10). ABEEólica calculates that, with the growth in the sector, there are now fifteen direct and indirect jobs per MW installed. This says little about the nature of the jobs themselves. A view of the possibilities is evident in another recent ABDI initiative. ABDI was inspired by a US Department of Energy study to create websites showing the many career positions available for wind (fifty-two positions) and solar (thirty-three) power, using Brazilian wage rates and training opportunities to motivate workers.[22]

The most detailed to-date study of actual outcomes used industry interviews and site visits to simulate the wind sector jobs that are likely given the contracted wind power from 2012 to 2016. It concluded that almost 90,000 jobs-year will be created over these years, or 11.7 jobs-year/MW installed, but that they will have a different makeup from the manufacturing-heavy European sector – which had substantial manufacturing exports, unlike Brazil (Simas and Pacca 2013: 35–38). In Brazil, 58 percent (Europe 13 percent) of the jobs were estimated to be in the construction stage and 16 percent (3 percent) in operations and maintenance, leaving 26 percent (83 percent) mostly for manufacturing (Simas and Pacca 2013: 38). The much larger amount of national manufacturing after 2014 means that that ratio is probably now low for Brazil, but many jobs are still low-skilled and temporary.

The Brazilian labor movement has been correspondingly agnostic on wind power. Using the language of the global labor movement's debates on green jobs (Stevis and Felli 2015: 37–38), the CUT has stressed that green jobs must be "decent work" and that the transition

---

[22] Interview with Boeira, ABDI, 2018; see http://sitesinteligencia.abdi.com.br/site s/carreiras-eolica/ and http://inteligencia.abdi.com.br/carreiras-solar/.

to sustainability must be a "just transition."[23] By 2016, expectations were lowered: CUT environmental secretary Daniel Gaio noted in a published interview that wind and solar power are being built "by large transnational conglomerates, where labor is subcontracted [*terceirizado*] and precarious, making workplace organization difficult."[24] While workplace organization is more difficult in the scattered installations of wind and solar power than in traditional large installations, the evidence shown earlier in this section does not support Gaio's simple image of domination by large transnational conglomerates. There is also significant traditional industrial production that he does not acknowledge. The CUT has engaged in international debates about a just energy transition, but there is much less discussion at home (Just Transition Research Collaboration 2018: 17–18). In interviews, only a few civil society groups were familiar with the term "just transition."

A final measure of industrial policy is the development of capacity to innovate and drive future developments in the global industry. Firms did file for 1,601 patents related to wind power in Brazil between 2000 and 2013. Most of these were filed before significant generation of wind power began there and the rate declined sharply after 2012. While the rate of filings is higher than that in South Africa and India, it is a small fraction of the 23,816 applications for patents filed in China during the same period.[25]

Despite ambiguous and incomplete results on jobs and innovation, the wind sector in Brazil shows many signs of robust growth and effective rent management. The large quantity of wind procured for the grid is a GIP achievement itself, which helped spur both deployment and manufacturing industries. The auction mechanism used for most of this procurement proved itself to be a powerful rent management tool, especially since auctions were highly competitive. The auctions did not promote localization, by design, but financial and other incentives did so. BNDES has both supported localization of production and disciplined firms not meeting its strict rules. While the localization requirements originally delayed deployment of wind power, there are strong indications that a green spiral has begun to settle in. State and industry

[23] www.cut.org.br/noticias/desenvolvimento-sustentavel-se-faz-com-enfrentamento-da-pobreza-justica-social-e-d18e/.
[24] www.cut.org.br/noticias/o-golpe-tenta-desmontar-a-agenda-do-meio-ambiente-a24f.
[25] http://inspire.irena.org/Pages/patents/Patents-Search.aspx.

have worked together to generate both demand for wind power and the supply to meet it.

3.2.3 Solar Power Policies and Outcomes in Brazil

Solar power was not included in the original Proinfa and its adoption continues to lag well behind wind power in Brazil. Brazil has many of the same interests in solar-powered electricity as in wind: solar installations can be assembled quickly, adding more capacity to the grid and supplementing the annual fluctuations in hydropower without creating new dependencies on imported or fossil fuel. Solar power's higher prices (Chapter 4) and the challenges to creating domestic production lines of solar components have been the major blocks (Empresa de Pesquisa Energética 2012a: 1), showing that GIP concerns can block as well as advance the development of new industries. BNDES's Build-Down local content measure, for example, simply did not work for the solar industry, as solar panels cost more than 40 percent of the total value of an installation and could not be manufactured in Brazil in the first decade of the 2000s (Empresa de Pesquisa Energética 2012a, 17–18).[26] Solar manufacturing is quite complex, requiring assembly lines of "very costly and sensitive high tech equipment" (Schmidt and Hueteneler 2016: 12). In addition, with solar power being added only after 2014, it is contemporaneous with the broader national government retreat from industrial policy after 2016, when the post-PT governments began. Thus, it did not benefit as much from the closer support, for example, from MDIC, that wind had received.[27]

Demand-side interventions to promote solar power are very recent in Brazil. An industry group began to meet in 2010 at the suggestion of the Ministry of Mines and Energy, to be its interlocutor. Its 140 members in 2012 wrote a set of proposals to the Ministry for development of their industry that pinpointed the lack of demand as the single largest obstacle (ABINEE 2012: 9). A successful auction in the state of Pernambuco in 2013 finally persuaded decision-makers that solar power's time had come.[28] In October 2014, Brazil held the first reserve auction that included solar power. Developers registered 400 solar

---

[26] Interview with BNDES group, Rio de Janeiro, 2012.
[27] Interview with Boeira, ABDI, 2018.
[28] Interview with Rodrigo Sauaia, Presidente Executivo of Associação Brasileira de Energia Solar Fotovoltaica, Absolar, São Paulo, 2018.

projects with over 10 GW of installed capacity, a sign of the pent-up deployment side awaiting government procurement demand (Empresa de Pesquisa Energética 2014a: 8). Thirty-one projects were selected, to provide 889.7 MW of installed power. The average winning bid price, US$88, was 18 percent below the bid ceiling set by the government – and well below the US$103 that had won in Pernambuco the year before.[29] This was the first real step toward developing solar power in Brazil, which has since been reinforced by more auctions after a gap in 2016 when economic growth slowed (see Figure 3.1). There was a strong concentration of winning builders in the first two auctions. The Italian Enel Green Power received contracts for almost as much as the next three combined (CEBDS 2018: 35).

On a parallel track, regulatory changes in 2012 established the possibility of distributed solar production through net-metering and further changes in 2015 facilitated its growth (Sebrae 2017b: 75–76). From May 2017 to May 2018, installations nearly tripled to reach 27,803 micro and mini generators.[30] This is still a very small number for a country with about 210 million people, but it shows a rapidly growing market for distributed solar as well as grid-scale. Unlike grid-scale wind and solar power, the demand side for distributed solar power is from individual consumers and so lacks the state control that would make it part of industrial policy. It is discussed in Chapter 4.

The timing of the demand-side incentives for solar production responds to the drop in global solar prices as world installed capacity soared and Chinese producers entered the market. That same drop in prices generated a heated debate about whether Brazil should adopt solar power by simply importing the ever-cheaper internationally produced components or by trying to localize production. The Ministry of Mines and Energy has come down hard on the side of ignoring localization, supported by the Ministry of Finance.[31] The same drop in component prices that motivates new demand for solar also makes competitive localized production correspondingly difficult. On the other hand, importing components leaves the industry vulnerable to currency movements when there is little of a domestic supply chain.

---

[29] Interview with Sauaia, Absolar, 2018.
[30] www.absolar.org.br/noticia/noticias-externas/energia-solar-fotovoltaica-atinge -marca-historica-de-500-mw-em-microgeracao-e-minigeracao-distribuid.html.
[31] Interviews with Ricardo Baitelo, Renewable Energy Project, Greenpeace Brasil, São Paulo, 2014 (JRT); Melo, ABEEólica, 2014; Boeira, ABDI, 2018.

Given the currency devaluations in 2015 that made their projects economically infeasible, all but Enel of the 2014 winners had to seek extensions and pay a fine.[32] Some dropped out altogether.

BNDES's solution was to copy and formalize the progressive local content process eventually worked out for the wind sector.[33] Instead of its usual flat requirement for local content, winning solar power developers in the 2014 auction and afterwards needed to commit to progressively nationalizing the manufactured components and production processes in their installations, with BNDES participation in the financing growing with the nationalized share. These loans are well worth receiving: 15 percent of the investment can be financed by BNDES's National Climate Change Fund, with a basic interest rate of only 0.1 percent annually, and up to 65 percent can be financed through its normal Finame industrialization line. Even so, the broader economic crisis and currency declines made BNDES's original schedule of increasing local content too hard to achieve. In consultation with Absolar, the solar industry association, BNDES made the requirements simpler and more flexible in June of 2017, extending a further carrot of up to 80 percent financing from BNDES.[34] Even the cheaper finance from BNDES still does not compensate for the higher prices of domestic inputs, so BNDES finance did not present equally strong incentives for localization of solar production as it had in wind.

BNDES also plays a much smaller role for solar power with four other public banks offering solar finance and multiple private banks doing so. Sebrae counted literally dozens of sources of solar finance (Sebrae 2017b: 89–129) and Absolar maintains an online database of more than seventy financial lines available for potential consumers.[35] Most of these lines are for small consumers wishing to install distributed solar systems. For example, the regional development councils of the North, the Northeast, and the Center-West agreed on an US$800 million credit line for distributed solar power in 2018. A few months later, access to BNDES's National Climate Change Fund was

---

[32] www.rechargenews.com/solar/1182915/brazil-allows-pv-developers-to-cancel-ppas-from-2014-tender.

[33] www.bndes.gov.br/SiteBNDES/bndes/bndes_pt/Institucional/Sala_de_Imprensa/Destaques_Primeira_Pagina/20140812_energiasolar.html.

[34] www.absolar.org.br/noticia/noticias-externas/bndes-muda-metodologia-para-facilitar-o-incentivo-a-geracao-de-energia-solar-no-brasil.html.

[35] www.absolar.org.br/financiamento.

extended to individuals and small consumers like condominiums, businesses, local governments, and others.[36] These were also given access to a second Finame line, Finame Renovável, which had an initial tranche of about US$500 million for distributed renewable energy systems and solar water heaters. Interest rates are as low as 1.3 percent. Another program finances households and microenterprises with about US$57 million, with interest rates varying by income. Since financing limits have been one of the most significant limitations to developing solar power, especially for distributed generation, these initiatives are critical to removing a major blockage.[37] Only BNDES systematically requires local content, so these additional sources of finance boost solar manufacturing mostly through the indirect route of increased demand.

Beyond financial incentives, there are a number of incentive systems for solar power at both national and state levels (Sebrae 2017b: 80–86), so this summary highlights just a few of the most important. For solar project developers, the 2007 REIDI law that exempted imports for infrastructure projects from the PIS and COFINS taxes was among the most important, although it created a disincentive for national production. For solar manufacturers, the PADIS incentive program for semiconductors was the most important. This 2007 law established a suite of fiscal incentives tied to successive development stages of semiconductors and displays that included solar PV cells mounted in modules. The PADIS was ruled an illegal subsidy by the World Trade Organization (WTO) in 2018,[38] before all the development stages were achieved. Finally, there were two laws in 2015 that relieved taxes on distributed generation along with stimulations for investment through the Program of Investment in Distributed Generation (ProGD) that same year (Portaria MME No. 538). In 2015 and 2016, the Ministry of Mines and Energy temporarily lowered import duties on capital goods for solar production lines from 14 percent to 2 percent to support distributed solar power as part of this.

ABDI contracted a survey of the solar sector in 2018 that found that 38 firms specialized in centralized installation and services while the

---

[36] www.valor.com.br/brasil/5410515/fundos-vao-financiar-uso-de-energia-solar-com-r-32-bi; www.canalenergia.com.br/noticias/53063571/bndes-muda-regra-e-pessoas-fisicas-podem-investir-em-energia-solar; www.bndes.gov.br/wps/portal/site/home/financiamento/produto/bndes-finame-energia-renovavel.

[37] Interview with Nahur, WWF-Brasil, Brasília, 2018.

[38] *Valor Econômico*, 14 December 2018.

large majority (188) focused on distributed services. A few did both (Agência Brasileira de Desenvolvimento Industrial 2018). A more detailed survey by Sebrae (Sebrae 2017b), which works with small and micro businesses, found 528 firms doing solar installation, 226 offering engineering services, and 176 equipment distributors, with some overlap. In contrast, just one to ten firms made each of seventeen materials and components in the solar production chain, although the survey found twenty making panel structures and trackers.[39] In order to be at all competitive in the current solar marketplace, manufacturers need to be large and able to take advantage of economies of scale, so it is likely that there will continue to be many fewer manufacturing firms than service sector ones.

This can also be seen in the response to BNDES's solar finance lines where just forty-six firms had at least one product credentialed with Finame in 2018.[40] Ten of these made only small wattage panels, but the list included ten firms making invertors, eleven with trackers, and many making larger panels – Globo Brasil, the first, set up in 2015 with help from São Paulo state's investment agency.[41] Essentially, all the products but the small solar modules are marked as eligible for BNDES finance only on a case-by-case basis, so that developers who want to use the product to meet their local content requirements have to prove that the minimal levels of local content were met for their purchases. There are few technology limits now to manufacturing solar modules in Brazil, but costs have become the major limit, especially with what is still small-scale demand for both centralized and distributed solar power installations. After the United States imposed a tariff on Chinese solar panels in 2017, Brazilian manufacturers demanded the same, but the government has been unresponsive.[42]

Turning to other indicators, IRENA estimated that quick job growth had appeared in the photovoltaic solar sector in Brazil, from zero jobs in 2014 (International Renewable Energy Agency 2015: 16) to 4,000 in 2015 and 2016 (International Renewable Energy Agency 2016b: 12;

---

[39] www.sebrae.com.br/sites/PortalSebrae/artigos/conheca-mais-sobre-a-cadeia-produtiva-de-energia,17ead6d4760f3610VgnVCM1000004c00210aRCRD.

[40] www.bndes.gov.br/wps/portal/site/home/financiamento/servicos-online/creden ciamento-de-equipamentos/consulta-fornecedores-produtos-credenciados. Search terms were "solar" and "fotovoltaico."

[41] www.investe.sp.gov.br/noticia/globo-brasil-inaugura-fabrica-de-paineis-solares-em-valinhos/.

[42] Interview with Boeira, ABDI, 2018.

International Renewable Energy Agency 2017: 21) and a big jump to 10,000 jobs in 2016–2017 (International Renewable Energy Agency 2018: 25). It does not break down the jobs by type, although BNDES estimated that there were 1,000 direct solar industrial manufacturing jobs in 2017.[43] An estimate by Greenpeace Brasil suggests that the current regulatory structure would result in 609,000 direct and indirect jobs by 2030 for distributed solar alone (Greenpeace Brasil 2016b: 9). With innovation, as with jobs, the evidence is still quite initial. Applications for patents for solar power in Brazil came several years before demand did, peaking in 2011, and the 1,653 total filings in Brazil were just 2.3 percent of China's 71,266.[44] It is obviously early to assess Brazil's solar power industry, but localization, if not innovation, appears to be beginning. Similarly, it is too early to expect a full green spiral.

3.3 State and Market in the South African Electricity Sector

The physical and socioeconomic electricity systems that predated wind and solar power in South Africa place one actor at the very center: the electricity parastatal Eskom. It has historically done 96 percent of the power generation in the country and still oversees its transmission, dispatch, and distribution, with municipal governments contributing to the last (National Planning Commission 2012: 141). In 2020, debates over its breakup and partial privatization continue. Eskom continues to hold much of the national expertise in electricity planning, modeling, and technical implementation.[45] The post-apartheid government began to consider reducing Eskom's role shortly after taking office in 1994, about the same time that Cardoso began to reform Eletrobras. But while Brazil quickly achieved significant reforms, Eskom fought back more successfully. It stymied several early efforts to introduce private actors into generation and to alter the distribution model (Eberhard 2007).[46] It did acquire a regulator, NERSA, in 1996.

In resisting change, Eskom has benefited from profound disagreements within the governing coalition (Ndletyana 2013). The ANC

---

[43] www.bndes.gov.br/SiteBNDES/bndes/bndes_es/Institucional/Press/Destaques_Primeira_Pagina/20170628_metodologia_de_acreditacion.html.
[44] http://inspire.irena.org/Pages/patents/Patents-Search.aspx.
[45] Interview with Fabricius, Eskom, Germiston, 2014. See also Chapter 2.
[46] Interview with Eberhard, an energy analyst, Cape Town, 2014.

party has won all national elections since 1994, parlaying its role in ending apartheid into party dominance while falling prey to factional disputes. Its governing Tri-Partite Alliance is with the South African Communist Party (SACP) and the trade union federation COSATU, partners in the anti-apartheid struggle (Seidman 1994). The Tri-Partite Alliance has been deeply divided over economic policy, with the SACP and COSATU arguing for statist and collective economic models over the market-friendly policies the ANC has followed since 1996. At the same time, the ANC has had sometimes contentious relations with the large white-owned conglomerates that dominate the South African economy (Nattrass 1994; Nattrass 2014; Seekings and Nattrass 2011; Taylor 2007). All of these divisions show up in hard-fought debates over electricity policy, where different parts of the government frequently push different strategies.

South African political economy has been further rocked in recent years by divisions within the labor movement and its changing relations with the ANC. One union at the center of many of the events was the National Union of Mineworkers (NUM), deeply entrenched in the traditional South African economy. NUM had been the largest union in South Africa, but membership dropped after it supported the police who killed thirty-four striking workers in the Marikana platinum mine in 2012 (Alexander 2013: 615). NUM has also suffered internal tensions since its membership, once a fairly homogenous grouping of low-skilled black miners, now includes the skilled and professional workers of Eskom as well (Beresford 2012; Buhlungu and Bezuidenhuit 2008). The whole union has a clear self-interest in the historic models of electricity generation in South Africa, dominated by coal and Eskom. NUM has also continued its support of the ANC and is a dominant actor in COSATU (Alexander 2013: 615).

Meanwhile, the National Union of Metalworkers of South Africa (NUMSA) was expelled from COSATU for failure to support the ANC in the 2014 election. It formed an alternative labor federation, the South African Federation of Trade Unions (SAFTU), in 2017. NUMSA is the South African union that has thought the most about a new electricity model for the country. It already organizes workers in steel, fiberglass, and other materials sectors that are important for renewable electricity, and had plans to organize workers "in all branches of the renewables sector" (NUMSA 2011: 7, 9). Despite their differences, both federations and their core unions began to express open opposition to procurement from wind and solar IPPs in 2017 that has helped block changes to Eskom (Cloete 2018; Deedat 2018).

As this brief survey of governing party and union positions suggests, divisions over the appropriate role of state and market in the electricity sector continued unresolved at the time when wind and solar power emerged as viable alternatives to Eskom's coal power infrastructure. Eskom was asked in the early 2000s to build wind and solar power, but it simply refused to do so (Tsikati and Sebitosi 2010). The turning points for both issues – state versus market, coal versus renewables – were significant shortfalls in electricity supply that caused extensive load-shedding in 2008. As in Brazil and many other places (Aklin and Urpelainen 2018), an electricity supply crisis opened the door for wind and solar power in South Africa. As already discussed in Chapter 2, these developments raised questions about Eskom's capacity to exercise its historic roles, making room for the proponents of market actors and of wind and solar power simultaneously.

In partial response, the 2008 National Energy Act made a number of changes, setting up a separate Department of Energy and moving some of Eskom's responsibilities there. While this was formally just a transfer of power from one state actor to another, the new Department of Energy was more open to including private actors in the electricity sector. It also had much less of a corporate interest in retaining the integrated electricity structure centered on Eskom than the organization itself did (Morris and Martin 2015).

Debates continued after 2008 on exactly how private actors and renewable energy would be introduced. Because the debates involve specific GIP choices for wind and solar power, they are discussed in Section 3.3.1 on the renewable energy programs themselves. In the end, South Africa also chose auctions where IPPs could bid to supply long-term government contracts as the best way to bring wind and solar power into the national electricity supply. At the same time, the South Africans continued to use Eskom and more traditional procurement practices for coal and nuclear power. This included, as we will see again, significant state capture (Chipkin and Swilling 2017; Southall 2016).

Despite important distributive aims in South African auctions and their GIP, social support has been weaker than in Brazil. Both Eskom and South African unions have continued to openly fight the addition of wind and solar IPPs, placing the question of state versus market provision of electricity at the center of national policy for an energy transition (van Niekerk 2020: 133–134). While unions once used the language of just transitions to make demands about how wind and solar power might be introduced, they have increasingly used that language to argue against introducing them at all: "The tradeoff of unemployment for workers in the coal sector and Eskom for non-carbon/renewable energy did not seem fair" (Deedat 2018: 11).

As Chapter 2 describes, routine electricity planning in South Africa has been stalled since 2011, with the question of who – Eskom or private firms – will build electricity as one of its sticking points. While past draft Integrated Resource Plans (IRPs) (Department of Energy 2013, 2016, 2017, 2018) all stressed the important role of private actors, the 2019 drafts have for the first time explicitly stepped back from the question of who will build the new plants. They are only directing the mix of electricity supply, while the presidency is to separately decide on Eskom's role (Department of Energy 2019a: 64) and a role for Eskom in new generation is urged (Department of Energy 2019b: 17).

3.3.1 South African Renewable Energy Programs and Incentives

When electricity supply crashed in South Africa in 2008, wind and solar power appealed as diversified electricity sources that could be built quickly, with the added benefit of reducing climate emissions (Ritchkin and Zadeck 2010). The larger political economy of widespread unemployment and an economy that still excluded many black South Africans made jobs and racial inclusion top priorities for all national economic initiatives. The electricity sector itself was dominated by the same white capital firms of the apartheid years (Fine and Rustomjee 1996) and coal mining remained one of the best jobs for black South African workers with few skills. As a result, industrial policy aims were an obvious add-on for the ANC with the main question being which specific industrial policy mechanisms to use. Black economic empowerment (BEE) initiatives have targeted Black African populations for special priority attention within these (Atwell 2013; Krüger 2011). Positions about the wind and solar industries map onto the large, contentious fault lines in current South African politics. This was visible in the ways in which different departments and ministries competed to fill the governance gap for electricity generation after Jacob Zuma became president in 2009. Chapter 2 has already introduced these, but here I stress their implications for industrial policy and the relationship between states and markets.

The South African Renewables Initiative (SARI) had a classic industrial policy profile, not least because it involved the Departments of Trade and Industry (DTI) and Public Enterprises (DPE). These tend to take the side of a larger state role in the economy, either actively promoting the private sector (DTI) or the SOEs that are the DPE's domain. SARI's proponents saw the possibility of an ambitious industrial policy that could make South Africa a producer rather than a consumer in the "third industrial revolution" of clean energy.[47] The DTI linked SARI to its official Green Growth strategy, with supporting initiatives in the Department of Economic Development's New Growth Path and Green Economy Accord. In Minister of Industry Rob Davies' vision, developing wind and solar power could "simultaneously enable the development of the industrial capabilities to design and manufacture renewable generation systems, provide jobs, protect and enhance the competitiveness of exports in increasingly carbon-sensitive international markets and contribute to the country's energy security and so the basis for a robust and growing economy" (foreword to Ritchkin and Zadeck 2010: 3). SARI had financial commitments from foreign governments, but it did not build ties to the ascending Department of Energy and the initiative was not developed.[48] Some participants, like WWF South Africa, have continued to try to develop an industrial policy grounding for renewable energy (e.g., Fakir 2017).

A second initiative came from the regulator NERSA, which used its tariff-setting role to justify establishing a Renewable Energy Feed-in Tariff, or REFIT, to bring private wind and solar IPPs into the generation matrix. REFIT did not have explicit industrial policy components, although it expected that demand could stimulate industry development. The REFIT program struggled, however, to set prices right. Initial prices set in 2009 were too low for developer interest and so were raised later that year, only to be abruptly dropped again in

---

[47] Observation of launch, December 2011, Durban. Minister of Industry Rob Davies claimed to be launching South Africa's participation in the "third industrial revolution."

[48] Interview with Fakir, WWF South Africa, Cape Town, 2013.

2011. Eskom also resisted signing agreements that would give the facilities access to the grid. The low rates and the uncertainty destroyed developers' trust in the program and no electricity was actually procured through this program either (Pegels 2014c: 130–131). There were persistent questions about whether a FiT would be too expensive and whether it met the constitutional requirement to have competitive bidding (Bischof-Niemtz and Creamer 2019: 44).

In contrast, the Department of Energy and the National Treasury decided that price competition should be incorporated from the beginning, both for electricity costs and as a way of managing rents in a setting where true costs were largely unknown. Their program, the Renewable Energy Independent Power Producers Procurement Programme (REIPPPP), is the one that has actually been used. The name shows the intention to contract electricity from private firms rather than depend only on Eskom for generation. It was paired with another plan that used similar IPPs to build coal plants on auctioned contracts with the state. These programs were a significant challenge to Eskom, whose economic model depends on controlling electricity generation (Morris and Martin 2015). The decision to use IPPs and auctions was taken inside the bureaucracy, and it was not in the original plan of former president Zuma or, certainly, Eskom, which had always resisted private generation.[49] The National Treasury, in particular, preferred private capital and could influence the decision-making as it was being asked to provide guarantees for the plants and their contracts (Bode 2013). The REIPPPP brings in IPPs through auctions where companies place tenders to supply electricity to the national grid under long-term contracts, similar to the Brazilian ones. A small, tight-knit team from the two agencies set up "one of the most sophisticated, complicated bidding processes ever seen in Africa" and has run it well (Eberhard, Kolker, and Leigland 2014: 10). The Treasury's participation is indicative of the intention to have strong rent management in the REIPPPP as it is known for its commitment to market disciplining (Pearson, Pillay, and Chipkin 2016).

Nonetheless, there has also been an expectation that renewable electricity should be added to the grid in ways that would benefit small, nontraditional firms and especially the historically excluded black population. Black-owned firms successfully lobbied to have the

[49] Interview with Levington, SAPVIA, 2018.

generation done by IPPs rather than Eskom, seeing the smaller scale of renewable electricity as more amenable to new market entrants like them. There has also been an increasingly explicit social contract that promotes renewable electricity in exchange for the jobs it will create, especially for black South Africans.[50] With formal unemployment levels hovering around 25 percent for the entire post-apartheid period, every economic policy in South Africa must address job creation.

The aims for black empowerment and job creation are built into South Africa's auctions in unique ways. Bids from developers must include BEE partners. Seventy percent of the evaluation of competing bids is based on a firm's proposed prices for the supply of electricity and 30 percent on the basis of local content and so-called community renewables proposals (Bode 2013; Tait 2012; Tait, Wlokas, and Garside 2013). The community renewables requirement asks firms to specify the numbers and types of job that will be associated with their projects and to propose benefits and ownership shares for local communities, defined as those within a 50 km radius of the project. Following the BEE aims of the requirement, jobs for Black Africans and communities are particularly important. The industry associations spend much of their time explaining these requirements to potential foreign participants, stressing that they are critical for wider social acceptance of renewable energy.[51]

The community renewables proposals operated as a kind of check-off requirement in the first two rounds. Bids with a proposal that fit the terms were considered above the threshold and allowed to compete in the auction, mostly on price. For the third and subsequent rounds, however, the community renewables portion of the bid became competitive: the firm with the most generous proposals was ranked highest for this part of the bid, and other proposals were evaluated against it. This made the obligation one that requires more strategizing and attention in creating a bid proposal.[52]

Even with the social and BEE components, many actors oppose the REIPPPP because it uses IPPs. Several of the more critical nongovernmental organizations (NGOs) who are in the Life After Coal campaign favor opening renewable energy generation to a much wider set of

---

[50] Interviews with Fabricius, Eskom, 2014; Fakir, WWF South Africa, 2013; Levington, SAPVIA, 2014 and 2018.
[51] Interview with Levington, SAPVIA, Johannesburg, 2014.
[52] Interviews with two IPP developers in 2013.

small-scale and community-based initiatives (see also Bode 2013).[53]
These have a harder time finding a role in auction systems than they do
with FiTs (Grashof 2019; Leiren and Reimer 2018). In order to phase
out coal more quickly, however, the Campaign accepts the use of wind
and solar IPPs, as do most of the civil society activists in South Africa.

Labor unions have more strongly opposed the REIPPPP on principle.
NUMSA has been a critic of the turn to private generation from the
start of the REIPPPP, decrying: "Capital[,] as is always the case, views
the introduction of renewables as a new site of accumulation"
(NUMSA 2011: 1; van Niekerk 2020: 142). Eskom has fanned the
labor movement's critiques, blaming its need to pay private firms high
prices for wind and solar power for its economic problems. Eskom even
refused to sign power purchase agreements with the firms that had won
bidding windows 3.5 and 4, bringing the whole REIPPPP to a standstill
from July 2016 until March 2018.[54] Eskom's then-CEO Brian Molefe
and other key figures in Eskom were vocal in their criticisms of renewable sources for their cost and especially irregularity of supply, stating
a clear preference for coal and nuclear power. Eskom also directly cited
the REIPPPP when explaining why it was closing five coal plants a few
years before they were scheduled to be retired in 2020.

Eskom's statements further galvanized organized labor (van Niekerk
2020). A Coal Transporters Forum brought and lost a case in the
Johannesburg High Court that asked the court to prevent Eskom
from signing more renewable energy contracts (Case 42887/2017).
Both NUM and NUMSA threatened job actions in March 2017,
against the loss of coal sector jobs. COSATU told the National
Economic Development and Labour Council (NEDLAC) in
June 2017 that it was planning a large protest as a result: "The purpose
of this notice is to stop government from buying renewable energy at
the expense of jobs and as an excuse to privatize Eskom" (COSATU
2017: 2). COSATU's filing to NEDLAC insists that while it favors an
electricity matrix with fewer fossil fuels, any resulting jobs should be in
the state, rather than private, sector (COSATU 2017: 3). While politically opposed to COSATU, SAFTU has made nearly identical arguments
on wind and solar power, using the language of just transition to reject

---

[53] https://cer.org.za/news/the-transition-to-a-low-carbon-future-must-be-rapid-
and-must-be-for-everyone; email interview with Loser, CER, 2018.
[54] www.engineeringnews.co.za/article/eskom-letter-sends-shock-waves-through-
private-power-sector-2016-07-21.

closing the coal plants and the IPPs altogether. Noting that capitalism had caused global warming, SAFTU warned that it could not be addressed with "[p]rivate companies which are only interested in making profits, [which] will do nothing to help the workers whose jobs disappear," counting 92,000 vulnerable jobs.[55]

Not surprisingly, the IPPs themselves and their industry associations immediately shot back defenses of the REIPPPP, and kept the issue in the news in 2016–2018 with press releases, interviews, and editorials in a remarkably public series of exchanges with Eskom representatives about state versus private generation. Key industry analysts and Greenpeace also weighed in.[56] Then-minister of energy Tina Joemat-Petterson appeared to end the debate with a statement that all forms of electricity would be part of the matrix, but skirmishes have continued through the years, as different parts of government made different statements about what kind of electricity should be procured and from whom. Chapter 2 has already traced the effects on energy-sector planning, where successive plans made wildly different statements about what kinds of electricity would be procured.

As this discussion shows, the question of whether state or private actors should generate electricity continues to be the subject of very lively debate in South Africa. Since almost all the private generation has been wind and solar power and almost all the wind and solar power is generated privately, the two electricity choices are strongly conflated. After Zuma was pushed from office in March 2018, new president Cyril Ramaphosa opted rhetorically for restarting the REIPPPP, with its private generation of renewables. Yet when the electricity plan was finally officially updated in 2019, it included a call for Eskom to be allowed to build new capacity of some kind (Department of Energy 2019b: 17), a clause added after the labor movement had delayed the agreement in national discussions of the plan. Given that the issue has been festering at least since 1998, it is unlikely that this will be the final word. For those who are not ideologically committed to particular resolutions of the state–market divide, the actual performance of the

---

[55] http://saftu.org.za/saftu-calls-on-workers-join-march-for-eskom-jobs-and-against-privatisaton/. See also Cloete 2018.
[56] The following are just a few of the contributions: www.sapvia.co.za/sapvia-media-statement-private-sector-investment-in-solar-pv-faces-risks/; www.bdlive.co.za/opinion/letters/2016/07/25/letter-populist-remarks-have-little-to-do-with-eskoms-structure?service=print.

REIPPPP and the success of rent management within it are important considerations, and those are the subject of Section 3.3.2.

3.3.2 *The REIPPPP As Industrial Policy: Rent Management and Outcomes*

The ongoing struggle over state versus private electricity generation has nearly overwhelmed public debate over the REIPPPP in South Africa. Both sides have put forward different facts about the program's outcomes that require some parsing. Now that Zuma and his associates are out of office, even Eskom uses data that is close to that consistently presented by the wind and solar industries, most academic analysts, and NGOs in the energy sector. That is used here, with a particular focus on the quality of the REIPPPP as industrial policy.

On the demand side, four auction rounds have now been conducted and the projects of the first round came online in 2014. The four rounds contracted a total of 2,660 MW of installed capacity of wind power and 1,899 MW of solar PV (all figures from Department of Energy 2015). This is more than the 3,275 MW initially contemplated for the program (Department of Energy 2011). As a tool for promoting a green end, producing wind and solar power, the REIPPPP can claim some success, especially in the coal-dominant culture of South Africa. As an industrial policy, the demand side of the REIPPPP is more mixed. The auction format has performed as an intended rent management tool, bringing costs down sharply over time (Bischof-Niemtz and Creamer 2019: 45). While there is more concentration among the winners than in Brazil, South Africa has retained enough serious participants for effective competition (Bayer, Schäuble, and Ferrari 2018). Yet the details of procurement have been less promising.

Figure 3.2 shows the annual procurements for wind and solar power, which not only are much lower than Brazil's but also reflect the hiatus when Eskom flatly announced that it would not, in fact, sign contracts for the quantities procured in the 2014 and 2015 auctions. Those quantities then reappear in 2018 when the contracts were finally signed, but it should be obvious that the demand side of South African GIP offers considerable uncertainty about the prospects of wind and solar power. The most recent electricity plans propose to return to more wind and solar procurement, but they also leave several years with minimal demand and continue to impose annual limits (Department of Energy

2018, 2019a, 2019b). This is a problem for the firms that do construction and installation, but it is even more problematic for the manufacturing side as manufacturing facilities cannot be simply shut down for a few years and then reopened. Industry associations and their allies have been pressuring to have a steady and larger demand in a revised plan. In the meantime, the REIPPPP has not yet offered enough simple demand-based benefits for renewable energy firms to expect significant industry development (Matsuo and Schmidt 2019).

To complete the picture of few industrial policy benefits for wind and solar power, South Africa does not have an actor that plays the financing or disciplining role of BNDES in Brazil. For wind and solar power, there has been little public funding, with or without rent management. The main state-controlled finance for the REIPPPP projects is from two national development banks. The Green Industries Sustainable Business Unit of the Industrial Development Corporation (IDC) has lent about US$750 million for renewable electricity projects. Twenty percent of that went to BEE initiatives.[57] It sees itself as playing a facilitating and catalytic role and lacks the resources to do much more.[58] The Development Bank of South Africa (DBSA) helped to set up the IPP office and advises on program management. It has also funded parts of thirty-three projects, targeting the BEE and community development components (Morgado, Taşkın, Lasfargues, and Sedemund n.d.: 56). Projects must otherwise be privately financed at market rates, which is a significant hurdle for would-be developers and makes the resulting electricity correspondingly more expensive. It is also a challenge for many of South Africa's banks, for whom these are large and risky loans (Baker 2015b). European project developers, who can use Eurobonds with low interest rates, have a significant advantage in the auctions.[59] Most installation contract winners are international firms, even if they have BEE partners (Bayer, Schäuble, and Ferrari 2018).

Conversely, Eskom was treated quite generously with little meaningful oversight for years. In 2015, the South African Treasury provided an extraordinary fiscal transfer to Eskom of US$1.64 billion. In 2019, the Ramaphosa government pledged another US$1.64 billion in transfers to Eskom in each of the next three years in his State of the Nation

---

[57] www.idcbackup.co.za/IR2012/green-industries.php.
[58] Interview with Raoul Goosen, Green Industries Strategic Business Unit, Industrial Development Corporation (IDC), Johannesburg, 2014.
[59] Interview with Levington, SAPVIA, 2014.

address and a total of US$10.7 billion over ten years.[60] This was many times the finance provided for wind and solar projects, despite Eskom's poor performance in both building its two new coal plants and providing electricity – but it equally reflected Eskom's central role in directing rents to the Zuma government and its allies (Chipkin and Swilling 2017).

In the industry's tally, it had brought far more to the table than the public sector had. The REIPPPP has been one of the few new industries to develop in South Africa's anemic economy and was a bright spot of private investment – 86 percent of all foreign direct investment in 2014.[61] In a blog posting, the South African Wind Energy Association's (SAWEA) then-president Johan Van den Berg listed private investment of US$17 billion in rural areas, with US$2.2 billion going into social and enterprise development in those communities. Almost US$8.9 billion was budgeted for local content, 12 industrial facilities had been set up, and SAWEA counted 111,835 job-years already created as a result. All of this was endangered by the delays in signing REIPPPP contracts and van den Berg warned of industry exits.[62]

Turning to the question of jobs created, several government-labor-business dialogues had promised abundant green jobs. The Green Economy Accord, signed in 2011, set a goal of 300,000 green jobs by 2020, to be achieved through "a localisation strategy that uses the enormous spending on climate-change induced technologies to create local industrial capacity, local jobs, and local technical innovation" (Economic Development Department 2011: 7–8). The Accord aspired to 75 percent local content for renewable electricity in particular, with 50,000 jobs by 2020, 6,500 of them for engineers and technicians (Economic Development Department 2011: 19). A civil society initiative with unions aimed even higher in its One Million Climate Jobs campaign, although most of those jobs would be for installation of solar water heaters (Aroun 2012).[63] As already described in Section

---

[60] www.dailymaverick.co.za/article/2019-07-04-floundering-eskom-ship-running
-out-of-ballast-as-treasury-prepares-special-appropriation-bill/.

[61] Interview with Levington, SAPVIA, 2018.

[62] www.energy.org.za/news/independent-power-producers-take-on-eskom-
through-national-energy-regulator; www.energy.org.za/news/eskom-delays-on
-ipp-signatures-are-costing-jobs; see also interview with van den Berg, SAWEA,
Johannesburg, 2014.

[63] climatejobs.org.za; interview with Trevor Ngwane of the One Million Climate
Jobs campaign, Johannesburg, 2014.

3.3.1, NUMSA has a strong preference for eventual public or collective ownership in all branches of the renewable energy sector (NUMSA 2012: 1). At the same time, it saw a reason for the engagement of a South African private manufacturing sector in the short and medium term, if only to keep multinational firms from flooding the country (NUMSA 2012: 11).

In principle, South Africa could successfully localize much of the supply chain for wind and solar power. The consulting firm McKinsey, in a study for the Department of Energy, concluded that 45 percent of the solar supply chain and 79 percent of the wind supply chain could be produced nationally immediately with wind readily climbing to 97 percent. These numbers compare favorably with those of coal (53 percent) and nuclear (36 percent) (cited in Bischof-Niemtz and Creamer 2019: 133–140). Overall, the study found many more potential jobs in wind and solar than in coal and nuclear power, for both installation and supplier jobs.

Table 3.1 shows that most of the bid localization numbers are much lower than these hypothetical numbers. Under the REIPPPP, firms must source a growing percentage of inputs from local sources, with a percentage of that from local Black African suppliers (Baker and Sovacool 2017; Rennkamp and Boyd 2015). Unlike Brazil, where the government and BNDES set specific levels to be achieved, the South African program allows firms to bid the levels as part of their competition with each other. Winning bids have steadily raised their local content pledges, rising from 21.7 percent in round 1 to peak at 46.9 percent in round 3 for wind bids. Solar bids have risen more steadily from 28.5 to 64.7 percent. In order to support these levels, international firms trained South Africans both in their home countries and by helping to establish the South African Renewable Energy Technology Center (SARETEC) with the South African government and universities (Matsuo and Schmidt 2019: 22–23).

Looking beneath the bids finds an even more complicated story. For wind power, initial bids included about 25 percent local content, mostly for the "balance of plant," or what goes into and above the ground to hold the tower. The local content floors of subsequent rounds have been higher, but industry representatives in 2014 put actual production capacity at the time below the round 3 bids.[64] In 2013, there was only one

---

[64] Interview with van den Berg, SAWEA, 2014.

Table 3.1 *South African REIPPPP electricity generation projects*

	Wind	Photovoltaic solar
Contracted installed capacity		
Round 1	652	635
Round 2	571	423
Round 3	787	435
Round 4	677	415
Job creation: construction* (per MW)		
Round 1	1810 (2.85)	2381 (3.77)
Round 2	1787 (3.17)	2270 (5.44)
Round 3	2612 (3.32)	2119 (4.87)
Round 4	2831 (4.19)	3825 (9.22)
Job creation bid: operation* (per MW)		
Round 1	2461 (3.88)	6117 (9.68)
Round 2	2238 (3.98)	3809 (9.13)
Round 3	8506 (10.8)	7513 (17.27)
Round 4	8161 (12.07)	9273 (22.35)
Local content percent bid		
Round 1	21.7	28.5
Round 2	36.7	47.5
Round 3	46.9	53.8
Round 4	44.6	64.7

Source: Contracted installed capacity from www.eskom.co.za/Whatweredoing/Pages/ RE_IPP_Procurement_Programme.aspx; other numbers compiled from Department of Energy 2015.

* Number is jobs-year, where one job-year = 12 person-months and 1 person-month is 160 hours. Figure in parentheses is jobs-year per MW installed.

local wind components manufacturer, which was liquidating because it could not supply the right blades for the new markets (Rennkamp and Boyd 2015: 10). Two firms subsequently opened operations in South Africa to build towers, adding another 15 percent of potential local content (Baker and Sovacool 2017). One of these was a joint venture between the DCD Group and the government's IDC, which built its first tower in 2014. Blades and turbines would be the next logical components, but small market size and obligatory international certifications make those a challenge in South Africa.[65] They are still imported (Baker

---

[65] Interview with van den Berg, SAWEA, 2014.

and Sovacool 2017: 8). The small market size made many components unprofitable and solar production in particular often imported cheap Chinese panels and exaggerated the value added in South African assembly to hit the targets (Matsuo and Schmidt 2019: 23). Finally, during the uncertainty around the REIPPPP in 2016–2018 and since, many firms closed shop or left South Africa. The IDC, which had financed many of them, also suffered.[66] For example, the DCD joint venture to build wind towers mostly closed operations in 2016, costing 115 jobs.[67]

Grid-scale solar power is an even greater challenge for localization, with 2014 manufacturing supporting only 22 percent of local content levels.[68] Three firms could produce solar modules in South Africa in 2013, although they were primarily assembly lines of international components, according to a consulting firm hired to survey the localization potential for solar power in South Africa. A total of only twelve firms including those three were producing components, although some potential for expansion was evident (EScience Associates, Urban-Econ, and Ahlfeldt 2013: xii). One firm, the German SMA Solar, made inverters. Another seven firms made panels and other inputs, according to a survey published in 2017 (Baker and Sovacool 2017: 8). The unreliable demand has affected the solar sector too: three of the seven companies listed by Baker and Sovacool (2017) did not have an internet presence in 2018. Many of the local content bids in the delayed rounds are above the current manufacturing capacity of local firms.[69] As in Brazil, the industrial policy effect is at best to localize some manufacturing in a new industry, and the South African industries are well behind the Brazilian ones. There has been minimal patent activity in South Africa related to wind and solar power, after some early solar patents.[70]

All of these developments have an impact on the jobs provided by the REIPPPP, another key industrial policy metric. The four rounds of the REIPPPP have resulted in 67,713 promised jobs (see Table 3.1). This paragraph takes those as actual jobs, even though the demand hiatus already described means that fewer jobs are likely to be created. In the

---

[66] Interview with Levington, SAPVIA, Johannesburg, 2018.
[67] www.fin24.com/Economy/South-Africa/idc-wants-to-revive-coega-wind-energy-project-20180126.
[68] Interview with Levington, SAPVIA, Johannesburg, 2014.
[69] Interview with Levington, SAPVIA, 2018.
[70] http://inspire.irena.org/Pages/patents/Patents-Search.aspx.

aggregate, this appears close to the 80,000 positions in the coal mining sector (Bischof-Niemtz and Creamer 2019: 147). Yet even among the bids, almost 20,000 of the jobs are construction jobs, which will last only the 18-month installation period. The operations and maintenance jobs are more numerous, but early analysis discovered that, because of missing skills, developers expected many of these jobs to be held by foreigners; very few would go to black South Africans in particular (Aroun 2013: 7). The levels of operations and maintenance jobs may be inflated in South Africa, as the percentage of jobs there per MW installed is substantially higher than in Brazil. The jump between the noncompetitive rounds 1 and 2 and the competitive rounds 3 and 4 also suggests that bidders padded their jobs totals to make competitive bids; one project manager volunteered that his company had done so to secure the contract.[71] IRENA counted 15,000 solar PV jobs in South Africa in 2017 and 10,400 in wind power (International Renewable Energy Agency 2018: 21). Virtually all of these are nonmanufacturing jobs (Bischof-Niemtz and Creamer 2019: 142). Thus, the quantity and the quality of the jobs fall far short of the labor movement's expectations.

COSATU has been one of the most radical participants in international debates on green jobs, helping to develop the international discourse about a need for a just transition to a low-carbon economy (Stevis and Felli 2015: 38). By 2017, COSATU was concluding that there would be fewer renewable energy jobs than estimated in South Africa and that coal workers would not be retrained for them (COSATU 2017: 3). The immediate trigger for a renewed just transition debate has been the proposed closing of five coal plants as REIPPPP contracts were signed in 2018 after a two-year delay.[72] South Africa has launched an extensive set of discussions about a just transition for workers, with some initiated by the government and others arising from civil society and unions themselves.[73] NUM and NUMSA have begun to articulate more specifics about what they

---

[71] Interview with IPP project manager, Cape Town, 2013.
[72] www.industriall-union.org/south-african-unions-call-for-a-just-transition-to-renewable-energy?utm_source=Newsletters+in+english&utm_campaign=b9dd11c8b4-EMAIL_CAMPAIGN_2018_11_22_03_22&utm_medium b9dd11c8b4-10713381.
[73] Interviews with Levington, SAPVIA, 2018; van Staden, EIUG, Johannesburg, 2018; Loser, CER, email interview, 2018.

would consider a just transition in their own national context. They are acutely aware that many of their members are not prepared for the next "industrial revolution" of renewable energy.[74] Some of the union demands would undermine the REIPPPP's basic state–market balance, asking for generation plants to be socially rather than privately owned (Cloete 2018). But others ask for provisions like those agreed in 2018 between Spanish unions and their government, including fair early retirement packages, environmental cleanup, and fuller training and absorption of coal sector workers into the renewable energy sector.[75] That plan has a US$280 million price tag, while an initial academic study of South Africa estimated labor-related costs of a just transition to be approximately US$140 million over twenty years.[76] The fact that South Africa already has distributive aims in its REIPPPP rules opens the possibility of adding more specific just transition solutions to them, like prioritizing projects in old coal and gold communities that already have a semiskilled workforce and few other options.[77]

Returning to the theoretical concerns about rent management, they do not seem to be particularly important for the South African REIPPPP. The program itself offers comparatively few rents, beyond those that can be gleaned in a competitive auction process with steadily dropping prices. Private finance must be found and there are few other incentives. In return, firms take on a rather formidable set of obligations meant to direct benefits of the program to black South Africans and host communities. Yet these gains were enough to make the emergent industries fight hard against Eskom's refusal to sign their contracts, perhaps the best sign of an incipient green spiral there. Whatever rents may exist in this sector, they are trivial compared to the corruption and state capture of the nuclear and coal industries (Chipkin and Swilling 2017).

It is less clear whether the distributive clauses most efficiently achieve their ends, but they are part of the wider South African debate about how to make up for the moral and economic damages of apartheid. It is worth pointing out that the benefits to communities in the REIPPPP do

---

[74] Interview with Levington, SAPVIA, 2018.
[75] www.ugt-fica.org/images/20101024_Marco_para_una_Transición_Justa_de_l a_Mineria_del_Carbón_DEFINITIVO.pdf.
[76] www.dailymaverick.co.za/article/2019-12-10-r6-billion-first-estimate-of-just-transition-in-south-africa/.
[77] Interview with Levington, SAPVIA, 2018.

not approach those available in systems where communities are encouraged to participate directly in generation (Bode 2013; Morris and Jungjohann 2016). Labor is also clearly dissatisfied with what it has gained to date, although some of its response to the REIPPPP is grounded in the broader and unresolved debates about the proper balance between state and market power and post-apartheid compensations.

3.4 Conclusion

The political economy of industrial policy focuses on the economic interests that states and private business actors might have in developing renewable energy as a new industry. Industrial policy for renewable energy implies both a large role for the state, which might act itself or at least sets incentives and limits for the private sector, and new private sector roles in countries like these where SOEs have done most electricity generation. This invokes broad debates about the appropriate roles of state and market actors in the electricity sector. It also involves potentially close relations between state and market actors as they work out those incentives and limits. Incentives that are too generous for too long allow private actors to gain private rents at the expense of public interests. Effective rent management better balances private and public returns. The quickest development of wind and solar power would simply import the cheapest components, so efforts to localize an industry could be seen as incompatible with renewable energy development. Conversely, industry localization might spur wind and solar power in the longer term by creating a broader base of political support among firms and labor whose self-interest creates a "green spiral" of sustained industry development. Existing national industrial structures obviously shape the possibilities too.

A key historical institutional contrast set the stage for differing national outcomes in this policy arena for Brazil and South Africa. Brazil settled the broad outlines of state and private roles in the electricity sector in the 1990s, taking a great deal of power from its electricity parastatal Eletrobras and giving some generation and distribution responsibilities to private firms while other state agencies under the Ministry of Mines and Energy took on Eletrobras's other roles. While discussion continued about these roles into the 2000s, it was mostly muted and did not have much impact on the development of wind and solar power. Conversely, contestation over the balance between state and private action is still very heated in South Africa and has had a large impact on the development of renewable energy there. Eskom had successfully defended its monopoly on the electricity sector until IPPs were allowed to build wind and solar power in its stead, starting in 2011. The reinforcing double cleavage – an SOE producing essentially all the coal and nuclear power while private firms produce essentially all the wind and solar power – has meant that the two debates are confounded in ways that have not been helpful to the latter. The difference between the two countries is an example of how existing institutions can shape different outcomes in the same policy arena. Questions about the state's economic ambitions and its relations with the private sector, including rent management strategies, must be answered against these different, historically grounded institutional backdrops.

The questions can be straightforwardly addressed for Brazil, and especially its wind power sector. The ambition to develop new national industrial sectors was clearly a major motivation for wind procurement in Brazil. Governments across multiple parties and administrations saw this as a modern growth sector worth supporting through localization policies of various kinds. The best explanation for the otherwise puzzling difference between wind and solar outcomes in Brazil is that it was so much easier, earlier, to consider developing a national manufacturing industry for wind power than it was for solar. Wind sector manufacturing drew on skills and materials already produced in Brazil – for its aeronautics industry, for example. That confidence seemed misplaced at first, when an initial small FiT program for wind power was actually delayed by the program's localization requirement. But after 2009, steadier demand and significant financial support from BNDES with other tax and tariff incentives began to put a self-sustaining green spiral in place, creating jobs, expanding manufacturing, and achieving many industrial policy goals short of novel innovation. Reduced demand in economic recession after 2015 has challenged those gains but not wholly undermined them. High levels of competition in cost-based auctions to supply electricity to the national grid disciplined rents, as did strict localization schedules by BNDES.

If industrial development ambitions spurred wind power in Brazil, the more limited opportunities to do the same in solar power help to account for its delay. Brazilian policy-makers were uninterested in procuring solar power, with its higher costs, when its different production requirements meant that a local industry would be much more difficult to create in the Brazilian context. As global prices dropped, some similar finance-driven incentives were offered to the solar power industry starting in 2014, although a greater array of financing options and the larger role for distributed generation diluted the industrial policy influence. In addition, the later start meant that most of the solar industry's development has been under the post-PT governments that began in 2016, which are less inclined to a comprehensive industrial policy strategy and are governing in economic downturns. A national solar installation industry has grown much faster than its manufacturing counterpart, and solar power was delayed overall because of its lower economic potential.

Many in South Africa also favored creating new wind and solar industries, and a flurry of government policies moved to do so after electricity shortfalls in 2008. When the REIPPPP was begun in 2011, promising steady procurement of wind and solar power through competitive auctions, many participants took part and manufacturers began to shift their operations to South Africa. But, as demand faltered at quite low aggregate levels in 2016 and contracts with auction winners went unsigned from 2016 to 2018, those developments reversed quickly. At minimum, this shows the critical role of procurement demand in motivating industry development. But the deeper issue was Eskom's refusal to sign the contracts and the Zuma government's unwillingness or inability to force it to do so. This made the government's indecision about its economic aims for renewable energy very clear and was highly destructive of the private sector confidence needed to launch a new industry. Yet this is one of the most successful of South Africa's post-apartheid efforts to develop new industrial initiatives with investment across the board limited by open contention in the dominant ANC about whether it wants to promote private industry.

The theoretical framework of rent management used in this chapter is really secondary to outcomes in South Africa because it assumes a commonality of state and private interests that was never fully evident. The REIPPPP itself, as a rent management system, is comparatively austere. Financing is almost entirely through private sources and there are few other incentives. The REIPPPP also uses highly competitive auctions. While they are not entirely cost-based, the remaining components make stringent demands for meeting South Africa's post-apartheid distributive aims through bids for local content, jobs, and community development. Those have contributed to some positive job outcomes, but the standstill on wind and solar power development has limited what can be expected. Labor unions are actively demanding a just transition for labor and coal communities in exchange for moving forward on wind and solar power. The industry associations agree. The anemic industrial development results for the sector so far do not help that discussion, but almost everyone hopes that they will improve.

The political economy of industrial policy is clearly a useful framework for viewing outcomes of wind and solar power in Brazil and South Africa. The framework is most illuminating in the Brazilian case, where state actors offer clear statements and corresponding action about their economic ambitions and strategies for developing what they call alternative renewable energies. Where industrial development has been more feasible, in the wind power sector, they were motivated to establish effective incentive policies while also disciplining industry recipients. It should be noted that these requirements did delay the rollout of wind and especially solar power in Brazil, which could have been accomplished more quickly and more cheaply without efforts to build a local industry. By their own recounting, however, policy-makers' decision to procure wind power in the first place would not have happened without the economic possibilities.

The puzzle left in Chapter 2 about the climate political economy, which could not account for the slow development of solar power in Brazil, is partially answered here. That chapter does add an important framing element to this one: the fact that contention around climate change largely skirts around wind and solar power in Brazil left the possibility of a more technocratic and low-conflict approach in other policy arenas, which also manifested in the industrial policy sphere. This chapter adds the historical caveat that prior settlement of most public–private roles in the electricity sector also contributed to that outcome. Both public and private generating firms were allowed to participate in the auctions to produce wind and solar power and competed on an equal basis.

In contrast, the high contentiousness around climate policy and its existential challenge to Eskom was redoubled in the industrial policy arena because the public–private balance had not been settled in South Africa. Because IPPs were selected to produce wind and solar power, they represented a double existential threat to it: phasing out coal threatened Eskom's historic generation role while ushering in IPPs threatened its future one. Electricity utilities rarely concern themselves with industrial policy, which is decided in other policy spaces, but it is not surprising that Eskom and its allies reached into this adjoining arena to contest it.

With the partial exception of Brazilian wind power, manufacturing and job gains from transitioning to wind and solar power were disappointing in both countries. Even Brazil's wind power industry looks anemic compared to the Chinese equivalent, which began at very nearly the same time (Lewis 2013). These results do clearly reflect the second-mover status of these countries, trying to build the industries when they were already well established elsewhere. These are the most industrialized countries in their regions, so it is not clear that other developing countries will do better. At the same time, South Africa's industrial development was clearly delayed by the long and unsettled fight over the appropriate roles for public and private actors in the sector. Whatever the theoretical possibilities, it seems obvious that it would have had better outcomes on all fronts if one or the other or both had simply been given the right to proceed. Many other countries, especially those without an Eskom equivalent, can try to develop industries without that debilitating fight. In addition, installation and operations and maintenance jobs seem within reach for many.

Reflecting on the more general possibilities of GIP in middle-income and developing countries, the limited success of these two regional powers is sobering. The advanced state of the global industries means that states must take specific steps to localize manufacturing, where their current capacities and skills allow. The contrast between the two countries shows that steady demand, often overlooked in favor of flashier and more expensive policies, is a critical first step of GIP in electricity. In both countries, well-designed and -administered auctions provided a strong framework for providing that demand (when they were allowed to happen) in ways that controlled rents by encouraging competition. The staged approach of Brazil's national development bank, which eventually developed a clear calendar of progressive localization requirements for wind and then solar power, appears to be a useful strategy for going beyond installation industries. It is worth noting that even there, the manufacturing firms found the schedules overly ambitious and they had to be revised. In addition, the localization desire slowed installation of both wind and solar power and seems even more likely to do so in less industrialized locations. For the politics of renewable energy, however, if not for the economics, locally active firms in the sector were irreplaceable advocates of energy transition through developing wind and solar power industries.

4 | Electricity Consumption in Brazil and South Africa: Distribution and Prices

Access to electricity is a significant benefit for everyone. While households can function without electricity, it is more efficient, often cheaper, and much healthier than the biomass or fossil fuel alternatives. Economic actors of all kinds depend even more heavily on reliable electricity sources, using them to power everything from hospitals to manufacturing to computers. Solar power offers significant new strategies for addressing gaps in access to electricity because it is readily used in isolated and off-grid locations (Sovacool and Drupady 2012: 1, 6). Even in urban areas, household and industrial consumers can generate much of their own electricity and feed extra electricity into the grid. Larger installations of both wind and solar power can add to the total amount of electricity available on national grids and contribute to energy security by diversifying fuel sources. Set against these benefits are the historically higher costs of wind and solar power, so high in the 1990s that no standard cost–benefit analysis could justify building them (Schlömer et al. 2014: 1332–1333). Their prices have come down substantially since 2009, however, prompting new considerations of their use.

In other words, there is a broadly shared individual and collective interest in having a secure, affordable supply of electricity. This sets a basic state interest in providing electricity services through legislation, regulation, and even direct provision, especially in democracies (Brown and Mobarak 2009). While this is true everywhere, it is felt especially keenly in middle-income and developing countries where many people might lack access to that supply. Where wind and solar power can meet those needs at acceptable costs, there is a general interest in adopting them. The basic political economy of distribution, then, is about setting any added costs of renewable energies against the benefits of using them to expand electricity services, especially for populations without adequate access.

132

Existing national electricity systems can strongly affect those costs and benefits as some subsets of consumers may have more concentrated benefits and costs. Consumers not yet on the grid have particularly intense interests in electricity access, but they also tend to be both highly cost-sensitive (because those not yet on the grid are most often poor) and more costly to reach. Industrial consumers in electricity-intensive sectors like mining have particularly concentrated interests in both the reliability and the cost of electricity. When electricity is scarce or expensive relative to incomes, the interests of all citizens and those of these subsets of consumers may enter into competition.

Electricity provision to consumers is not just a technical task of building generation, transmission, and distribution capacity; it responds to how the state manages and organizes the economy and how it views its citizens. Electricity provision also reflects which political coalitions and actors can make effective demands to have their electricity consumption needs met in conditions when not all do. Those not on the grid are usually politically weak, while industrial consumers are likely to be politically as well as economically influential. Yet ordinary consumers will have strength in their numbers in democracies. Similar concerns arise on the revenue side of electricity services, since it is common for different categories of consumer to pay varying prices for electricity so that some cross-subsidize others. These are distributive questions that go to the heart of the central political questions of who gets what and when: who benefits from electricity policies? Do the electricity regimes in Brazil and South Africa consolidate or reduce socioeconomic inequalities? Do wind and solar power amplify or dampen those effects? Electricity provision is a particularly visible manifestation of for whom the state cares.

The state–society relations of particular relevance in this chapter are those that put the state in the role of service provider and regulator while viewing society as consumers. The provision of basic services like electricity is part of the governing pact between modern states and their societies, being one part of states' transformation into "institutions predominantly preoccupied with the production and distribution of social well-being" (Esping-Anderson 1990: 1; see also Golden and Min 2013; Min 2015). Citizens provide political support and revenues through taxes and fees for the state. In return, they expect that states will provide the basic infrastructures of security, energy, transportation, and the like, which are the foundations of modern economic life.

Yet real states deliver on these promises more and less well and unequally. These services matter for all – "no one prefers fewer hours of electricity, less reliable supply, or higher rates" (Min 2015: 6–7) – but poorer populations are especially dependent on state provision of them. As a result, electricity services bring real consequences for the well-being of their citizens as well as for the legitimacy and effectiveness of states and rulers. Equity of access, quality of service, and affordability are all just transition concerns. These general considerations will map differently onto the existing consumption patterns and distributional institutions of Brazil and South Africa. If wind and solar power can offer affordable solutions to the distributive dilemmas, more will be built.

Electricity has been at the very center of clashes between state and society in South Africa, as was clear in earlier chapters and reappears in this one. The apartheid state built a racially differentiated electricity grid that prioritized its minerals-energy based economy, organized in a few large conglomerates. A few large industrial consumers continue to consume outsize shares of the national electricity supply (Fine and Rustomjee 1996). In contrast, households were and are under-served, with Black African households still lagging systematically behind other consumers. Almost 20 percent of households are not yet even on the national grid. Struggles over service provision and payments became a key tool in the anti-apartheid fight and they continue to today, as the post-apartheid government has failed to meet consumer expectations since coming to power in 1994 (von Schnitzler 2016). Wind and solar power have been growing contributors to the central grid since 2011, but distributed power has played only a small and unmeasured role. The debate over the role of wind and solar power is growing more, rather than less, contentious, as previous chapters have shown. Cost and equity concerns are central in the disputes, but the backdrop to them all is the question of just whose interests are served by the state's service provision efforts.

In contrast, electricity provision has been nearly universal since the 1990s in Brazil with many of the remaining households brought online since 2003 in the "Light for All" program (*Luz para Todos*). While there is a group of industrial and extractive firms who rely heavily on electricity, it takes much less of the total supply than do South Africa's equivalents. There has been comparatively little social mobilization over provision or prices. The electricity system that wind and solar power encounter in Brazil has again been more bureaucratized than openly politicized. As costs allowed, grid-scale wind was added to diversify the electricity supply; it now approaches 10 percent of the total. The government's prioritization of cost calculations helped keep grid-scale solar out of the picture until 2014. A small group of technical bureaucrats spurred distributed power generation, mostly solar, through regulatory changes in 2012 and 2015 (Bradshaw 2018), and it is now expanding quickly. As wind and solar power expand, questions about subsidies to them and their impact on the overall grid are becoming more contentious.

Section 4.1 introduces theoretical debates around the distributive politics of electricity, focusing on who is seen to be likely to benefit from the state's role as service provider. Section 4.2 examines how experiences in South Africa and Brazil inform those debates, beginning with a brief comparison of access to electricity in the two countries. In the rest of Section 4.2, broader questions about the ways in which wind and solar power affect the political economy of access to electricity and the quality of that supply in each country (4.2.1 for South Africa and 4.2.3 for Brazil) precede analysis of the contestation around prices and subsidies (4.2.2 for South Africa and 4.2.4 for Brazil). The conclusion in Section 4.3 addresses the core themes of the book: Do consumer interests, as expressed through the coalitions that are built in each country, provide incentives or disincentives for expanding the share of wind and solar power in the national electricity supply in Brazil and South Africa? And – a just transition question – do these alternative renewables improve or reinforce existing inequities in electricity distribution in those countries?

4.1 The Distributive Politics of Electricity

The existing social science literature on power infrastructure has tended to focus on the supply side of electricity, and especially the question of public versus private provision and related public regulation (e.g., Murillo 2009; Post 2014; Victor and Heller 2007c). While these are obviously important issues (and covered in Chapter 3), this chapter focuses on the distribution and consumption of electricity. This side of infrastructure has been less studied by social scientists, and so I also draw here on the more general literature on service provision and distributive politics. Electricity is a public good, but actually providing it, especially as the service is extended toward universality, involves "finely targetable benefits" (Min 2015: 5). Significant inequality of access and costs is a plausible outcome.

There are two broad families of theories that have been used to explain states' distributional choices: voter-based models and power resources/constellations theory (Huber and Stephens 2012: 10–11). In one version of the voter-based models, the expectation is that patterns in service provision result from politicians' calculations about how they will be electorally rewarded for their public expenditures. Politicians are thought to respond to the ways in which specific sets of constituents will hold them accountable, so that services are expected to be allocated to core constituents or other population subgroups, perhaps timed to electoral cycles (de Kadt and Lieberman 2020; Golden and Min 2013: 74; Kramon and Posner 2013; Kroth, Larcinese, and Wehner 2016; Min 2015). Alternative approaches focus on the benefits to voters rather than to politicians, examining whether service provision matches the more equitable, welfare-maximizing expectations of the median voter (Brown and Mobarak 2009: 193; Golden and Min 2013: 74–75; Henisz and Zelner 2006; Keefer and Khemani 2005). Even as the model posits that politicians respond to median voter preferences, especially in democracies, it also acknowledges that powerful special interests might cause politicians to deviate from equitable or fair allocations. The share of electricity in a constrained electricity supply that goes to household consumers versus industrial consumers is an important measure of this outcome (Brown and Mobarak 2009).

The power resources theory approaches similar questions about who benefits from state electricity provision from a macropolitical framework that expects power inequalities to lead to inequitable service distribution (Esping-Anderson 1990; Huber and Stephens 2012; Wood and Gough 2006). This more sociological perspective examines the political histories of whole socioeconomic systems, pointing to the varying power of political class coalitions to explain variations in welfare outcomes. The approach has been most commonly used to explain social policy (e.g., Haggard and Kaufman 2008), but it can be easily extended to basic infrastructural provision like electricity. The power resources tradition has usually focused on class interests, socially constructed and dependent on historical constellations (Huber and Stephens 2012: 26). In addition, regional and racial interests are inescapable with these cases (Lieberman 2003; Marx 1998).

There is little systematic data available over time for either Brazil or South Africa that would allow proper adjudication of the causal claims of the various approaches. Instead, the chapter seeks to document the empirical patterns themselves as much as possible. Electricity has two major dimensions that can be assessed for their distributive outcomes. The first is actual access to electricity: Do households and businesses have electrical service at all? If electricity service is not universal, who has it and how is it extended to new consumers? While many studies stop here, the next obvious issue is whether they have access to electricity in the quantity and quality they need. The second dimension asks who pays how much for that service. The electricity infrastructures in Brazil and South Africa already embodied answers to these questions before wind and solar power were added to their electricity supply. Those answers – the stark inequality of access to and the increasingly unaffordable costs of South Africa's electricity and the more moderated inequities of Brazil – are outlined in the rest of this chapter along with consideration of whether wind and solar power aggravate or ameliorate them. Solar power in particular has qualities that might change the character of electricity outcomes.

In general, proponents point out that solar power (less so wind power) is among the most flexible of electricity sources in scale, being usable at both grid scale and at the scale of single buildings or even a single water heater. The latter, distributed scale of generation opens up the possibility of concentrated new benefits that counter any higher costs: individual consumers can be serviced with electricity even if the grid does not reach them or they can opt for self-provision of electricity (Garcez 2015: 18; Sovacool and Drupady 2012). For this reason, distributed solar power is often prized for democratizing electricity access and control (Abromovay 2014; Brass, Carley, MacLean, and Baldwin 2012: 108–109; Burke and Stephens 2018). Viewed more closely, however, there are two possible scenarios for distributed solar power that carry quite different distributive implications for middle-income and developing countries.

On the one hand, there is the scenario most often discussed, which is that distributed solar power offers new ways to bring electricity to under-served populations, especially those that live in rural and remote locations, where building traditional transmission and distribution grids is very costly (Brass et al. 2012: 108–109). Whether this service delivers on all of its promises is a major area of debate (e.g., Slough,

Urpelainen, and Yang 2015). The quality of distributed solar power may be lower than consumers expect, offering minimal power or proving difficult to maintain (Aklin, Bayer, Harish, and Urpelainen 2017). Overall, however, distributed solar used in this way reduces service inequities even if there is debate over how much it does so.

In the alternative scenario, wealthier paying consumers may opt off the grid in response to high costs, poor service quality, or ideological priorities from environment to autonomy (Abromovay 2014). This becomes a parallel move to their choice to pay for private education, security, and health care over poor-quality public services. Even in developed countries, there are concerns that this phenomenon contributes to a "utility death spiral" as the public service is left with the costly burden of maintaining the whole grid infrastructure for fewer paying customers (Castaneda, Franco, and Dyner 2017; Graffy and Kihm 2014). In middle-income and developing countries, existing consumers – typically comparatively economically privileged – are also helping to finance grid and generation expansion, exacerbating the difficulty of reaching previously unserved groups and possibly undermining public provision altogether if they leave the system.

Turning to their costs, wind and solar power have been more expensive than the large hydropower and coal plants that are the incumbent electricity sources in these and many countries. Wind and solar power are also intermittent sources, available only on some days and at some times. Both of these characteristics mean that greater use of wind and solar power introduces new costs, often broadly diffused across consumers. Although those costs have been dropping since 2009, for particularly large or poor electricity consumers, they may still appear prohibitive. The extra costs have been a major concern of public electricity planners (Tolmasquim 2016), who must choose to absorb them at grid scale or arrange cross-subsidies so that some consumers pay the costs of others. Elected politicians as well as bureaucrats may get involved in these decisions, bringing the distributive politics of electricity directly into the state. Arguments about who pays for wind and solar power are increasingly heated in both countries.

4.2 Electricity Service in Brazil and South Africa

Brazil and South Africa share a historical starting point in the development of their electricity systems: mass electrification from the 1940s to the 1980s was linked to developmentalist policies that expanded electricity infrastructure in the service of national industrial ambitions (Fine and Rustomjee 1996; Tendler 1968). Household consumption was a secondary consideration during this period and was unevenly achieved. Electricity provision was closely associated with other markers of economic and social privilege, reflecting and reinforcing divisions in the rest of society. The dominance of regional inequalities in Brazil and racial differentiation in South Africa matches other topics, like taxation (Lieberman 2003: 18).

In Brazil, electricity was Target No. 1 of Juscelino Kubitschek's developmentalist government of the 1950s, with its principal purpose being to support industrialization (Evans 1979: 92; Sikkink 1991: 136). Industry got the largest share of the limited supply, with only 53 percent of households supplied with electricity in 1972 (Baer 1976: 52). Even this was unequally spread across the regions, as 85 percent of households in industrial São Paulo had electricity while only 25 percent of the poor, rural Northeast region did (Baer 1976: 59). Electricity provision and other social benefits also went first to the formal, mostly industrial labor force that lived in formal parts of cities (Hunter 2014: 20). Only 54 percent of the individuals in Rio de Janeiro's informal housing areas, or *favelas*, had electricity around this time, with provision closely tied to socioeconomic status and race (Perlman 2006: 162–165). When unions were repressed under the military government of 1964 to 1985, labor activists joined with emerging community organizations to challenge both the military government itself and its indifference to citizen benefits like electricity (Seidman 1994: 197–198).

In South Africa, electrification was tightly linked to its Minerals-Energy Complex (MEC), which rests on manufacturing based on the primary sector (Fine and Rustomjee 1996). Power plants sat on top of coal mines and sent their electricity mostly to other mining and manufacturing operations held by a few large conglomerates. Electricity distributors only gradually added household consumers, and only 36 percent of the population was on the grid in 1993 (Winkler 2009: 34). Following the apartheid government's explicit policies, these were mostly white and urban consumers. Before the late 1980s, the state-controlled electricity utility Eskom was not allowed to provide electricity for black communities, leaving services to poorly-resourced Black Local Authorities in the townships (Kroth et al. 2016: 8–10).

The infrastructure of service provision and nonprovision became a central terrain for the struggle over apartheid in its final years, laying legacies for the post-transition period. The anti-apartheid struggle targeted electricity and other services, with coordinated boycotts against paying for them.[1] Joined with petty sabotage, protests, and sometimes acts of violence, the "rent boycotts" became a central means for showing that residents did not acknowledge the authority of the apartheid state and helping to undermine it (von Schnitzler 2016: 20). The reappearance of protests and rent boycotts after 2000 raises uncomfortable questions about what they signify now.

Brazil transitioned to civilian government in 1985 and wrote a constitution with many new citizen rights in 1988. By 1989, when it directly elected its president for the first time in more than twenty-five years, the formal transition was complete. Similarly, South Africa saw its first racially inclusive election in 1994 and wrote an expansive new constitution in 1996, completing its formal transition. In both countries, citizens' ability to really take command of the rights promised in their new constitutions lagged behind the formal transition by some years and is still incomplete.

With respect to electricity provision in particular, however, Brazil has now achieved nearly universal access to electricity – even if all of its citizens and industries are subject to rising prices and sometimes limited supplies. In South Africa, in contrast, electricity access continues to be a marker of social and economic inclusion and exclusion, and several waves of protest have not changed that outcome. Figure 4.1 shows how much more slowly South Africans have gained access to electricity services. Just 86 percent had at least a basic electricity service by 2013 (Scharfetter and van Dijk 2017: 15). Sections 4.2.1 to 4.2.4 show how the outcomes were rooted in distinct political economies of access and price – and how wind and solar power have affected those outcomes.

4.2.1 South Africa: Political Economy of Access and Quality

Wind and solar power have entered the South African electricity system primarily through large, grid-scale installations, helping to meet the

[1] Interview with Trevor Ngwane, Soweto Electricity Crisis Committee, Johannesburg, 2014.

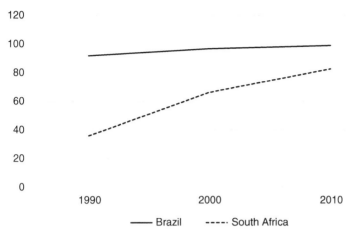

Figure 4.1 Percentage of the population with access to electricity
Source: World Development Indicators (WDI; an online database, https://dataca
talog.worldbank.org/dataset/world-development-indicators); the 1990 percentage
for South Africa was given as 65 percent in the WDI, but the figure uses the more
generally accepted percentage of 36 percent in 1993 (Winkler 2009: 34).

post-transition demand surge. In fact, by the mid-2000s, it was clear
that electricity demand would be outstripping supply in the near term.
Eskom responded by starting to build new capacity in the form of two
giant coal-powered plants. Even if the plants had been finished on time,
supply would have been short, but the projects have run years behind
schedule and are still unfinished in 2020. The Department of Energy
responded by opening auctions for private operators to supply wind
and solar power to the grid starting in 2011. The first projects were
already operational in 2014. Their comparatively quick addition to the
grid eased the zero-sum nature of electricity supply after 2007, limiting
the cuts that historic consumers needed to make as access continued to
be slowly extended. Demand for electricity unexpectedly began to fall
in 2012, however, bringing coal and renewables into open price-based
competition, which is discussed in Section 4.2.2.

Nearly all South Africans with electricity service receive it from the
same national grid. In this context, the consumption shares of different
categories of consumer are a good starting point for understanding the
distributive politics of electricity. Given the low but increasing access to

grid services for households, it is not surprising that this is matched by similar patterns among consumption shares. South Africa's consumption shares require some data reconstruction, but the residential share was only roughly 15 percent in 1990, rising slowly to 18 percent in 2000, 20 percent in 2010 and a bit above in 2015.[2] The rise reflects a pattern commonly seen in democracies, which tend to distribute more electricity to households than authoritarian governments do (Brown and Mobarak 2009), although the residential share remains quite low after twenty-five years.

Most of the balance of the electricity supply goes to manufacturing and commerce, which held a fairly steady 55–60 percent share over these years. The mining sector's share of electricity first flatlined and then actually dropped after 1990, from 25 percent to 13.9 percent.[3] These aggregate numbers mask even greater concentration among electricity users. In 2018, the twenty-eight members of the Energy Intensive Users Group (EIUG) consumed over 40 percent of the electricity in the country, down from thirty-one members using 44 percent in 2014.[4] EIUG members are large industrial and mining firms. They are also the primary private employers, critically important in a country with chronic 25 percent unemployment rates. They almost all use constant electricity supplies, twenty-four hours per day, seven days per week, and built their business models on the historically low costs of South Africa's coal-based electricity.[5]

Not surprisingly, the EIUG is a very powerful actor in the South African electricity sector. It has already shown up in earlier chapters of this book as it is an active participant in most debates about electricity, whether technical or political. The government often turned to the EIUG for information about the shape of future electricity demand and has included representatives on all of its special electricity commissions. EIUG representatives also participated in all routine electricity planning until the 2018 IRP draft (see

---

[2] Calculated from data compiled by the Council for Scientific and Industrial Research; see www.energy.gov.za/IRP/irp-update-draft-report2018/CSIR-annual-elec-demand-forecasts-IRP-2015.pdf. For comparison, Brazilian households consumed 24 percent of the national supply in 2007 and 28.8 percent in 2017 (Ministêrio de Minas e Energia 2007: 91 and 2017: 41).

[3] www.energy.gov.za/IRP/irp-update-draft-report2018/CSIR-annual-elec-demand-forecasts-IRP-2015.pdf.

[4] Interviews with Piet van Staden, EIUG, 2018; Morgan and Nel, EIUG, 2014.

[5] Interview with Morgan and Nel, EIUG, 2014.

Chapter 2).[6] The EIUG's knowledge about the electricity sector and its own central place in the sector make it an agent in its own right rather than just another lobby. Its predominant position also makes the EIUG pay attention to the sustainability of the entire electricity system in ways it might not if it were a smaller actor.

One consequence of its weight is that the EIUG is also asked to take costly actions that facilitate grid operation. Notably, the national grid regularly did not generate enough electricity to meet consumer demand from 2007 to about 2015. EIUG consumers are the first targeted when electricity is in short supply, asked to make cuts as large as 10 percent in their use of power before other consumers do (Bischof-Niemtz and Creamer 2019: 9). In 2014, prospective new and expanding business operations had to apply to the Ministry of Trade and Industry for an approved electricity supply and even the Ministry's top-ranked choices faced a two-year wait before they could begin to draw on the grid.[7] As industrial demand dropped with rising prices – among other things, large aluminum smelters left the country – these restrictions eased.

The EIUG gains policy attention because so few actors consume so much of the electricity supply. Conversely, the household share of total consumption is small, but the sheer number of connections – already 95 percent of the connections to the distribution grid in 1998 (McDonald 2011: 71) and a larger share now – have gained households much of the political attention to electricity. Grid-based electricity is part of a suite of promises the ANC made to regularize the living situation of black South Africans after apartheid (Von Schnitzler 2016). In 1994, the African National Congress (ANC) program said, "An accelerated and sustainable electrification programme must provide access to electricity for an additional 2.5 million households by the year 2000, thereby increasing the level of access to electricity to about 72 per cent of all households (double the present number)" (cited in Kroth et al. 2016: 11). The party's manifesto for local elections in 1995 and 1999 also promised services, while other parties focused on crime (Kroth et al. 2016: 11). After winning large majorities in the national and most provincial elections every year since 1994, the ANC is the actor most clearly responsible for the policies guiding electricity outcomes.

---

[6] Interview with van Staden, EIUG, 2018.
[7] Interview with Morgan and Nel, EIUG, 2014.

The ANC's original economic planning document, the Reconstruction and Development Programme (RDP) of 1994, laid out an ambitious agenda for the new government which it quickly replaced with the more market-oriented Growth, Employment and Redistribution Strategy in 1996 (Wenzel 2007). Even so, electricity provision – set at 250,000 additional households annually – was the only one of the Reconstruction and Development Programme's objectives that was not only met but exceeded (Winkler 2009: 32). The first phase of the National Electrification Program in 1994–1999 made 2.75 million connections, bringing coverage to 66 percent of the population, but the remaining unconnected households were rural ones that are more difficult and expensive to connect (ibid.: 34). The original plan was to reach full coverage by 2012, but only 85 percent were connected in 2018. The National Planning Commission now assessed that full coverage could be reached only by 2030, with 10 percent of that off-grid (National Planning Commission 2018: vii). Black South Africans make up a disproportionate share of those still unserved (Monyei, Adewumi, and Jenkins 2018: 154).

One complication in expanding coverage was the question of who would be responsible for distribution, connections, and other investments. PricewaterhouseCoopers helped to develop a plan in the late 1990s that would have unbundled and partially privatized the electricity sector, including a plan to create six independent regional electricity distributors instead of the current arrangement where municipalities buy bulk electricity from Eskom and resell it. The plan was sidelined in 2003–2004 after opposition from local municipalities that use profits from reselling as part of their normal budgets, as well as principled opposition to privatization from trade unions (McDonald 2011: 77–79). This left Eskom responsible for connections in impoverished rural areas, at the same time that demand was now finally outstripping supply. The 278 (257 after 2016) existing municipal distributers covered urban connections, with widely varying capabilities (Baker and Phillips 2018).

Using national statistics and geo-referenced nightlight satellite imagery, a study has found that the South African case provides support for the general association of democracy with electrification (Brown and Mobarak 2009; Kroth et al. 2016). There are also more specific political effects. In the parts of the country where municipalities connect people to the grid, connections follow median voter theory expectations independent of the partisan makeup of the local council. In areas where Eskom is making connections, however, "newly enfranchised voters in the ANC's core constituencies were prioritized" (Kroth et al. 2016: 6).

The connection successes mask the fact that many households who gain access to the grid subsequently lose it as they move around the country or are disconnected for nonpayment. In 2008–2010, years of economic recession, 840,000 households lost access to the grid even as 700,000 gained connections (Harris, Collinson, and Wittenberg 2017: 20). Not surprisingly, these were disproportionately poor households (ibid.: 25). Even more are invisibly disconnected since they have prepaid electricity meters that they often lack the money to feed (von Schnitzler 2016: 5). Informal urban households are also difficult to track, with hundreds of thousands of backyard shacks either unserved and uncounted or illegally connected through other consumers (Sustainable Energy Africa 2014).

Another view of the quality of South Africa's electricity service can be seen in the 2011 municipal-level statistics, the most recent detailed data available.[8] In 2011, an average of 80.3 percent of the residents in each municipality used electricity for lighting, but only 66.3 percent used it for cooking and 48.1 percent for heating. Wood continued to be the first or second fuel for cooking and heating in more than half of the municipalities. By 2016, 91.1 percent of households in South Africa used electricity for at least some purposes and 81.8 percent had refrigerators (Statistics South Africa 2016: 80–81). Because refrigerators are only useful if they can run continuously, they are a particularly good measure of the quality of supply.

Beyond sheer physical connections, the ANC administration developed two strategies to offer poor households affordable access to electricity, a long-time activist demand. Since 2003, poor households can receive 50 kWh free per month, a quantity that allows running four lights for four hours daily plus a small radio or TV (Dugard 2014: 279–280). Since 2001, a similar plan offers small-scale non-grid solar home systems with similar service standards, updated to include cellphone charging (Department of Energy 2012). The off-grid program is strictly for consumers who are in areas outside the three-year grid

---

[8] www.statssa.gov.za/?page_id=993&id=emfuleni-municipality. These calculations are my own, based on the municipal-level data.

expansion plan and it is the second way in which solar power enters the national electricity supply. By design, monopoly concessionaires in only three provinces (KwaZulu Natal, Eastern Cape, and Limpopo) offered the systems through 2012, with Northern Cape and Western Cape added since. About 93,000 households had received these off-grid systems by 2015.[9]

In 2013, the Cabinet adopted the Department of Energy's New Household Electrification Strategy to try to reach the final 14 percent of consumers not yet supplied with electricity. The plan anticipated that the last 10 percent would receive nongrid electricity, opening up the options to include any technology that would be cost-effective and including urban areas where connections were difficult (Department of Energy 2013). Implementation of the off-grid system so far has shown multiple flaws, from inconsistent governmental support to a failure to update the service requirements for technological developments from storage to LED lights (Aitken, Thorne, Thorne, and Kruger n.d.: 39–40).

While these programs obviously provide important benefits to poor households, it should be equally clear that these are very low levels of electricity provision by design. Grid-connected households can (if they can afford it) access more electricity, but households with the solar systems must supplement their electricity with other energy sources for heating and cooking. Many households refuse the alternative systems in fear that they will never get on-grid service if they accept them (Sustainable Energy Africa 2014: 50). The first extended analysis of the solar home systems also finds that their provision is even worse than it appears, as only a third of the households were in areas with enough sun to get the targeted quotas (Monyei et al. 2018: 156). The article concludes that the off-grid provision is unjust, and it confirms the assumptions of many consumers that only on-grid electricity is really adequate service provision.[10]

All of these dynamics have generated waves of mobilization that vividly express the population's frustrations. From March 2004 to February 2005, there were 5,085 legal protests with permits and 881 illegal ones across metro areas in all the provinces (Booysen 2007: 23).

---

[9] www.energy.gov.za/files/WOESA/2015/easterncape/Non-Grid-Electrification-Programme-DoE.pdf.
[10] Interview with Ngwane, Soweto Electricity Crisis Committee, 2014.

Known as service delivery protests, they focused on prices and access to services, showing a shift "from blind loyalty to the governing ANC to a critical, even confrontational stance" (Booyson 2007: 22). The ANC responded to the first waves by promising electrification for all households by 2010, but, obviously, it has not delivered. There were an estimated 10,000 annual protests after 2010. They had a sharper tone, reusing the anti-apartheid movement's calls to make South Africa ungovernable (Alexander and Ffath 2014: 208; Mottiar 2013: 603–604). Called "popcorn" protests because of the way they popped up and quickly subsided, they tended to target local governments rather than the national ANC and won few of their demands (Mottiar 2013: 606–607).

For a time, a subset of community organizations was gathered in the Anti-Privatisation Forum, which encapsulated service demands in a broader anti-capitalist discourse (Runciman 2015: 971). While its vision was broadly similar to that of the labor activists in Chapters 2 and 3, the Forum was focused not on the REIPPPP and electricity generation but on questions of price and consumption. "Struggle" electricians implemented the Forum's demands by creating illegal connections and helping households bypass their prepaid meters to claim what the Forum called their right to electricity.[11] After technology changes made that more difficult and Eskom threatened to remove cables altogether, continuing nonpayment was the strategy of choice, especially in Soweto where the Anti-Privatisation Forum was strongest. Divisions over how to relate to the ANC and organizational problems meant that the Forum had substantially disintegrated by 2010, even as the problems it had tried to address remained acute (Runciman 2015; von Schnitzler 2016).

Another kind of "protest" came from higher-income consumers already connected to the grid, including some commercial and industrial consumers. As the reliability of electricity supply deteriorated after 2007, some of them opted off the grid entirely or in part, through distributed solar systems that they bought and installed themselves. It is not clear how many have done this, in part because the government has not yet established national regulations for distributed solar systems. Electricity plans simply guessed that about 200 MW will be added annually after 2018 (Department of Energy 2018: 40), rising

---

[11] Interview with Ngwane, Soweto Electricity Crisis Committee, 2014.

to a guess of 500 MW the next year (Department of Energy 2019a: 39). Even without actual data, it is clear that these are upper-income consumers, as the capital costs are well beyond those of most consumers and there are no public subsidies. Nongrid-scale solar power may be becoming part of a pattern of private self-provision by wealthy consumers at the expense of public provision networks.[12] There are also thirty-seven South African firms sourcing their own, renewable sources of energy, more than in any other developing country (International Renewable Energy Agency 2018: 20). South Africa thus shows some incipient set-in of the "utility death spiral" where wealthy paying consumers opt for off-grid consumption through solar power, leaving a smaller number of consumers to pay the fixed costs of the grid and electricity provision.

Eskom has responded in part by declaring all grid connections for small and micro installations illegal for "safety, tariff and technical reasons" until the regulations are completed.[13] Municipalities are slightly more welcoming: 34 of 164 of them allow distributed generation installations and 18 have agreed feed-in tariffs (South African Local Government Association 2017: 4). In 2014, the National Energy Regulator (NERSA) drew up a set of regulations for connecting micro-generators to the network, and a revised set of regulations followed in 2018.[14] The proposed rules are not permissive, as they ask for every single solar system to be registered with the centralized distribution system, with installations over 1 MW capacity – suitable for a shopping center or large manufacturing or agricultural facility – requiring as much licensing as a full-scale power station. The rules have gone through multiple revisions since 2014, including major rounds in 2017 and 2018, but without final formulation. The solar industry association SAPVIA estimated that 1,000 MW of such small installations had been built by 2019 but could not be licensed and used, although a determination from the Minister of Energy will finally license 500 MW of that, consistent with the 2019 IRP draft.[15]

[12] Interview with Euston-Brown, Sustainable Energy Africa, 2013.
[13] www.eskom.co.za/Whatweredoing/Pages/SmallMicroGeneration-.aspx.
[14] www.nersa.org.za/Admin/Document/Editor/file/Consultations/Electricity/Documents/Consultation%20Paper-Rules%20for%20Registration%20of%20SSEG.pdf.
[15] www.businessinsider.co.za/nersa-licence-change-jeff-radebe-eskom-sseg-renewable-energy-projects-flood-2019-5.

Income inequality in South Africa is probably even more unequal after the end of apartheid than before (Skillings and Nattrass 2005). As this summary suggests, electricity provision is not less equitable now than before, but South Africans who are black, poor, and rural still disproportionately continue to lack access to quality supplies of electricity. So far, neither formal democratic transition nor their own mobilizations have changed that. Section 4.2.2 examines the role of costs and subsidies in debates about bringing wind and solar power into the South African electricity supply.

4.2.2 *South Africa: Political Economy of Costs and Subsidies*

Expanding access to electricity has been relatively uncontroversial in post-apartheid South Africa. Questions about prices and costs, on the other hand, find many of the same actors of Chapters 2 and 3 once again in open contention over why Eskom's electricity prices have risen so fast and how they can be lowered. After tracing those debates, I also discuss the less contentious topics of subsidies for poor consumers and the role of municipalities in price-setting. Throughout, I consider how wind and solar power might have changed price outcomes.

Everyone who consumes electricity through the South African national grid is affected by the prices that Eskom charges. Eskom provides about 60 percent of the electricity supply directly to consumers and sells the rest to municipalities that pass it on to their consumers (Baker and Phillips 2018: 2). The South African government negotiated with Eskom to lower prices by almost 20 percent from 1992 to 1996 and by 15 percent more from 1994 to 2000 (Bischof-Niemtz and Creamer 2019: 2). But since 2001, prices have risen well above the rate of inflation. Tariffs rose 3.78 times between 2001 and 2011, while Black African incomes rose just 2.7 times during that period (Electricity Governance Initiative of South Africa 2013: 13). Average prices rose 200 percent from 2008 to 2016 (Baker and Philips 2018: 7). No consumers pay the average price and Eskom's 2017 customer categories show the variations. In that year, industrial consumers paid just R0.68 per KWh, less than the R0.81 Eskom charged to municipal distributors. Eskom charged the households it services directly R1.19 and commercial customers R1.90. The mining sector was charged R0.85, closest to the actual cost of generation that year (Vermeulen 2017: 72).

The rising tariffs are obvious to everyone, but the costs that drive them up (and thus the opportunities to reduce the rate of increase) are what South Africans debate. This is not just an abstract exercise. Eskom is entitled to have all of its appropriate costs covered by revenue and it meets regularly with NERSA to discuss its expected costs and revenues, to work out a schedule of tariff increases three to five years in advance. It can also ask to have mid-agreement changes for unexpected developments on either side. In 2016, for example, Eskom submitted an analysis that it had incurred R22.8 billion in justifiable variations in costs and revenues, but NERSA recognized only R11.2 billion of them as legitimate. These are highly technical discussions once largely ignored except by actors like EIUG, but they have drawn public attention and even protests and court cases post-2011.[16]

The influence of some costs is undisputed, including the doubling of the estimated cost of building the Medupi and Kusile coal plants and the much higher cost of borrowing, as Eskom has sunk from AAA to near junk bond status. The most important debates have been about the impact of wind and solar power, the relationship of price and demand, labor costs and conditions, and the rising cost of coal and its association with possible corruption in Eskom. These involve the price side of disputes that have already appeared in this book, so it is not surprising that they involve many of the same actors.

In the government's electricity planning, wind and solar procurement began for climate reasons even though planners knew that renewable energy cost more than coal (Department of Energy 2011). The first procurement auctions confirmed this, but prices for solar power dropped 83 percent from the first round in November 2011 to the fourth in November 2015 and wind power prices fell 59 percent. At that point, they were 40 percent below the price of new coal installations (Bischof-Niemtz and Creamer 2019: 45). The earlier high prices continued to be relevant since auction winners were offered twenty-year power purchasing agreements, but Eskom is entitled to fully recover the costs of the IPP production from NERSA (Bischof-Niemtz and Creamer 2019: 44).

Even so, as it became increasingly clear after 2015 that South Africa would have to choose between building nuclear power or building

---

[16] www.sapvia.co.za/power-tariff-to-rise-by-9-4-after-nersa-allows-eskom-a-par tial-r11-2bn-clawback/.

wind and solar power (see Chapter 2), Eskom's leadership began to argue vehemently about comparative prices. In multiple documents and presentations, Eskom and other advocates of nuclear power used the price figures from 2011 to insist that wind and solar power were too expensive. Former head of Eskom generation Matshela Koko was particularly insistent that all of Eskom's financial and generation troubles stemmed from the need to pay IPPs for wind and solar power, arguing this in the media even after being fired from his position.[17] The 2016 and 2017 NERSA hearings on proposed tariff increases for Eskom were particularly intense, coming as Eskom itself was refusing to sign REIPPPP contracts on the grounds that renewable energy was too costly. Labor unions, which worry that their industrial employers will fail if electricity is too expensive, have continued the critique, even after Eskom dropped it when Zuma was pushed out of the presidency in 2018.[18] The National Union of Metalworkers of South Africa (NUMSA), for example, criticized the new contracts signed in 2018 as though they cost as much as the 2011 contracts when they are a fraction of the earlier prices.[19] The minister of energy was firm in rejecting these arguments, saying that the assertion that "Eskom incurs losses as a result of the IPP program is without foundation, misleading and false."[20]

The opposite side of the argument was about the true cost of nuclear power. Eskom's leaders and allies in the Zuma administration contended that nuclear power would be cheaper than wind and solar power. Nuclear costs are difficult to estimate as few utilities have built new nuclear power plants for decades, with fewer still after the Fukushima disaster in Japan. Nuclear plants are also notorious for their time and cost overruns (Sovacool, Gilbert, and Nugent 2014). Extensive Treasury modeling exercises had shown that the nuclear build was completely financially infeasible, even without the probable cost overruns, but the finance minister was forced out in 2015 after showing these calculations to the ANC leadership according to his

---

[17] For example, see www.iol.co.za/news/politics/matshela-koko-questions-eskoms-failure-to-meet-demand-18883577.

[18] www.numsa.org.za/article/numsa-statement-on-eskom-s-selective-re-opener-of-the-third-multi-year-price-determination-mypd3/.

[19] www.numsa.org.za/article/numsa-statement-on-the-ongoing-dispute-at-eskom/.

[20] Media interview in February 2019, online at www.ee.co.za/article/the-status-of-electricity-generation-in-south-africa.html.

testimony to parliament's state capture hearings.[21] The corrupt deals now documented as part of the nuclear procurement process make nuclear power's cost in South Africa almost certainly much higher than its proponents argued (Chipkin and Swilling 2017).

As in Chapter 3, labor allied with Eskom as other cost-cutters began to target growing Eskom labor costs as another possibly inappropriate cost. NERSA picked up on a World Bank study that compared employment and supply in the electricity sector in Sub-Saharan Africa, according to NERSA concluding that Eskom was overstaffed by 66 percent for the electricity it was producing and that it paid more than four times the average African wage per worker. NERSA's own study in response showed that Eskom had produced 7.26 GWh per employee in 2007/2008 but was expecting to produce only 5.3 GWh per employee in 2018/2019. It calculated that it meant an excess of 6,232 employees (National Energy Regulator of South Africa 2017: 86, 87). The labor movement has reacted strongly and negatively to any hints of job cutbacks, including 1,000 jobs at 5 coal-powered plants long known to be reaching the end of their lifespan (Department of Energy 2011). Instead, NUM and NUMSA joined Eskom in blaming the wind and solar producers again, even while now (inconsistently) acknowledging that they were cheaper. These are the just transition dilemmas discussed in Chapters 2 and 3, reappearing as arguments about prices (Deedat 2018: 11–12). Former president Zuma helped fan these concerns as part of his electricity plans, but Cyril Ramaphosa's government has made hints that the cuts will come.

Other actors that are more single-mindedly focused on actual prices have shifted positions as prices moved, rather than fighting the rearguard battle with Eskom and organized labor. As late as 2014, as prices of new build of renewables and coal were reaching parity, the EIUG was still wary about the expense and unreliability of wind and solar power. Prices had risen 300 percent in six years for the EIUG's member firms.[22] By 2018, when the renewables were clearly much cheaper than the increasingly costly new coal installations, the EIUG was more accepting of wind and solar power and even envious of how bursts of wind power could provide essentially free service for heavy users in

---

[21] Nene's complete testimony is available at www.scribd.com/document/390031857/Minister-of-Finance-s-Statement-at-the-State-Capture-Inquiry#download.

[22] Interview with Morgan and Nel, EIUG, 2014.

Europe.[23] Price increases had already driven smelters out of South Africa to new locations with cheaper electricity. EIUG members are now explicitly weighing in against new nuclear plants on cost grounds and because small wind and solar plants offer more flexible supply than large nuclear installations.[24]

The Organisation Undoing Tax Abuse (OUTA), also focused on prices, agreed with the EIUG's comparative price calculations. OUTA engaged in the NERSA-Eskom discussions in 2016 and afterwards in trying to force Eskom to sign the IPP agreements and refrain from building expensive new coal and nuclear plants. It organized 8,000 written comments on Eskom's 2016 costs submission, compared to just 300 in 2015.[25] NERSA itself has warned that Eskom has begun to enter into the "utility death spiral" where ever-higher prices drive consumers from the grid, leaving a shrinking customer base to pay even more (National Energy Regulator of South Africa 2017; see also Department of Energy 2019a: 16).

Some of the other costs behind that spiral are traceable to the problematic and even criminal mismanagement of Eskom, already tracked in studies of state capture, and reflected in twelve criminal charges, nine for senior managers (Chipkin and Swilling 2017; Public Protector 2016).[26] These include comparatively routine mismanagement that has excessively enriched individuals with bonuses and other special payments (National Energy Regulator of South Africa 2017). There are also larger schemes already discussed in Chapter 2 that have led to serious overpayment for coal of dubious quality and kept nuclear power on the build agenda when it is not cost-competitive (Bischof-Niemtz and Creamer 2019). Eskom's balance sheet also shows systematic failure to collect debts that it is owed by municipalities. While this paragraph lists very serious failures, most stem from Eskom's having been made the site of corrupt initiatives for the benefit of small groups of individuals. In addition, elected officials and partisan actors prevented Eskom from following its own institutional interests in

---

[23] Interview with van Staden, EIUG, 2018.
[24] Interview with van Staden, EIUG, 2018.
[25] www.dailymaverick.co.za/article/2016-02-08-nersa-hearings-thousands-oppose-eskoms-price-increases/.
[26] Several important reports are linked here, in OUTA's complaint to the Competition Commission: www.biznews.com/energy/2017/02/21/eskom-molefe-outa/.

a number of cases. Multiple presidents have hesitated to support policies that would be politically disruptive, like layoff plans or forcing municipalities to pay their arrears, even when inaction makes South Africa's electricity more expensive.

Groups that pay more for electricity also see differential prices for other consumer groups as an avoidable cost. Differential pricing is not necessarily a subsidy, however, as different consumers represent different costs of service. Industry has a flat load profile, often requiring electricity constantly, which is the cheapest to service.[27] Meanwhile, household consumers pay more in part because they create the most expensive peak demand times as they come home from work or school, prepare dinner, and turn on consumer electronics. Since 1982, residential customers have been 15–18 percent of the total load, but they were 75 percent of the variable load already in 1998 (McDonald 2011: 71). That higher cost is not equally distributed among households. Remarkably, only 16 percent of households in South Africa pay for their electricity, meaning that there is a large subsidization of poor and nonpaying electricity users by paying customers (Kambule, Yessoufou, Nwulu, and Mbohwa 2019: 375). Yet subsidies to households are an integral part of the expanding access discussed in Section 4.2.1.

The Integrated National Electrification Programme (INEP) subsidizes connections to the households that did not have the service at the end of apartheid. These are virtually all poor or remote consumers and mostly Black Africans. Poor households on and off the grid also have their electricity use subsidized. Both of these subsidies have been handled since the early 2000s through special allocations, so they are not part of the Eskom-NERSA debates over cost. This makes them virtually invisible to most people, although taxpayers, of course, ultimately pay for these programs. The Department of Energy spends 85 percent of its INEP budget on planning, managing, and making connections for new consumers. Allocations for 2016 to 2020 were to cover the costs of bringing 723,000 households onto the grid and to offer off-grid

---

[27] One exception to this generalization is the special long-term prices that BHP Billiton had arranged for its smelters in South Africa and Mozambique. These priced electricity by the dollar price of aluminum rather than by any links to the cost of generation, which amounted to a major subsidy as electricity prices went up after 2001. Eskom began to contest the deal in 2010 and a court case in 2013 finally revealed the scope of the secret subsidy: Billiton was paying approximately 22.6 cents per kilowatt hour (Manuel 2013). Two of the smelters involved with the deal and Billiton itself have since left the country.

installations to 60,000 more (National Planning Commission 2018: 42). While most public services are supplied on a cost-recovery basis in South Africa, the government acknowledges that rural electrification is a "purely social program" that will never make back its costs, as rural consumption is very low (Aitken et al. n.d.:18).

A few municipalities began supplying small amounts of free electricity to grid-connected consumers in 2001, and since 2003, the federal government supplies 50 kWh/month free per household through grants to the municipalities that actually provide it. Without this program, electricity costs averaged 18 percent of household expenses, a percentage that dropped to 12 percent with the subsidy (Winkler 2009: 69). When the Free Basic Electricity (FBE) program began, the government erased US$1.2 million in consumer debt, but household electricity debt has returned to nearly that level. Soweto alone was more than half of the new debt and the government is planning to have all provision prepaid by 2020 (Kambule et al. 2019: 375).

The national government funds the FBE through unconditional bulk transfers to municipalities based on the number of indigent households thought to be in the municipality. Overall, this is about 59 percent of households (Sustainable Energy Africa 2014: 49). The municipality itself determines which households are indigent, with most using either an indigent register or the amount of total electricity used. The latter will miss the many illegal backyard dwellers who increase the total consumption of their legal partner, while the registers are often incomplete and out of date. In addition, the unconditional nature of the transfer means that municipalities never report on who receives these funds, making it impossible to know if the FBE is actually going to the poorest households (Sustainable Energy Africa 2014: 40–44). In 2014, Statistics South Africa estimated that just over half of the households that should have received the FBE actually did, while the National Treasury estimates that just a third of them do (ibid.: 46–47). Another 2 percent receive the solar subsidy, so it makes a very modest contribution to electricity affordability (ibid.: 49–50). The solar subsidy is even more difficult for providers to administer and monitor.

A final wrinkle in the political economy of electricity distribution in South Africa has to do with the role of municipalities. These currently hold the legal rights to distribution and many of them depend heavily on electricity charges for revenues, using them to cross-subsidize other municipal activities and functions. Not more than 10 percent of the electricity department's revenue is to go into the municipal budget, but the share is always more than that.[28] This is an added cost to the electricity too. In 2013–2014, electricity sales were 30 percent of municipal revenue on average, and up to half of revenue for smaller municipalities (Baker and Phillips 2018: 10). Their markups over the price of bulk supplies from Eskom are 20–150 percent, but the sharp increases in Eskom's prices have limited what they can add (Baker and Phillips 2018: 11). Poor municipalities with little industrial activity and many consumers who either consume only at free levels or evade payment are accruing large unpaid debts with Eskom as the electricity revenues are diverted to other purposes (Vermuelen 2017: 72).

While there is an inclining block tariff that formalizes progressive prices for larger amounts, any paying customer is clearly also paying for the many South Africans who do not. Since the latter are often actually not able to pay, it is politically impossible to challenge these racially marked outcomes. Increasing numbers of households are opting to go off the grid and generate their own power as a result (van Niekerk 2020: 144). The government is developing national rules for distributed generation, but municipalities rejected the first draft of the regulations as protecting Eskom's monopoly interests more than their own. In particular, they want all consumers to be required to pay network access charges and greater attention to be paid to the timing of demand (Vermeulen 2017: 73–74).

Otherwise, municipal government representatives were surprisingly sanguine about the coming changes, which they expect to arrive whatever they do.[29] Twenty percent had independently set up their own regulations (South African Local Government Association 2017: 4). A representative of City Power Johannesburg noted that most municipalities think that consumers have a right to reduce their electricity bills if they want – by choosing energy-efficient options or investing in household solar systems – provided they continue to pay the costs of network access (Vermeulen 2017: 67, 74). Since the buy-back rates that NERSA approves are lower than the bulk rates that Eskom charges, the generation of one household is easily sold on to its neighbors with

[28] Interview with Sarah Ward, Head of the Energy and Climate Change Division, Environmental Resources Management Agency of the City of Cape Town, Cape Town, 2013.
[29] Interview with Ward, Environmental Resources Management Agency of the City of Cape Town, 2013.

fewer energy losses, making a net gain for the distributor. Municipalities would like to do some of their own generation as well – like on municipal buildings – and the City of Cape Town has sued NERSA and the Ministry of Energy for this right (ibid.: 71). These dynamics mean a different price logic for the municipal distributors than for Eskom, for whom they mean a market that shrinks even further. They also divide the large and technically competent municipalities like Cape Town and Johannesburg from more marginal municipalities.

In summary, a myriad of issues has made the price of South African electricity both high and contested. Some of that contestation has spilled over from conflict in other political economies that now takes the form of arguments over the real price of things. Other issues reflect the bitter dilemmas of a country that spent decades preventing most of its citizens from getting access to electricity services on racial grounds. While the benefits of electrification are high, the costs are even higher. Wind and solar power have pushed them above where they would have been historically, but they should be comparatively cheap in the future. Still, the costs of building out extensive infrastructure for a large number of consumers who cannot afford to pay connection or monthly charges are very high. Cost-cutting solutions like reducing the workforce or collecting arrears are politically difficult. Distributed solar power allows comparatively wealthy consumers now on the grid to escape the rising prices, exacerbating inequality. South Africa is more like its Sub-Saharan neighbors in facing these dilemmas than it is like Brazil, which has benefited from a more equitable starting point.

4.2.3 Brazil: Political Economy of Access and Quality

As in South Africa, Brazilian electricity planners have added wind and solar power mostly through large clusters of plants connected to the national grid. Wind power came first, added to help meet supply shortfalls in 2001 when Brazil's traditional hydropower reservoirs dried up. Chapter 3 has already addressed the industrial policy motivations for this addition, which the cost considerations of this chapter reinforce. Solar power was left out until its price dropped to nearer that of other sources in 2014. The main virtue of wind and solar power in Brazil was less their sheer generation capacity, as in South Africa, than their providing energy security by helping to diversify a hydro-heavy supply. Wind power is particularly useful as it complements the seasonal availability of ample hydropower, flourishing in the dry times of the year (Tolmasquim 2016). In general terms, then, wind and solar power affect access to and quality of electricity service in Brazil by replacing hydropower on a seasonal basis and more permanently as their socioenvironmental costs make new hydropower dams difficult to build. Policy and regulatory changes also made distributed solar an increasingly attractive option for both remote and conventional urban electricity access.

Most Brazilians receive their electricity from a single national grid. It is harder to see that democratic transition boosted consumer access to electricity here, as 91.1 percent of Brazilian households already had electrical service in 1990. Households had a more robust share than they did in South Africa, consuming 24 percent of the national electricity supply in 2007 and 28.8 percent in 2017 (Ministério de Minas e Energia 2007: 91, 2018: 41). The rise came largely as industry's share dropped from 45.8 percent to 35.8 percent over the same decade, through unwanted deindustrialization of the economy in a decade of economic ups and downs. Brazil also has a group of electricity-intensive industries, joined as ABRACE. It is much less dominant than the South African EIUG, with fifty-seven firms using about 12 percent of the national supply. ABRACE is correspondingly less influential, gaining few free passes for participation, but it maintains an active lobbying team.[30] Commercial (15.7 to 19 percent) and agricultural and other consumers (14.5 to 16.4 percent) round out the consumer profile (Ministério de Minas e Energia 2007: 91, 2018: 41).[31]

Questions of access and quality of service for Brazilians have mostly focused on that last 9 percent of consumers. Brazil had three primary categories of consumer without regularized access to the national electricity grid in 1990. One set was in the informal areas of the large cities of the South and Southeast, where several decades of internal

[30] Interview with Iocca, ABRACE, 2018.
[31] Reforms under the Cardoso government created two formal categories of end-consumer. Smaller "captive" users like households and small businesses are connected to particular distribution grids and must buy electricity from them, while large "free" consumers can choose their own suppliers and negotiate bilateral contracts for electricity. The number of these free consumers grew from 69 in 2003 to 687 in 2007 (Leite 2009: 73). While this was a crucial change in the broader distribution dynamics of electricity in Brazil, it has little direct impact on wind and solar power, so it is not discussed here.

migrants had set up *favelas* (slums). Others were in rural areas across the country and especially in the North (Amazon) and Northeast regions. They were divided in turn between those close to the national grid and a truly remote group. The urban group, closer to the centers of both political and electrical power, was brought on the grid first, while those reachable through rural grid expansion came next. Developments in distributed generation are now bringing the final remote groups electricity even as they are also allowing the wealthy, urban consumers who have had electricity services for the longest time to opt off. This section takes up each of those groups in turn.

Urban movements demanded the upgrading of their informal settlements with electricity and other services beginning in the 1970s, as part of the broader opposition to the then-military government. Full response to their demands did not come until greater democracy did. Many of the newly elected governments made building infrastructure like electricity for the *favelas* a priority (Gay 1990: 105; Jacobi 1987: 16). By the time Janice Perlman returned to reinterview Rio residents in 1999–2003, even those who had remained in the *favelas* had essentially universal electricity access (Perlman 2006: 160, 165). The levels of coverage are reflected in their possessions: 98 percent owned televisions, 97 percent owned refrigerators, and 88 percent had telephones, while about two-thirds of respondents also had stereos, washing machines, and video cassette recorders (VCRs) (Perlman 2006: 166). At this later time, socioeconomic status – and presumably access to electricity – was no longer correlated with race (Perlman 2006: 162).

Electricity grid coverage expanded from 91.9 percent of the population in 1990 to 96.7 percent in 2000 (see Figure 4.1). A 30 percent increase in total system capacity and 10,000 km of transmission lines made this possible (Presidência da República 2002: 174). The new lines brought grid electricity to 600,000 residents of the Amazonian state of Pará, while a network of four transmission systems in the Northeast improved coverage there. Some of these would have previously had access to electricity through small, isolated diesel-based grids, but they now joined the national network. The lines also linked the North and the South of the country, establishing a route to bring hydropower from the water-rich areas of the Amazon to the rest of the country and improving the resilience of the grid to regional and seasonal variations (Presidência da República 2002: 176).

Even with these expansions, 31 percent of rural households still lacked electricity in 2000, with the highest rates still in the Northeast (39 percent) and the lowest in the Southeast (12 percent). Lower-income households in rural and peripheral urban areas in all regions continued to use wood for cooking, contributing to heavy demand for fossil and biomass fuels (Costa, Cohen, and Schaeffer 2007: 12). Rural areas have traditionally had little popular mobilization, but Brazil's contentious Landless Rural Workers' Movement (MST) eventually counted over a million members in more than 2,000 settlements. They had achieved land distribution of more than 3.7 million hectares by the mid-2000s and demanded resources to actually cultivate their land, including electricity (Carter 2015: 8–9; Carter and de Carvalho 2015: 230; Wolford 2003).

When the Workers' Party (PT) reached the presidency in 2003, responding to such demands from allies like the MST was high on its agenda. The PT's Light for All program of that year aimed, in the words of the Ministry of Mines and Energy, "to promote the reduction of poverty and hunger rates using electricity as a vector of economic and social development" (Ministêrio de Minas e Energia 2009: 2). The program targeted not just low-income communities without electricity but also farming communities and rural settlements, citizens around conservation units, communities of racial minorities, and local development initiatives including schools, clinics, and water supply. It also gave priority to communities affected by hydroelectric dams – which it began to build in large numbers while in office. This addressed a clear environmental injustice as such communities had often historically borne the costs of hosting the dams without receiving electricity (Instituto Energia e Meio Ambiente 2018b: 6).

An accompanying law (10,438) set the parameters for universalization of electricity services, requiring the dozens of distribution companies to have annual targets and plans for connecting any remaining unelectrified consumers. The distributors' priority was to reach those who could be connected to the existing grid, with government subsidies through the Light for All program in the North and Northeast (Slough et al. 2015: 317).[32] Almost all of the most complicated areas to service had remained under state control through the electricity parastatal Eletrobras, whose own planning for expansion was delayed and

---

[32] Interviews with Knijnik, PAC, 2014 and 2018.

disrupted as the post-PT government finally privatized its troubled distributors at the end of 2018 (Instituto Energia e Meio Ambiente 2018b: 8–9). The impacts of privatization are still unclear, but the prospect itself had already introduced considerable uncertainty into electrification plans.

Before privatization, Eletrobras installed 773,000 km of distribution lines, reaching 16.3 million people with 3.4 million connections while adding just 3,500 individual solar systems and 17 collective ones. The subsidies discussed in Section 4.2.4 and distributors themselves covered three-quarters of the approximately US$8 billion cost.[33] A plurality of early recipients (42.3 percent) were households headed by rural workers (Ministêrio de Minas e Energia 2009: 4) and 97 percent earned up to three minimum salaries, indicating successful targeting of the poor (Ministêrio de Minas e Energia 2009: 5; but see Slough et al. 2015). Over half (55.1 percent) consumed 80 kWh/month or less and almost half (46.9 percent) still reported using other sources of energy (Ministêrio de Minas e Energia 2009: 10, 9), suggesting that beneficiaries cannot afford or do not have access to adequate supplies of electricity.

The PT government originally envisioned Light for All as a four-year project (2004–2008), but it kept extending it to cover previously unidentified populations. Since 2013 (still under PT president Rousseff), its annual budgets have been halved, but the post-PT governments have also continued the program.[34] Decree 9357 (2018) extends it to 2022. These extensions have happened on largely technical grounds. Communities can and do ask to be in the program, but they have not typically mobilized in other ways for service. In 2018, only about 3 million Brazilians still lacked electricity connections and they tended to be among the most remote consumers in the Amazon.[35] Law 12,111 of 2009 made access to electricity a right that distributors must provide to people wherever they are. The Light for All phase initiated in 2010 was the first to contemplate distributed generation, but it became a major priority in the 2015 program (Decree 8943) for really isolated consumers (Bezerra et al. 2017: 3).

---

[33] http://eletrobras.com/pt/Paginas/Luz-para-Todos.aspx.
[34] www.aneel.gov.br/informacoes-tecnicas/-/asset_publisher/CegkWaVJWF5E/content/conta-de-desenvolvimento-energetico-cde/654800?inheritRedirect=false.
[35] Interview with Knijnic, PAC, 2018.

Regulations to build distributed systems depended on developments in other, more technical parts of the electricity system, starting with the National Electricity Agency (ANEEL). In Amanda Bradshaw's fascinating telling of ANEEL's role, just four or five technical bureaucrats pushed initial discussion in the agency about creating a space for distributed generation (Bradshaw 2018: 128–129). They experimented with bioenergy on a pig farm that was polluting the giant Iguaçu hydroelectric reservoir, and then looked for how they could remove regulatory barriers for other distributive generation, such as the solar cells eventually placed on the 2014 World Cup stadiums. The National Congress and the Ministry of Mines and Energy also had the capacity to enable distributed generation, but neither showed any inclination in this direction, so ANEEL's technical staff moved into the gap. The bureaucrats deliberately chose strategies that would not require or provoke other actors to join in. Their initial regulation in 2012, for example, chose net-metering rather than a feed-in tariff, since the latter was a subsidy that would require a law that seemed politically infeasible (ibid.: 134–135). The regulation itself stressed that it was removing obstacles to distributed generation rather than actively promoting it. This also followed the preferences of the national PT government, which did "not want to be seen as promoting an elitist policy, with little or no chance for the poorest segments of the population to take advantage of it" (Garcez 2015: 75).

Once ANEEL's bureaucrats wrote the first regulation, other actors stepped in to help push it further. A new industry association, Absolar, immediately became a part of all conversations on solar power after 2013, drawing on its expertise and its willingness to partner broadly.[36] Chapter 3 has already traced the solar industry's discussions with BNDES and with agencies for industrial development and small business administration starting around 2012. These led to literally dozens of public and private finance lines for distributed solar (Sebrae 2017b: 89–129) which proved critical for removing one of the most important barriers to consumer adoption of distributed solar systems in Brazil.[37]

Other promoters of distributed solar power came from the nongovernmental sector. For the Socioenvironmental Institute (ISA), support for distributed solar power in the Amazon is a key part of its "positive

[36] Interview with Sauaia, Absolar, 2018.
[37] Interview with Nahur, WWF-Brasil, 2018.

agenda" where the organization makes recommendations of outcomes and policies it would like to see. (Blocking large hydroelectric power plants, in contrast, is part of its "negative agenda.")[38] Greenpeace Brasil has a strong commitment to distributed solar generation for all consumers, not just the isolated ones (e.g., Greenpeace Brasil 2016b). The organization has approached the topic through dialogues with the Energy Research Enterprise (EPE) and with distributors and ANEEL, trying to develop a model that gives the distributors themselves a stake in expanding distributed solar generation.[39] Other organizations have also contributed to the debate, including by preparing reports on the solutions that distributed generation can provide for consumers (e.g., WWF-Brasil 2015a; Instituto Energia e Meio Ambiente 2018b).[40] A Working Group on Infrastructure and Energy and the Front for a New Energy Policy in Brazil provide broader forums for NGOs and social movements to discuss energy policy, take joint positions, and issue joint reports.[41]

When ANEEL opened up consultations for a new regulation on distributed generation in 2014 and 2015, all of these showed up in force. Just some 1,000 systems had been installed when the consultations opened. Distributors were essentially alone in resisting a new regulation that would more openly promote distributed generation of all kinds, including solar power. They challenged whether the regulation was in ANEEL's mandate and accused the program of making all consumers pay for the consumption choices of a wealthy few (Bradshaw 2018: 144). Even so, ANEEL decided deliberately that this was the time to accelerate adoption (ibid.: 150). The new regulation, No. 687 of 2015, came into effect in 2016. It tightened the deadlines for distributors to approve and connect distributed systems and removed network connection charges. The Ministry of Mines and Energy backed up ANEEL's legal case with a new program in support of distributed generation in 2015, the Program of Distributed Generation (ProGD).

---

[38] Interview with Ciro Campos de Souza, Campaigner for Instituto Socioambiental in Roraima, São Paulo, 2014 (JRT).
[39] Interviews with Ricardo Baitelo, Leader of Renewable Energy Project, Greenpeace Brasil, São Paulo, 2014 (JRT) and Lima, Greenpeace-Brasil, 2018.
[40] Interviews with Nahur, WWF-Brasil, 2018 and André Ferreira, IEMA, 2018.
[41] Interview with Lima, Greenpeace-Brasil, 2018.

With these regulatory changes backed by the rise of grid-scale solar power and the decline of solar cell costs, installations began to sky-rocket. From 1,768 installations (16.4 MW installed) in 2015, the total climbed to 27,803 (250 MW) in May of 2018. While this was still a tiny part of the total electricity supply, EPE began to include extended discussion of distributed solar power in its plans in 2017 (see Chapter 2). Before this, it had been just a paragraph in EPE's demand projections. The ten-year plan for 2017 now suddenly expected 770,000 installations (3.3 GW) by 2026, numbers that EPE had scaled up to 1.35 million and 11.9 GW in the next year's plan (Ministério de Minas e Energia 2017: 221, 2018: 209). The latter numbers assumed that ANEEL would decide in its third version of the regulations that the time for acceleration was over and would heed distributors' requests to add a network charge for distributed generation customers. This decision is to be made by the end of 2020. If the permissive framework remains, EPE expects 21 GW of distributed generation by 2027 (Ministério de Minas e Energia 2018: 209). While solar installations are modeled to be just 82 percent of the microgeneration installations and 55 percent of all the electricity produced, the distributed solar market has clearly risen and begun to mature very quickly from its modest beginnings just a decade before in the musings of a small group of technocrats.

These developments did not in themselves reach the remote Amazonian consumers. As the national regulatory, finance, and supply systems changed to promote distributed generation elsewhere, however, they also made the remote solar programs somewhat more viable. They still competed with the diesel systems that are more characteristic (71.8 percent) of electricity services in isolated and remote services (Bezerra et al. 2017: 5). For small, isolated networks, auctions had selected the potential suppliers since 2009. Solar power's profile, with expensive infrastructure but no fuel costs, competes poorly with diesel's opposite characteristics in the auctions. Diesel suppliers and local politicians even have vested interests in the ongoing diesel costs, which represent revenue to them (Instituto Energia e Meio Ambiente 2018b: 11–16). Where diesel is a long journey away, solar power is more attractive. It will need to be installed and maintained properly, unlike in Brazil's earlier experiments with distributed solar systems in the Amazon (ibid.: 43). In implementing the remote programs, Eletrobras uses a similar standard to South Africa's for its distributed systems, requiring that they guarantee monthly generation of 45 kWh for a household. However, households and communities can also request larger supplies, which Eletrobras and the Ministry of Mines and Energy consider on a case-by-case basis (Eletrobras 2017: 9). With just 3,500 remote solar systems installed by 2018, actual implementation is still developing.

The net result of these policy developments in Brazil is that grid-scale wind and, more recently, solar power helped add capacity to the national grid that was needed to allow both household and industrial consumption to grow in the twenty-first century. Wind power is especially important for complementing Brazil's dominant hydropower. Distributed solar generation began a sudden takeoff in 2016, as more permissive regulations and supporting developments are spurring quick adoption. All observers agree that these are mostly the middle- and upper-class consumers typical everywhere (Abromovay 2014), but successive governments have also planned to use distributed generation to help reach the last unserved households in remote Amazonian regions. With most Brazilians on the national electrical grid and paying for their electricity, the policies used to introduce wind and solar power to the electricity matrix in Brazil have thus generally not yet worsened inequalities of access and quality of electricity supply, although they might, if distributed solar continues to develop as it has without regulatory changes like network charges.

4.2.4 Brazil: Political Economy of Prices and Subsidies

Since 1993, Brazil has followed a general policy of electricity pricing based on cost recovery, accompanied by policies that place low prices second only to security of supply (Garcez 2015; Tahnka 2008: 159–160). Both existing and new generators of electricity of all fuel types compete in auctions to supply electricity to the grid, with selection based only on price. Occasional reserve auctions for particular fuel types are scheduled primarily to ensure a balanced supply; solar power has so far been procured only through these. Daily dispatch of individual generation plants is also based on price, with the large hydroelectric dams historically going first. Tariffs are very responsive to the current cost of generation, and the heavy use of expensive thermoelectric plants in drought conditions brings rapid automatic increases in rates. Consumers can see these automatic adjustments through the utilities' use of color bands to show current prices.[42] This section examines electricity prices in themselves and as they relate to the entrance of wind and solar power in Brazil. While the new renewables generated little controversy in procurement policies, an increasingly heated debate over subsidies to them may affect the future trajectory of both grid-scale and distributed wind and solar power generation and consumption.

Through policies like those just outlined, the Brazilian government has cultivated the appearance of technocratic pricing policies for electricity. Even in the face of price volatility, very few household consumers or consumer NGOs attend ANEEL's tariff hearings – although ABRACE and the regulated agencies do (Castro 2013: 1079–1080).[43] There has been little consumer mobilization on the issue outside of the hearings either, in contrast to South Africa. For poor consumers, the government's own policy choices, especially after 2003, have helped to reduce their electricity costs, even without much mobilization. A "social tariff" was introduced in 2010 (Law 12.212, regulated by Decree 7583), which provides a 65 percent discount for the first 30 kWh consumed per month by poor families and smaller discounts up to 220 kWh.[44] This has helped to insulate poor consumers from the full price increases. The fact that the Brazilian government chose to cover three-quarters of the cost of Light for All with federal budget outlays and subsidies (R$16.8 billion of R$22.7 billion), rather than attempting direct cost recovery, also helped poor consumers.[45]

At the same time, one specific political choice on prices has roiled the sector, uniting everyone in opposition from unions (DIEESE 2015) to both large electricity users and distributors.[46] Then-president Dilma Rousseff used negotiations with concessionaires in 2012 to force a temporary 20 percent drop in electricity prices heading into her reelection campaign in 2014 (MP 579, Law 127831/2013), only to have tariffs surge after she was reelected. An official of CPFL Renováveis, a major firm in the renewables sector, called these price changes "the 9/11 of the energy sector" since they were announced on

---

[42] www.energia.sp.gov.br/2018/04/aneel-aprova-mudancas-no-mecanismo-das-bandeiras-tarifarias/.

[43] Large consumers are allowed to exit the common electricity pool to negotiate their own deals directly with suppliers when broader policies do not suit their needs.

[44] www.planalto.gov.br/ccivil_03/_ato2011-2014/2011/decreto/D7583.htm.

[45] MME Press Release, 31 December 2014.

[46] Interview with Iocca, ABRACE, 2018.

the same date as the devastating attacks on the World Trade Center in the United States.[47] Other interviewees were similarly distressed. While the low prices lasted only a short time, they were extremely costly for Eletrobras and distorted all of Brazil's price-based system for electricity during that time. Afterwards, annual prices rose well above inflation, multiplying the pain of several dry years in 2014–2015 that required using the expensive diesel plants. ABRACE estimated that average prices rose 44 percent between 2014 and 2018, well above the pace of inflation.[48] Both prices and price increases have been highest in the North and Northeast regions where quality and access are worst.

Wind and solar power are not directly blamed for the price increases. A feed-in tariff brought a small amount of very expensive wind power into the grid between 2002 and 2011, but it was an emergency response to severe droughts in 2001 that showed the need to quickly diversify the grid. All distributors are required to purchase a small amount of the electricity from the Proinfa program, so its costs are diffused. EPE has called for adding larger amounts of wind and solar power to its ten-year procurement plans for the national grid only as their prices seemed likely to be competitive (see Chapter 2). Wind power came first, in an experimental 2009 auction reserved for it. The winning bids were so low that EPE's tone changed completely in the next year's plan. EPE now called wind power highly competitive (Ministério de Minas e Energia 2010: 13) instead of just a vague possibility whose potential was unknown (e.g., Ministério de Minas e Energia 2007: 141). The average winning bid of the first auction was R$235 per KW, much lower than Proinfa's R$404. Prices reached their bottom in 2012 at R$117 before rising a bit in later auctions (Sebrae 2017a: 51).

EPE noted in its plans for years that solar was too expensive to even consider, but a surprisingly inexpensive auction in Pernambuco state in 2013 led to a 2014 auction.[49] This once again wiped away EPE's price skepticism as hundreds of projects competed (Ministério de Minas e Energia 2015: 138–139). The average winning bid price, US$88/MWh, was 18 percent below the bid ceiling set by the government – and well below the US$103

---

[47] Interview with official of CPFL Renováveis, São Paulo, 2014.
[48] Interview with Iocca, ABRACE, 2018. These increases are significantly below those in South Africa, of course, even with the higher inflation rates in the latter.
[49] Interview with Sauaia, Absolar, 2018.

that had won in Pernambuco the year before.[50] Winning bids were half that being paid in European FiTs (Ministério de Minas e Energia 2014: 18). Industry lobbyists helped secure a large jump in the planned procurement of solar power between EPE's 2020 and 2023 planning documents.[51] Wind power is now often the cheapest option even in auctions open to different kinds of electricity, and EPE expects that solar will join it. In the 2018 auctions, the price of solar power was down to US$35.2/MWh, already cheaper than biomass and new hydro.[52]

The basic contracting and pricing of grid-scale wind and solar power – the generation side – have not been particularly contentious in Brazil. However, consumers pay an array of subsidies through their electricity tariffs, some of which go to wind and solar power, and there is increasingly sharp conflict on those subsidies. The subsidies had a fairly innocuous beginning as a way of paying for the 2002 Proinfa FiT through an Electricity Development Fund (CDE). Since then, governments and politicians of all the major parties have used the CDE as a way to pass all kinds of charges on to consumers. The compensation for distributors after Rousseff's tariff cuts, for example, passed through the CDE as did costs for restructuring Eletrobras for privatization.

In 2018, the more permanent subsidy lines in the CDE included the cost of universalization – mostly the Light for All program – and the cost of the social tariff for low-income consumers.[53] National coal is subsidized through the CDE until 2023, as is the cost of diesel and other fuels used in isolated systems. The diesel charges have vied with a set of grid connection discounts to be the largest single items in the file. The connection discounts are part of the original Proinfa, designed to give small (under 30 MW) electricity installations that use alternative fuel sources – originally wind, bioenergy, and small hydro, but now also solar and others – discounts of 50–100 percent on their connections to the national grid. Distributed solar installations can also have subsidized connections. Since 2002, governments have added other categories of consumer to receive discounts. Rousseff's Decree 7891/2013 added

---

[50] Interview with Sauaia, Absolar, 2018.   [51] Interview with analyst, EPE, 2014.
[52] Interview with Sauaia, Absolar, 2018.
[53] www.aneel.gov.br/informacoes-tecnicas/-/asset_publisher/CegkWaVJWF5E/co
ntent/conta-de-desenvolvimento-energetico-cde/654800?inheritRedirect=false.
Interview with Knijnic, PAC, 2018.

rural consumers, water and sanitation companies, and irrigation and agriculture for various reductions in the cost of grid connections.[54]

This last line item of connections discounts is the one that has grown most quickly, from R$4.46 billion in 2013 to R$8.36 billion in 2018, or from 31.6 percent of the whole CDE (R$14.12 billion) to 43.5 percent of a much bigger CDE (R$20.05 billion). To gain some sense of scale, the giant Belo Monte hydroelectric dam will cost R$33 billion to build. Rousseff's Provisional Measure in 2015 (MP 706) already asked for attention to the CDE in the wake of numerous legal challenges, but the real debate came after she was irregularly impeached in 2016. Her market-oriented vice president, Michel Temer, moved quickly to reorganize the electricity sector with an eye to privatizing Eletrobras's distributors, again using a Provisional Measure (MP 735, June 2016). Brazilian presidents can issue almost any Provisional Measure (*Medida Provisoria*) without congressional approval for two sixty-day periods, after which it must be passed by Congress into law to continue.

As part of preparing Eletrobras for privatization, MP 735 passed its control of the CDE to the body that controls the electricity market, the Council of the Electricity Market (CCEE). It also asked the CCEE to present plans to limit the annual payouts of the CDE. The congressional debates around this Provisional Measure were heated, with members of parliament adding a wish list of projects in dozens of amendments or moving to squash it altogether. President Temer used his line-item veto to take coal off the list of incentivized alternative fuel sources in the eventual legislation, for example (Law 13.360/2016). The discussion has continued, especially since the plans to limit the CDE imply that some subsidies will be pitted against others (Instituto Energia e Meio Ambiente 2018b). In this debate, there are many disputes over just who and what are being subsidized, in addition to whether they should be. The National Congress has tried to settle the debate several times since 2016, attaching it to other legislative projects, but arguments are still pending. Even as most argued to reduce the CDE, industry analyst Claudio Salles counted forty projects in the Congress that would raise it.[55]

[54] www.aneel.gov.br/tarifas-consumidores/-/asset_publisher/zNaRBjCLDgbE/co ntent/descontos/654800?inheritRedirect=false.
[55] http://acendebrasil.com.br/media/imprensa/20180905_OGlobo__Contapesada .pdf.

Victor Iocca of ABRACE has perhaps the most straightforward vision: without entering into much dispute about the merits of particular subsidies, he suggests that electricity prices (the first and permanent concern of ABRACE's members) should not be used to pay for social aims unconnected to electricity.[56] Others, including those concerned with wind and solar power, are more attentive to the details. Absolar, for example, argues that the debate misses the much, much larger historical subsidies to the oil and gas industry. It also objects to the common grouping of wind with solar power (e.g., Instituto Escolhas 2018), since almost all of the CDE's connection discounts have been associated with wind power so far, with solar only now being added to the grid.[57] This is yet another point where the later entrance of solar power means that wind power benefited from advantages that solar has not, if the discounts are in fact taken away soon. In any event, the CCEE will be making a proposal on the CDE and its discounts in 2020 without an obvious winner in sight.

Distributed solar power has generated its own set of disputes about taxes, prices, and credits. Two especially important ones are the tax regime around distributed solar power and the familiar question of whether these micro and mini generators will pay for the cost of maintaining the overall electricity network. ANEEL's 2012 regulatory framework was designed to remove barriers from small generation systems of all kinds without necessarily incentivizing them. Micro and mini solar producers received credits for the value of the amount of electricity they produced that they could use for their own present and future consumption. Taxes on the electricity service are an important source of revenue for multiple levels of government. In 2015, 51.6 percent of total electricity charges were attributable to various taxes, with state-level taxes taking the largest share at almost 22 percent of the total (Acende Brasil and PricewaterhouseCoopers 2016: 10). Only the state of Minas Gerais exempted consumers from paying state taxes on the electricity they generated themselves in 2012, reducing the economic gains of joining the net-metering system.

Revised regulations in November and December 2015 improved the terms and taxes associated with net-metering and introduced several mechanisms to share the net-metering credits beyond the producer unit

[56] Interview Iocca, ABRACE, 2018.   [57] Interview with Sauaia, Absolar, 2018.

(Ministério de Minas e Energia 2017: 221).[58] For example, an apartment building could now put in a solar system of up to 5 MW and distribute the credits among all its tenants. By May 2018, all states and the federal district had finally exempted consumers from paying state-level taxes (on the circulation of merchandise and services) on their distributed generation, following a 2015 federal decision to exempt net electricity from the tax. Already in 2016, the cheaper solar prices and more expensive electricity tariffs had made the levelized cost of distributed solar comparable to distributors' charges in about half of the distribution areas (Tolmasquim 2016: 370–371).

These dynamics led to the surge of distributed solar power already discussed. ANEEL is taking comments on a proposed new regulation for the time period after 2020, which would ask all consumers to pay a tariff for network access even if they then generate electricity equal to all their consumption. NGO promoters of distributed solar power are arguing against this so-called binomial tariff, which would double the amount of time needed to pay off installation.[59] Absolar argues that the network charges would come too soon for industry development. Distributors had already argued hard to prevent the 2015 changes and have been even more insistent in the current round of public consultations. EPE modeled the proposal's effects and estimates that there would be nearly twice as much distributed solar produced (21 GW instead of 11.9 GW) by 2027 if the binominal tariff were not adopted. Average tariffs for those who remain on the network would rise up to 20 percent (Ministério de Minas e Energia 2018: 209–211).

Everyone engaged in the debate over distributed solar production in Brazil agrees that consumers who pay for their own installations are middle and upper class. A household system costs about US$2,500, an investment too large for poorer households even if the savings will pay it off in five years (or ten with the binomial tariff). Proponents of the binomial tariff make this point a central part of their arguments. Victor Iacco of ABRACE, for example, argues that all consumers should pay their share of the network costs and that this is especially critical because it would be wealthier consumers opting off.[60] NGO proponents of solar power are sensitive to the just transition dimension, although

---

[58] www.renewableenergyworld.com/articles/2016/02/new-developments-in-brazil-s-solar-power-sector.html.
[59] Interview with Lima, Greenpeace-Brasil, 2018.
[60] Interview with Iocca, ABRACE, 2018.

they note the usefulness of distributed solar generation for remote locations. WWF-Brasil sees household solar's major role as a way to mobilize support for the grid-scale solar power that will have a bigger impact on the electricity supply.[61] In the wake of strong contestation, ANEEL's regulators will strike the final balance on these issues.

4.3 Conclusion

Cost and distributional calculations obviously permeate the discussion of wind and solar power in both Brazil and South Africa. Newly democratic governments in both countries have expended considerable effort to extend electricity to households, even in remote and difficult locations. Grid-scale wind and solar power have helped make that possible, but they have also generated debates about the costs and subsidies involved in procuring them. Distributed solar power makes a double entrance in both, offering electricity to underserved remote populations and also enabling wealthy consumers to opt out of supporting public distribution networks. Overall, wind and solar power make modest, if mixed, contributions to reducing social inequities. Notwithstanding the similarities, the two countries also show that the details of preexisting conditions and regulatory choices can have a significant impact on how wind and solar power affect consumer interests.

In South Africa, apartheid-era policies left a difficult legacy for the post-transition government. Two-thirds of households, mostly Black African, did not have access to electricity, while a small number of large industrial consumers took a disproportionate share. Wind and solar power helped expand the pool of electricity available as Eskom and municipal distribution companies made millions of connections to eventually reach 85 percent of households. Plans to reach the remainder include solar and other forms of distributed power but are still incipient beyond a small program begun in 2001. Frustrations with the slow pace of connections and the cost and low quality of electricity service have led to large numbers of protests starting in 2004 and expanding after 2010, which the government seems unable to address. Wealthy consumers have begun to opt off the grid with distributed

---

[61] Interview with Nahur, WWF-Brasil, 2018.

solar systems even before national regulations allow it, reducing resources for an already precarious system.

There are few disputes around expanding access, but some of the same actors from Chapters 2 and 3 reappear in cost and subsidy debates. The debates are highly contentious, as participants are locked into a wider contention about the future of coal and the electricity parastatal Eskom. Eskom and its frequent partner trade union confederations have strongly challenged wind and solar power on cost grounds. They selectively used the expensive prices of early auction rounds to argue that wind and solar power should not be contracted at all. The dominant consumer group EIUG shifted to become more supportive as prices for renewable energy dropped, however, although it had been more aligned with coal producers and workers earlier. Overall, questions of costs and subsidies underline the fragility of electricity provision in South Africa, where neither large majorities of individual households nor the state have resources to support universal, high-quality electricity provision. Wind and solar power have not substantially changed that equation, whose inequities still reflect the racial separations of the apartheid years.

In Brazil, successive governments have been much more effective in approaching universal electricity service provision, in good part because they started from much higher levels of coverage – 91.9 percent of the population in 1990, versus South Africa's one-third covered. Most of the rest gained access through grid extension to first informal urban and then rural households. Wind and solar power formed increasing amounts of that grid electricity. Planners added a limited FiT for wind power for the grid in 2002 to complement hydropower after a year of drought and electricity. More procurement came only in 2009 after prices had dropped, and planners considered solar too expensive to add before 2014. So, price considerations were central to the timing and quantity of procurement of each. The timing of the change of government in 2016 to a more market-oriented one undermined some of solar power's expansion. Wind power had expanded and received extensive subsidies before those subsidies became highly controversial – just as solar installations began to receive them. Thus, the issues discussed in this chapter also contribute to the different fates of wind and solar power in Brazil, reinforcing those of Chapter 3, which discussed the more extensive use of industrial policy and public finance for wind power than for solar.

Distributed generation plans have offered many more alternatives for solar power in Brazil, however. The Light for All program used solar power as theorists have suggested, to offer electrification to remote consumers not reachable by grid-based electricity. It could not do so until a small group of technocrats in the electricity regulator ANEEL set up regulations to first allow and then promote distributed generation. At first working deliberately below broader political notice, they are now overseeing a classic debate about whether consumers with distributed generation installations must help to pay for the network costs of electricity provision overall. Meanwhile, the adoption of such installations is proceeding at rates so rapid that even supporting NGOs and the solar industry itself did not anticipate them. Depending on the outcomes of that debate, wind and solar power may move from their current modest contribution to improving the equity of access to electricity to destabilizing the distribution system.

A chapter on electricity access probably would not appear in a book on the first adopters of wind and solar power. For middle-income and developing countries, the appeal of renewable energy is often associated with the ability of distributed solar power to bring electricity to unserved populations. Yet both Brazil and South Africa added most of their wind and solar power at grid scale. Those calculations were based in part on cost and efficiency of provision, other themes of this chapter. South Africa also found that many of its consumers insisted on grid provision for quality reasons, arguing that the small systems that the state offered were not adequate for their needs. In Brazil, distributed solar power was a strong option only for unserved communities that were truly remote. It was wealthy urban populations already served by electricity networks who were the most enthusiastic adopters of distributed solar power. These observations together show the crucial role of this political economy's calculation of literal costs and benefits of electricity service, but they suggest that those calculations might not look the way that the academic and policy literature suggests they will – at least for these middle-income countries with significant electricity infrastructures already in place.

5 | *People and Place: Siting Wind and Solar Plants in Brazil and South Africa*

Rotating wind turbines are an instantly recognizable sign of the growth of renewable electricity worldwide, as are banks of solar power cells, on rooftops or in fields. This chapter reflects the fact that all electricity infrastructure projects are sited in particular places. Each of these communities will have local social, economic, and environmental conditions that will be affected by a new infrastructure project. Parallel academic literatures offer strikingly different expectations about whether those impacts will be positive or negative, with clear implications for the interests at stake and the anticipated future trajectories of wind and solar power. After sketching those different approaches, I present the relevant institutional frameworks in Brazil and South Africa. I then investigate whether site-based resistance to wind and solar electricity infrastructure has occurred in the two countries and whether the responses of host communities and activists to new installations can account for the differential outcomes for wind and solar power in them. I ground the analysis of community responses in studies of collective action in general and mobilization on energy and infrastructure in particular.

Unlike other policy arenas covered in this book, there is considerable disagreement about the structure of interests around the siting of renewable energy in particular communities. For environmental economists and many energy scholars, having a wind or solar power installation nearby should bring significant economic benefits to host communities, beyond any national and global gains, a win–win scenario. They expect to see local construction and manufacturing jobs, land payments to local landowners, and indirect increases in local economic activity, among other economic gains (e.g., Brown, Pender, Wiser, Lantz, and Hoen 2012; Copena and Simón 2018; Xia and Song 2017). In democracies in particular, politicians are expected to encourage decentralized power generation since it can bring economic benefits to rural constituencies, redressing regional inequalities and rural decline (Bayer and Urpelainen 2016: 604).

Local economic benefits, expected for any renewable energy installation, should be even higher for the grid-linked community-owned installations found mostly in Europe. In those, communities also pocket the revenues from generous feed-in tariffs and other benefits of ownership, including the ability to prioritize local benefits in their decision-making. Local economic gains were as much as eight times higher from these experiments in "energy democracy" as from commercial installations in Germany, for example (Mey and Diesendorf 2018: 115; see also Morris and Jungjohann 2016; Seyfang, Park, and Smith 2013). Community involvement and commitments to local electricity installations in developing areas have also been shown to be critical for the ongoing use of the installations, or they fall into disrepair (Brower Brown 2011: 346–347).

The overall picture of the siting interests involved in these literatures includes both concentrated (local economic) and diffuse (national economic and global climate) benefits from wind and solar power installations. These positive spillovers are seen to create a win–win scenario that promotes environmental and developmental aims at the same time. That interest structure should result in significant local community support for renewables except for narrow NIMBY (not-in-my-backyard) mobilizations (Dear 1992; Petrova 2013; Stokes 2013; Warren, Lumsden, O'Dowd, and Birnie 2005). This view of the siting political economy would expect to see siting logics promoting more renewable energy production.

Yet local communities have often resisted renewable energy installations, and not always on grounds easily seen as narrow (e.g., Ogilvie and Rootes 2015: 875; Ralston-Paton, Smallie, Pearson, and Ramalho 2017). At least two other major storylines contest the *win–win* one, with both arguing that this is an overly simplistic view of the interests involved and that the overall merits of wind and solar power should not be assumed to outweigh their local costs (Avila 2018).

A growing literature on "green versus green" dilemmas recognizes that macro and micro environmental dimensions may give different directives for electricity projects (Lombard and Ferreira 2014; Warren et al. 2005; Yonk, Simmons, and Steed 2013: 2). That is, wind and solar power are part of the solution to global climate change, but the *environmental conservation* storyline stresses that there may be significant costs for wildlife conservation and landscape protection in specific locations (Avila 2018: 601–602; Visser, Perold, Ralston-Paton, Cardenal, and Ryan 2019). Birds and bats are most immediately at risk in nesting areas and migratory corridors, especially from wind turbines, but other local environmental impacts from construction and maintenance are also cited as reasons to keep wind and solar installations out of particular places. Many activists who point out these costs resist a characterization of the interests they defend as local and narrow (Yonk et al. 2013: 27), seeing broad interests in species, habitat, or sociocultural preservation. This is a storyline that in many ways preserves the hope for win–win solutions but acknowledges compelling reasons to avoid some sites.

Finally, an *environmental justice* storyline casts a wider critique of wind and solar power infrastructure, grounded in critical geography and anthropology literatures. Not only does it see significant local harms, notably in the disruption of local land-use patterns and social and economic ways of life, but this storyline goes on to argue that it is not coincidental that the benefits and harms are distributed as they are (Avila 2018: 602). Unequal power relations place the most significant harms of such infrastructure projects squarely on marginal populations with uncertain land claims and precarious livelihood strategies (e.g., Brannstrom et al. 2017; Dunlap 2019; Huesca-Pérez, Sheinbaum-Pardo, and Köppel 2016; McEwan 2017). In this view, technical fixes like the mapping, environmental impact assessment (EIA), and compensation processes discussed in this chapter are likely to reinforce unequal power relations rather than to challenge them (Gorayeb, Brannstrom, de Andrade Meireles, and de Souza Mendes 2018; McCarthy and Thatcher 2019). Even moving a plant to another location will not overcome the fundamental dynamics, although giving communities substantial control and even veto power, as in the community-owned projects, might (Bode 2013). While the environmental justice storyline is not against wind and solar power per se, it is critical of how they are usually deployed, in centralized, top-down modes that further challenge already disadvantaged groups. As should be clear, this is a view of the relevant interests that sees primarily local costs from renewable energy infrastructure and expects community responses to block expansion of the sector where they can. However, the very lack of power of impacted communities works against such results.

These storylines were largely developed through research on how local communities in advanced industrial democracies responded to wind power installations. There are many fewer studies of how such communities respond to solar power and fewer yet on communities in middle-income and developing countries, beyond some case studies. This chapter therefore breaks new ground in systematically evaluating how local communities in Brazil and South Africa have shown their assessment of the local impacts of wind and solar power installations by mobilizing against them, or not. Those results offer inconsistent evidence about how well the three storylines capture a clear political economy of siting.

To preview the cases, Brazil's regulatory structures around wind and solar power have not encouraged the community-owned installations common in early adopters. Wind and solar power installations have tended to be fairly large commercial operations that have clustered in a few towns and regions of the country. The institutions of environmental licensing and land use were originally quite permissive of the earlier wind power plants, assuming their local impact to be small and/ or positive, although changes in 2014 provided disincentives for placing wind farms in sensitive areas like dunes. In a striking contrast to the other chapters of this book, contention is higher around siting wind power in Brazil than in South Africa, with about a quarter of the locations of Brazil's 600 wind farms mobilizing in some way to contest the plants. These protests are especially common in Brazil's poor Northeast region, and a strong environmental justice argument threads through these cases. Solar power, in contrast, has generated very little reported response from host communities. At the same time, the fact that there is so much more wind power than solar power in Brazil suggests that the logic of the siting political economy has not had a strong impact on outcomes.

South Africa made similar choices that also blocked community-owned projects of the kind familiar in Europe, although its auction system does require and reward developers for offering local communities a small ownership stake and local jobs. Regulations around environmental licensing and land use were originally comparatively restrictive, overwhelming the Department of Environmental Affairs. They have since been loosened in areas thought to have fewer environmental impacts. Neither wind nor solar power has generated much response from local communities, which have neither attacked the installations nor mobilized in defense of their benefits, as when Eskom and its allies, as described in other chapters, refused to expand wind and solar power. BirdLife South Africa has closely monitored and blocked the location of wind farms and even individual turbines; it worked closely with a local community partner in only one middle-class tourist-oriented community. This is the only chapter where the status quo coalition that played such a large role in the other political economies does not appear. For both countries, in fact, the siting logic seems quite separated from both the other political economies and the larger outcomes for wind and solar power.

5.1 Assessing Local Benefits and Costs: Analytical Strategies

The three storylines in the introduction are in part analytical constructs, reflecting the starting points and assumptions of different social science approaches and disciplines. But there are empirical claims underlying them as well. They have different views of the nature of the interests involved in wind and solar infrastructure projects and correspondingly different expectations about the nature and frequency of contestation of them. Reviewing the specific costs and benefits of wind and solar power in Brazilian and South African communities and how those communities have responded to the arrival of wind and solar power infrastructure projects can illuminate the siting logic in a more concrete fashion. While the storylines tend to emphasize the substance of community responses to wind and solar installations, it is important to note that citizen responses may also reflect procedural claims about the quality and nature of consultation and the conditions of participation – as well as whether they feel heard by decision-makers (Aitken, McDonald, and Strachen 2008; Walker and Baxter 2017: 161).

Whether or not communities object to the presence of wind turbines or solar panels, their ability to insert those preferences into electricity decision-making depends both on whether key institutions are open to them and on whether they can organize themselves to make collective demands. Neither of these conditions should be taken for granted. These considerations turn individual and community responses to the trade-offs associated with renewable electricity into political questions about the possibility and likelihood of collective action, rather than simply preferences. The perception among policy-makers and activists is that collective resistance has had a large and dampening effect on global wind power in particular, yet there has been much less research on actual campaigns and their outcomes and almost none on developing countries beyond a few case studies. In addition, there is little agreement about outcomes among the few review studies that exist (Ogilvie and Rootes 2015: 875; see also Aitken et al. 2008; Toke, Breukers, and Wolsink 2008). Thus, this chapter fills several large holes in the study of the actual local political economy of wind and solar energy.

In addition, very nearly all of the literature on mobilized responses to renewable sources of electricity focuses on wind power, where community resistance has more often been intense and well documented. In fact, all of the articles cited so far in this chapter are on wind power. Solar power impacts are a "black box," with the best-known local impacts in mining of inputs and manufacturing and later in waste disposal (Mulvaney 2013: 232–233), possibly skipping the installation level considered here. Solar power is less visually intrusive and can more easily be sited in nonsensitive locations, but it will also require large tracts of land to use at scale. In addition, locations can be poorly chosen, as when the US Bureau of Land Management opened to solar power public land that included extensive sacred ancestral homes for native American tribes (Mulvaney 2013: 234–235; see also Frate and Brannstrom 2017). The few empirical studies on the topic have concluded that communities have tended to accept solar installations unless they are very large (Peterson, Stephens, and Wilson 2015: 3), but this conclusion is not based on the extensive research devoted to wind power and opposition to solar may appear as it scales up (da Silva, Magrini, Tolmasquim, and Castelo Branco 2019; Mulvaney 2017). Thus, this chapter is unusual in adding evidence on community responses to solar power installations as well.

My study of community mobilization and its impact on wind and solar power outcomes can draw on a large literature on mobilized engagement with infrastructure projects, itself part of an even larger literature on social movements and collective action. Below, I use these literatures to generate a set of expectations about when and why communities might mobilize to try to block or challenge wind or solar power – or, indeed, to encourage it. Even before community responses to specific proposed projects, however, institutional and regulatory choices set parameters for the kinds of project likely to be introduced into communities.

In both Brazil and South Africa, community choices are situated within regulatory frameworks that have discouraged community ownership of the kind common earlier among wind and solar pioneers in Europe. The cost-based auction systems that both countries chose for procurement reward bids from large and efficient firms that typically come into local communities as outsiders (Grashof 2019; Leiren and Reimer 2018), although South Africa has added unusual community development requirements to its auctions that may work against these patterns. In both countries, local impacts are managed primarily through project-level EIA processes to evaluate the environmental and social effects of specific wind and solar installation proposals. Both countries have also engaged in some larger strategic planning for the sectors that draws on the regulatory traditions of strategic environmental assessment and land-use planning. Thus, an initial section for each country examines the provisions for assessing the impacts of wind and solar power at the project level and at a more holistic regional level.

These institutions and regulations create what is referred to in Sections 5.2 and 5.3 as the formal political opportunity structure for community mobilization around wind and solar power. The EIA processes in both countries include – differing – mechanisms to consult with local communities, but the communities are not limited to these formal opportunities. Such formal consultations may be deformed in various ways (e.g., Abers 2018; Gorayeb et al. 2018) and communities often opt to pursue other strategies to influence outcomes, from protest to direct negotiation with developers to the court system. In addition, strategic planning processes have also spurred collective action by civil society groups that draw on broader regional, national, or even global perspectives to consider local community impacts. The theoretical discussion moves beyond political opportunity analysis to consider additional possible explanations of other collective responses, discussed in more detail in Section 5.2.

Section 5.4 introduces the methodology I use to analyze the actual responses of communities in both countries to wind power installations and then solar power ones. Studies of social movements often select case studies of notable mobilizations for analysis. Five of eight known studies of community mobilizations about wind power in Brazil analyze the same emblematic community, Aracati, where wind farms in coastal dunes interrupted livelihood strategies of local populations as well as the physical ecology of the region. The research strategy here, in contrast, examines a fuller set of 600 Brazilian wind farms in 77 cities in order to see broader patterns of community response. The same strategy is used for South African wind and for solar power in both countries. While missing the depth of the case study approach, this research strategy gives a much better answer to the question of whether community responses might be shaping aggregate outcomes for wind and solar power. If all potential wind power sites in Brazil faced the opposition that the Aracati projects have, wind power would have a doubtful future there. But they do not, and wind power thrives accordingly. Section 5.5 presents the results of the study of resistance to wind farms in both countries, while Section 5.6 is a much shorter analysis of nonresistance to solar power installations. The conclusion (Section 5.7) returns to the question of the aggregate implications of community responses for renewable energy outcomes in the two countries.

5.2 Planning and Siting Power Infrastructure Projects: Explaining Community Action

In earlier adopters of renewable energy like Germany and Denmark, local communities led the way as producers of wind and solar power, harvesting the benefits of their experiments in energy democracy (Morris and Jungjohann 2016). Brazil and South Africa belong to a later generation of host communities, where wind and solar installations are built by outsider firms that have won competitive national auctions. To understand responses to these, I draw on a well-developed sociological literature that approaches these kinds of infrastructural incursion with a presumption that communities might resist them through social movements (McAdam and Boudet 2012). Earlier studies have shown that with their local "site fights" against power infrastructure projects, communities can potentially block projects or reorient entire segments of the energy industry (Aldrich 2008; Rucht 2002; Sherman 2011). This section examines existing arguments about when and why communities and civil society organizations mobilize around power infrastructure: How often and when does that mobilization take the form of site-based oppositional mobilization, whether an effort to block an individual project altogether or to make a demand for compensation or mitigation of impacts? What kinds of strategy do citizens use and how much influence can they have? Do they always resist the plants?

The classic answers of theories about social movements often begin by pointing to varying political opportunity structures. These are the more stable, exogenous factors that either increase or decrease the likelihood that prospective activists will take action and be successful (Meyer and Minkoff 2004; Tarrow 2011; Wright and Boudet 2012: 745). Analyses can start with basic political characteristics like the presence or absence of democratic institutions, but typically they also look for more specific constellations of formal participatory opportunities, the presence of allies, especially elite ones, and similar factors. Together, they reflect the observation that the emergence and success of collective action depend in part on the larger political context in which actions emerge, which can encourage or constrain possible mobilization as well as shape the response of authorities.

Here, I compare Brazilian and South African activists' ability to influence EIA as the most relevant formal participatory opportunity associated with project siting decisions in this sector (Hochstetler and Tranjan 2016), as already introduced in Section 5.1. Since wind and solar power are low in energy density per land unit, they require large tracts of land to be used at grid scale (Scheidel and Sorman 2012). Therefore, institutions for strategic land-use planning and land claims also form a part of the opportunity structure. These institutions and processes create very specific opportunities for participation while effectively constraining others. In South Africa, for example, individuals and organizations are allowed to present written comments on environmental impact reports and to appeal licensing decisions to the minister of environmental affairs, while Brazilians can write comments and also participate in public hearings on the specific projects where they can ask questions of developers,[1] but they can appeal decisions only in the courts rather than administratively.

Inside such formal participatory opportunities and especially outside them, the ability of communities to organize is seen to rest in whether they can find allies to support their efforts. While the sociological

---

[1] I am not claiming here that such public hearings are necessarily effective ways of communicating community positions. See Abers (2018) on the perfunctory quality of a set of community consultations on infrastructure projects in Brazil and Gorayeb et al. (2018) on how EIA processes were deliberately undermined by governmental and firm participants in licensing a wind plant there.

literature calls these political opportunity structures, the most important allies will often come from outside the political sphere itself. Active support from national and international environmental NGOs was particularly important for Brazilian communities facing a variety of different kinds of energy infrastructure project, for example, in addition to support from local Workers' Party (PT) governments (Hochstetler and Tranjan 2016: 510). Such allies can supply information about strategic options and likely impacts of projects or offer concrete legal or scientific assistance. Beyond other social movements and NGOs, the national governments of both Brazil and South Africa during the years of renewable energy expansion had historic links to social movements, which had partially frayed after years in power (Hochstetler 2008; Southall 2013), so those might or might not also be relevant partners. Finally, legal actors like Brazil's Ministério Público (a public prosecutor; see McAllister 2008) and legally oriented NGOs like South Africa's Centre for Environmental Rights (CER))[2] and Legal Resources Centre have played important partnering roles for communities in both countries.

In addition to the political opportunity dimensions, scholars have also highlighted that communities often respond with resistance to the potential physical hazards and risks of the projects themselves (McAdam and Boudet 2012; Wright and Boudet 2012). Specific electricity types all present different mixes of costs and benefits for both specific host communities and the country as a whole. These have measurable qualities, but the symbolic framing of them is also important for community responses. To highlight some of the most obvious implications of developing wind and solar power versus fossil fuels, these fuel sources stand out as low-carbon alternatives, although that comparative benefit may appear quite distant in time and scale to local communities (Sjöberg 1997). Conversely, fossil fuels have the advantage of having much higher energy density – the wattage produced per area of land – than wind (three times) and photovoltaic solar power (two times) (Scheidel and Sorman 2012: 591), so the renewables increase the likelihood of conflicts over land use and associated potential livelihood and environmental costs.

---

[2] The CER has been particularly active on coal cases and in enabling a just transition to renewable energy systems, discussed in more detail in Chapter 3. Interview with Loser, CER, 2018.

Beyond the electricity type, large projects are inherently more visible and generate mobilization more readily, even when multiple small projects may have a similar collective impact (Hochstetler and Tranjan 2016: 508–509). The site itself may also present particular environmental or socioeconomic hazards and risks. For example, it may be recognized as a protected area for plant or animal, especially bird, species. Use of the site for wind or solar power may also directly compromise livelihood strategies from fisheries to tourism. In general, greater hazards and risks should be more likely to generate a negative community response, although the link between hazards and risks and actual collective action depends on the other conditions of mobilization.

Finally, the resources of potential activists condition their ability to take advantage of any opportunities. Collective action is often difficult for social groups to organize because of the misfit between individual and collective incentives (Prakash and Gugerty 2010). The literature on community responses to infrastructure projects suggests that poor and/or socially disadvantaged communities are especially unlikely to resist even damaging projects (Aldrich 2008; McAdam and Boudet 2012; Wright and Boudet 2012). In part, this is because mobilization is expensive in terms of time and other resources that are scarce in poor communities. Effective resistance may also require legal or scientific expertise that local communities do not have. Poor and disadvantaged communities may also be more willing to overlook the costs of hosting infrastructure projects if there are accompanying benefits or compensations (García, Cherry, Kallbekken, and Torvanger 2016).

While the critical social movements literature has tended to focus on the costs of infrastructure projects for hosting communities, this final point about accompanying benefits or compensations is a reminder that there may be significant local benefits as well. The South African auctions were in fact designed to ensure that hosting communities within 50 km benefited from the new infrastructure projects (Bode 2013; Tait 2012; Tait, Wlokas, and Garside 2013), although the Brazilian ones were not. Even so, communities might well face complex packages of costs and benefits.

In summary, the literature on community mobilization identifies multiple possible correlates of when communities might resist having a wind or solar power plant located nearby: the extent of political opportunities from institutional structures and the presence or absence of allies; levels of physical and biological hazards and risks; and community resources. To them, the environmental and energy economists would add the possibility of actual economic gains. All of these have both objective and subjective dimensions to them, and part of the work of mobilization is to create a plausible framing of the issues. The explanations are not necessarily opposed to each other, and they clearly interact. For example, high levels of objective hazards may make communities feel more negatively toward a wind power plant, but they will actively resist it only if the other factors make them able to actually create a protest against the plant. Poor communities may face higher barriers to participation, but they may overcome them with the support of elite allies.

5.3 Institutional Frameworks Governing Wind and Solar Power

For the country case studies, I begin by describing the major institutional and regulatory frameworks that govern the placement of wind and solar power installations in Brazil and South Africa. I pay particular attention to how these frameworks might create opportunities for communities and civil society organizations to influence decision-making about where to place the large number of plants typically associated with these kinds of electricity, with corresponding implications for the local benefits and costs of hosting infrastructure projects like wind and solar plants.

Variations in community experiences with renewable energy begin with very basic choices about how the wind and solar projects that will be built are selected. Feed-in tariffs (FITs) require electricity utilities to pay comparatively high prices to anyone interested in generating renewable energy. In the early adopters, FITs encouraged even local communities to develop – and benefit from – their own generation projects and generally allowed broader, decentralized participation in generation (Grashof 2019; Leiren and Reimer 2018; Morris and Jungjohann 2016). Patrick Bayer and Johannes Urpelainen argue that this gives democracies in particular an incentive to adopt FITs because they benefit dispersed rural constituencies (Bayer and Urpelainen 2016).

In contrast, the auctions used by both Brazil and South Africa to select most of their renewable electricity projects place cost considerations at the center. This institutional choice tends to select large existing utilities and firms, including international ones, that can build on a cost-efficient scale (Bayer, Schäuble, and Ferrari 2018: 312; Bayer and Urpelainen 2016: 615). Host communities are not only unlikely to win auctions to produce electricity themselves; they will also probably see fewer direct benefits. Expenses must be tightly controlled and winning firms have regional, national, or even global conceptions of their interests, rather than locally oriented ones (e.g., Meckling and Hughes 2017). Each national subsection (Sections 5.3.1 and 5.3.2) therefore begins with a brief description of the auction process eventually used for project selection and how it largely foreclosed the possibility of the community-driven projects common in Europe.

Much of the discussion then focuses on the relevant EIA processes that more actively manage local impacts of electricity projects in both countries. Since being introduced in the United States in 1969, EIA has become the most common environmental regulation worldwide (Morgan 2012: 6). It is often joined with other kinds of social and economic impact assessment, either in parallel or as part of the same process. Impact assessment generally tries to identify the effects of a proposed economic project on local environments and communities in advance, considering alternative formulations and possible mitigation action to reduce negative impacts. Compensation of some kind is usually offered for unavoidable harms (Glasson, Therivel, and Chadwick 2012). Most impact assessment is carried out as a technical exchange among developers, their consultants, and the reviewing governmental agency (typically an environmental agency), but there is usually some provision for consultation with affected communities as well (Hochstetler and Tranjan 2016: 500). The end result of EIA may be an environmental license or permit to proceed, a conditional permit, or denial of permission to carry out the project. It is also sometimes called environmental licensing.

Both Brazil and South Africa have also engaged in larger planning processes and debates that have aimed to influence siting decisions beyond individual plants. In South Africa, many actors participated in a strategic environmental assessment that aimed to identify lower-impact corridors where wind and solar installations could be channeled. Despite wide participation, perceptions of the usefulness of the process for identifying the most important impacts vary and are discussed in more detail in Section 5.3.2. In Brazil, the Energy Research Enterprise (EPE) has taken the lead in carrying out comprehensive energy planning and conducted some mapping analyses of potential wind and solar power sites. The Ministry of Environment carried out its own analyses, leading to a revamping of the EIA process for wind power in 2014 and further mapping of bird populations beyond protected areas (see Section 5.3.1).

Finally, both countries have additional institutional frameworks that are not specific to wind and solar power or even environmental impacts that are relevant for local communities. A full view of land-use and land-tenure policies is beyond the scope of this chapter, but I identify some of the most relevant pieces. In addition, the legal systems in the two countries offer different levels of access to and use by communities, giving Brazilian communities a stronger array of legal options, although larger South African organizations have been able to use legal strategies as well.

5.3.1 Brazil: Institutional Frameworks for Community Responses to Electricity Projects

In this section, I first discuss how Brazil's choices for electricity procurement largely excluded the possibility of the community-owned projects that benefited host communities in early adopters. EIA has been the predominant institutional framing involved in the siting of wind and solar projects, so it is covered next. Finally, the section concludes with a brief look at some of the larger policies around land use, particularly those affecting the descendants of slave communities, who are especially likely to be present in the areas where wind power is built.

Brazil's first wind power plants were built in response to a FIT – the Program of Incentives for Alternative Energy in Electricity (Proinfa) – created in 2002 to respond to an electricity supply crisis following a drought in 2001 (see Chapter 3 for more details). Although it was a FIT program, Proinfa already prioritized lower costs – solar power was excluded for this reason – and had significant requirements for national production of components. Only twelve corporations were ever certified to build projects through this FIT, and all the installations were at least 30 MW in size (Bayer, Schäuble, and Ferrari 2018: 312), well beyond the capacity of local communities. Some national production facilities were established, but they generated jobs and benefits at a regional level rather than in the particular communities where the projects were, which saw only short-term jobs in construction and many negative impacts (Brower Brown 2011).

Notwithstanding the acquisition of 1,100 MW of wind power through this FIT, the PT government that began in 2003 eventually chose the auction system for further electricity procurement, including of wind and solar power. Concerns about the negative development implications of high electricity prices led to an auction system based entirely on cost along with a balance of kinds of electricity sources for energy security (Tolmasquim 2012). As recounted in Chapter 3, there were technical discussions inside the Ministry of Mines and Energy that expanded into the National Congress before a special committee selected the cost-based auction mechanism. Despite wide political debate in a democracy, there is no evidence that concerns about rural constituencies influenced the debate about policy instruments, as has been argued (Bayer and Urpelainen 2016). While rural constituencies were very important to the PT, the constituencies wanted land reform and grid access (Sauer and Mészáros 2016; see also Chapter 4). When regulations were changed in 2015 to allow small collectives to generate solar power together, take-up was slow, with just sixty-four units in 2017. Fourteen of these were rural (Böckler and Pereira 2018: 535).

Neither the FIT nor the auction systems in Brazil contemplated any systematic benefits to be paid to host communities. This is in contrast to hydropower, where 6.75 percent of the value of the electricity generated is distributed among host municipalities that have been flooded (from an original 25 percent share of that 6.75 percent in 1990 to 65 percent of the total since 2017), states, and federal administrative units.[3] These royalties are grounded in the 1988 Constitution's Articles 20 and 21 that make water resources a national patrimony. A federal deputy from the Northeast region, home of many wind plants, proposed a constitutional amendment in 2015 that would add wind resources (PEC 97/2015). The amendment has been making its way only slowly through an overcrowded legislative agenda ever since.[4] Beyond this quixotic bill, discussions of costs and benefits for local host communities appear primarily in the environmental licensing process.

[3] www.ana.gov.br/noticias/nova-lei-altera-rateio-de-distribuicao-da-compensa
cao-financeira-pela-utilizacao-de-recursos-hidricos/@@nitf_custom_galleria.
[4] www.camara.leg.br/proposicoesWeb/fichadetramitacao?
idProposicao=1584970.

Brazil instituted a national requirement for EIA in 1986, well before most of the developing world. Its three-license process (one for planning, one for construction, and one for operation) involves more scrutiny than the single license that most countries use. Since most documents related to national EIA have been online since 2005, along with many state-level documents, the Brazilian process is also unusually transparent (Hochstetler 2018). At the same time, activists see the process as fundamentally flawed, allowing many dangerous impacts to go unexamined at the expense of host communities (Gorayab et al. 2018; Zhouri and Valencio 2014). Flaws in consultation with local communities are the weakest part of Brazilian EIA, according to a survey of 131 academic papers on the subject (Duarte, Dibo, and Sánchez 2017: 275–276). Many policy-makers and project proponents challenge these critiques, arguing instead that Brazilian EIA functions as a major stumbling block (*gargalo*) to national development plans, offering few compensations for its delays and costs (Bragagnolo, Lemos, Ladle, and Pellin 2017).[5] In light of this heated debate, it is perhaps not surprising that speeding up environmental licensing is a priority for President Bolsonaro, who came to office in January 2019.

Licensing for wind and solar plants has operated somewhat outside of the larger debate on EIA in Brazil, but that debate continues to shape the orientation of participants. Most licensing for these projects is done at the state level, where capacity and procedures can vary considerably[6] and national changes would trickle down only eventually. In addition, as Brazil faced major electricity shortfalls in 2001, the standard-setting National Environmental Council (CONAMA) smoothed the way for expansion of generation with its Resolution 279/2001.[7] This Resolution simplified environmental licensing procedures for electricity projects with small impacts, with the scale of impact determined by a quick (ten-day) decision based on initial impact reports submitted. Environmental agencies granted most wind installations this procedure, meaning that they had just seventy days to complete the EIA. Individuals could make comments in writing or fifty people could request an Informative Technical Meeting, but the public hearings

---

[5] Interview with Knijnic, PAC, 2014.
[6] Interview with licensing analyst for ABEÉolica, São Paulo, 2014 (JRT).
[7] CONAMA has had substantial state- and federal-level representation along with business and civil society representatives (Hochstetler and Keck 2007: 32–36).

common in Brazilian EIA were otherwise set aside (Article 8, CONAMA Resolution 279/2001).

After the initial rounds of wind power procurement and licensing, the Ministry of Environment surveyed state environmental agencies in June of 2009 to review their regulatory experiences and the gaps they identified in licensing wind power (Secretaria de Mudanças Climáticas e Qualidade Ambiental 2009). Many state agencies, especially in the Northeast, were looking for stronger regulatory guidelines for the kinds of impact to assess as well as help identifying the areas that had strong wind potential but fewer potential socioenvironmental impacts (ibid.: 9). The lack of uniform licensing requirements across states also caused problems for firms, as did the fact that the complexity of the documents requested was often too high or too low for the socioenvironmental complexity of the location (Bezerra, Melo, Nunes, and Mesquita 2013: 46–47).

In response to such technical problems – as well as the frequent community resistance described in Section 5.5 – CONAMA issued a new set of regulations for wind power in 2014 (Resolution 462/ 2014). The overall theme of the new regulations is to try to induce private companies to decide themselves to place wind plants in the right locations, by continuing to require just the simplified licensing for low-impact installations.[8] In contrast, full EIA and public hearings became required for wind plants in high-impact locations: dunes, fluvial plains, and mangroves; the Atlantic Forest; the Coastal zone; within 3 km of a restricted protected area (*unidade de conservação de proteção integral*); in migratory bird areas; in areas that would have direct sociocultural impacts that would endanger communities or completely remove them; and in areas with species in danger of extinction (Article 3). ABEEólica estimates that a full EIA for a wind installation is six times more costly than an abbreviated study (Agência Brasileira de Desenvolvimento Industrial 2018b: 32).

In developing the regulation, CONAMA also considered including areas with indigenous and other traditional peoples on the list of high-impact locations that require full EIA, but it finally decided to rely on existing informed-consent requirements since some of these communities

---

[8] Interview with João Paulo de Faria Santos, Director, Department of Support for CONAMA, Ministry of Environment, Brasília, 2014.

actively want the plants.[9] Given the timing of this new regulation, it is worth noting that 78 percent of the 600 Brazilian wind projects considered here took place in the old permissive regime, with another 15 percent in 2014 and only 7 percent of them clearly under the new rules.[10]

The new regulation for wind plants led directly to another mapping exercise of migratory bird areas, which had never been fully identified. The conservation branch of the Ministry of Environment, the Chico Mendes Institute for Conservation of Biodiversity (ICMBio), quickly developed a map based on conservation areas and some existing studies (ICMBio 2014). For its 2016 update, ICMBio used a broader range of sources to identify migratory bird areas as well as areas of bird concentration and the presence of endangered species in a 250 km² grid of the entire country. This more detailed mapping showed that many of the existing and planned wind power plants in two states, Rio Grande do Norte and Rio Grande do Sul (despite the names, thousands of kilometers apart), were built in migratory bird areas, although many fewer were in Bahia and Ceará (ICMBio 2016: 35–36, 41, 51). In the future, this requirement is likely to strongly channel wind power plants out of some areas and into others, as the full EIA in migratory bird areas will require a minimum of a year-long study of bird presence and use (ICMBio 2016: 54). However, the hundreds of plants that were already readily located in areas with few migratory birds suggests that alternative sites are available. The national affiliate of BirdLife International, Save Brasil, does not have a specific program for wind power plants, being more focused on creating and maintaining conservation areas for birds.[11] This is strikingly different from the South African experience.

Another potential licensing strategy could be to require strategic environmental assessment (SEA), which examines the impacts of policies, plans, and programs and can be used to study cumulative impacts (Malvestio and Montaño 2013: 7–8). SEA is not mandatory in Brazil and has rarely actually influenced decision-making (Malvestio and Montaño 2013: 6; Margato and Sánchez 2014: 17). The most comprehensive socioenvironmental assessments of the electricity sector are done by EPE, a semiautonomous planning agency associated with the

---

[9] Interview with Santos, CONAMA, 2014.

[10] While individual projects were often licensed quickly, the licensing process for transmission lines to link them to the grid were slow, delaying operation (Bayer 2018: 2650).

[11] www.birdlife.org/americas/partners/save-brasil.

Ministry of Mines and Energy. Created in 2004, EPE is responsible for producing regular ten-year plans for electricity supply expansion based on optimization exercises that include a large number of variables from price to carbon emissions to the physical potential (Chapter 2). A significant part of the job has been to accumulate and create the underlying data required. In 2009, a team of about twenty career technical staff, most of them biologists and natural scientists, worked in EPE's environmental division, collecting data on economic, environmental, social, and institutional impacts.[12]

In 2006, EPE wrote an initial guide for socioenvironmental analysis of its projects (Empresa de Pesquisa Energética 2006); this was replaced by a more systematic methodology in 2012, reflecting a number of years of experience in planning (Empresa de Pesquisa Energética 2012b). In the 2012 methodology, EPE takes the proposed results of its optimization calculations and first maps them on national maps that show both physical characteristics and anthropogenic uses. It also considers a set of nine socioenvironmental themes and considers which of its kinds of electricity projects (e.g., hydropower, wind power, and alternatives) cause "interferences" with the theme and also maps the interferences onto Brazil's five major geographical regions (Empresa de Pesquisa Energética 2012b: 4–7). The result is a very large-scale assessment of where certain kinds of socioenvironmental problem are likely to emerge. For wind power, for example, the analysis suggested that the plants were likely to cause interferences with protected areas like coastal dunes, landscape concerns (especially tourism potential and views), and would run into the history of irregular land occupation and use patterns typical of the coastal area (Empresa de Pesquisa Energética 2012b: 10–12). All of these problems were expected to be especially sharp in the Northeast region, although the South also had likely conflicts with protected areas. Solar, barely in existence in Brazil in 2012, was not included in the analysis (Empresa de Pesquisa Energética 2012b: 10). Given that there are socioenvironmental challenges associated with every other source of electricity, EPE chose in 2012 to prioritize reducing problems like impacts on indigenous populations and native vegetation in the North (Amazon) region rather than the specific problems of wind power (Empresa de Pesquisa Energética 2012b: 20–21).

---

[12] Interview with Furtado, EPE, Rio de Janeiro, 2009.

The route from EPE's planning exercises to the final electricity plants commissioned is indirect.[13] This is partly because an interministerial body makes the final choices but also because Brazil's Ministry of Mines and Energy selects many of its electricity projects through competitive auctions (see Chapter 3). Even in auctions for single sources of electricity, as have happened for wind and solar power, developers pit potential sites against each other and the final choices come in the price-based auctions. In order to compete, developers must show that they have secured an initial environmental license and contracted land (theoretically addressing the problems identified here), but these requirements have not eliminated the possibility of problematic installations, especially in the years before 2014. Finally, there is no requirement that EPE's maps be followed, and the engineering reports for EIAs in the Northeast often cite state-level wind atlases whose quality may be poor (e.g., Gorayeb et al. 2018).[14]

The final institutional frameworks in Brazil that are directly relevant for community responses to wind and solar installations are those established for consultation with special local communities that are seen to have especially strong territorial links. Given the sociocultural makeup of many of the communities that host wind and solar projects, the most relevant framework is the 2007 National Policy for Sustainable Development of Traditional Peoples and Communities (Decree 6040/2007), which protects rights to territory and resource use for a broader variety of (self-recognized) cultural communities. Many Brazilian wind farms in the Northeast region, the center of Brazil's historic slave region, are located in *quilombolo* areas. These are formally communities that were formed by runaway slaves and the 1988 Constitution (Article 68) explicitly recognizes the land rights associated with such communities and slates them for demarcation by the Palmares Cultural Foundation (*Fundação Cultural Palmares*), a government agency (Boyer 2014). Despite this narrow definition, the practical definition of *quilombos* has expanded to include rural black communities more generally. The PT's 2004 Brazil Quilombolo Program (*Programa Brasil Quilombolo*) recognized this practice and allowed community self-identification as *quilombolos* to start the lengthy demarcation process (Boyer 2014; Torre 2013). As a result,

[13] Interview with technical analyst of EPE, Rio de Janeiro, 2012.
[14] Personal communication, Christian Brannstrom, May 2018.

whether or not a community is designated as a *quilombolo* community is partly a matter of the identities that particular communities decide to adopt – sometimes following extensive contention internally – and their ability to mobilize themselves through the lengthy demarcation process, rather than an easily mapped set of known locations (Boyer 2014; French 2009).

5.3.2 *South Africa: Institutional Frameworks for Community Responses to Electricity Projects*

As detailed in Chapter 3, South Africa also briefly introduced a feed-in tariff before replacing it with an auction system that governed all actual renewable energy procurement. Decision-makers were aware that the shift would favor larger and international actors rather than smaller, community-based systems, but the lower costs and simpler logistics of large installations swayed all key actors (Bode 2013: 77–81). Instead of avoiding auctions, the South African government chose to add socioeconomic development elements to them. Besides the local content requirements already discussed in Chapter 3, winning bids need to promise that host communities within 50 km of the plant will own at least 2.5 percent of the project, with a target of 5 percent, with national development banks stepping in to fund that portion. Most bids proposed a community trust structure for this share (Bode 2013: 88–89). Jobs for local community members were also part of the evaluation process. Small shares of the total procurement were also to be reserved for small projects (100 MW of the initial 3,725 MW total), but implementation of this was delayed (Bode 2013: 90). In Section 5.5, I discuss actual outcomes from these provisions, showing that they made modest contributions to host communities but did not approach the more systematic advantages of full community ownership.

In South Africa, EIA was also the major institution assigned to regulate the impacts of wind and solar plants on local communities. South Africa's experience with EIA is not as old as Brazil's, with mandatory EIAs beginning only in 1997. Perhaps for this reason, wind and solar power have been much more transformative of the broader framework of environmental assessment, both in its project-based EIA form and in several experiments in SEAs. Some of these changes have been contentious, but the participating civil society actors have rarely been the organized community actors that we will see in

Section 5.5 on Brazil. Instead, industry associations and national environmental groups have engaged with environmental licensing, along with scattered other actors. Land issues have festered in South Africa since a 1913 Act pushed black Africans off their land, but not, to date, in ways that commonly intersect with wind and solar power installations.

The apartheid government had ignored the impacts of its economic development projects on a largely Black African population, displacing residents at will and leaving them subject to air pollution and other environmental impacts. The post-apartheid government, in contrast, introduced mandatory EIA in 1997, part of its larger effort to modernize and normalize the South African state by adopting ideas like sustainable development and the need to consult local residents (Patel 2014: 170–171). The National Environmental Management Act of 1998 followed the post-apartheid constitution of 1994 in stressing equity and nondiscrimination along with environmental rights (ibid.: 174–175). The new government also had a strong mandate for generating economic growth and employment, which sometimes clashed with the new environmental regulations. In Durban, for example, already-mobilized communities took their fights against industrial pollution and displacement from the apartheid to the post-apartheid period, generating strong organizations and an influential discourse about environmental injustice (Leonard 2014; Scott and Barnett 2009).

Over the ensuing decades, EIA has become routine in South Africa. More than 43,000 EIA applications were submitted between September 1997 and March 2006, most of them at the provincial level. This was in part because of weak screening that sent too many projects through analysis, causing delays and encouraging hasty treatment (Retief, Welman, and Sandheim 2011: 154). The larger picture is too often one of "box ticking," with South African EIA tending to be "a lifeless and bureaucratic exercise" (Morrison-Saunders and Retief 2012: 38; see also Leonard 2014; Patel 2009). An administrator in Cape Town contrasted the elaborate guidelines for EIA in South Africa with large gaps in implementation capacity, calling the guidelines "Cadillacs for gravel roads."[15] The Department of Environmental Affairs and Tourism (DEAT) streamlined the process in 2006 and 2010 (Department of Environmental Affairs and Tourism 2010). For

[15] Interview with Andrew Hall, CEO, Heritage Western Cape, Cape Town, 2013.

example, the DEAT added time frames in 2010 after consultations with developers and other stakeholders.[16] Time frames and direct costs for EIA are close to international practices, even though the government would like them reduced (Morrison-Saunders and Retief 2012: 39).

Once again, the environmental licensing of wind and solar plants stands outside the broader patterns of EIA in the country. Most EIA in South Africa is done at provincial level, but renewable energy undergoes environmental assessment through the national Department of Environmental Affairs (DEA).[17] In 2009, this was because it was a new program that was a national priority and the national level had more capacity to carry it out. After South Africa signed the Copenhagen Agreement on climate change in 2011, the international commitment also required national-level control over licensing. Even at the comparatively capable national level, the renewable energy program introduced stresses that eventually required a complete reworking of EIA for the sector.

In the original approach, all firms that wanted to bid to build wind and solar projects had to have full EIAs completed before bidding, which brought about 900 new projects in for assessment in just three years. Given their need to meet auction deadlines and uncertainty about being selected in the auctions (only 90 of the 900 were chosen), companies often wrote EIA applications that were hasty or needed to be modified. On average there were seven EIA reviews of each of the 900 projects; there were up to nine on some. The sheer volume of the assessments and the quality problems overwhelmed the DEA. Having begun with a regulation that required a full EIA for all bidders, the DEA considered reforms that would have lifted some or all of the requirements for EIAs. However, industry representatives objected to a plan to exempt them from individual EIAs, arguing that it exposed them to possible risk, not least from financiers. All of the private and public banks that regularly finance wind and solar power in South Africa follow the Equator Principles (Wright 2012), which require EIAs as a standard of best practice. Meanwhile, the national government had also developed a new National Development Plan (National Planning Commission 2012) and was seeking to promote

[16] Interview with Fischer, DEA, Johannesburg, 2018.
[17] Interview with Fischer, DEA, 2018. The remainder of this paragraph and the next also draw on this interview unless otherwise noted.

strategic clusters of projects like major infrastructure installations to implement the Plan.

The result of these cross-pressures was a decision to do SEA that would identify less-sensitive Renewable Energy Development Zones (REDZ) that could be linked to five corridors marked for transmission infrastructure expansion. In the eight final REDZ, proposed installations are allowed a simplified (post-scoping) site-specific basic assessment rather than a full EIA. The DEA contracted with a government-linked applied science agency, the Council for Scientific and Industrial Research (CSIR), to conduct the strategic mapping studies in 2013. These studies generated sensitivity maps that classify land for potential wind and solar power sites using maps of environmental constraints, technical constraints, and socioeconomic activities (Department of Environmental Affairs 2015). For socioeconomic activities, for example, the CSIR group was looking to identify high social need areas with low incomes and few services that needed economic stimulation but that were also in close proximity to areas with basic service sectors that could be developed. Concentrating infrastructure projects in such areas allowed better skills transfer and skills development in the node, in their view.[18] The REDZ and the transmission corridors were officially published for implementation in February 2018. The DEA is still developing a final checklist of sensitivity indicators that will determine exactly which assessments developers must complete for a particular site.[19]

The CSIR scientists acknowledged that the basic databases they drew on were of very different quality. The infrastructure databases were good and the social ones were adequate, but the environmental databases allowed only a first cut with broad areas of feasibility indicated.[20] This gap opened up a serious line of criticism of the REDZ from BirdLife South Africa and eventually led to something of a parallel additional impact assessment process. The Birds and Renewable Energy Project of BirdLife South Africa is particularly focused on

---

[18]   Interview with Lydia Cape-Ducluzeau, Coordinator of Solar Strategic Environmental Assessment, CSIR, by Skype, 2014. Other CSIR participants in the interview included Cornelius van der Westhuizen, Coordinator of Wind Solar Strategic Environmental Assessment and Paul Lochner, Manager of Environmental Management Services.

[19]   Interview with Fischer, DEA, 2018. See also https://egis.environment.gov.za /redz.

[20]   Interview with van der Westhuizen, CSIR, 2014.

developing guidelines on how to do wind installations correctly and working with industry and government to achieve that, even as it is broadly supportive of wind and solar power.[21] After participating in the SEA process leading to the REDZ, BirdLife South Africa eventually sent a letter of objection to the DEA saying that it did not believe that the REDZ process had adequately identified areas where the natural environment would not be harmed.[22] It considers large areas within the REDZ to have potentially large impacts on bird and biodiversity areas as well as on four specific threatened and range-restricted species.

Not even a regular EIA (157 days) would give enough time for the studies of bird impact that BirdLife South Africa views as necessary, which include a full year of study. The shorter (107 days) environmental assessment foreseen for the REDZ was even less adequate. BirdLife South Africa's solution was to work with the industry association SAWEA to guide developers to undertake the bird study first before even starting the governmental environmental assessment process. A few strategic challenges to early wind farm environmental permits by BirdLife South Africa underlined that the lack of a site-specific bird study would bring an expensive veto point for a project as banks will not close the finance without the environmental permit.[23]

SAWEA has acquiesced to these demands, but developers see the expensive costs (R1 million/year for each of the bird and bat studies) and the time-consuming and complicated procedures as adding significant hurdles to developing wind power in South Africa: "Birds are the biggest risk to wind farms in this country."[24] The Cape vulture's wide range in KwaZulu Natal and the eastern Eastern Cape has made those areas virtually off limits for wind developments, even though the provincial governments are in favor. The wind industry is angry about BirdLife South Africa's large role, even while it acknowledges the importance of considering environmental impacts and has been able to negotiate compromises for many sites.[25] When BirdLife South

---

[21] Interview with Samantha Ralston-Paton, Birds and Renewable Energy Project Manager, BirdLife South Africa, by Skype, 2017.

[22] Letter from BirdLife South Africa to Ms Edna Molewa, Department of Environmental Affairs, May 21, 2017. Copy provided by Samantha Ralston-Paton.

[23] Interview with Ralston-Paton, BirdLife South Africa, 2017.

[24] Interview with Ben Brimble, former chair of SAWEA Environmental Working Group, Johannesburg, 2018.

[25] Interview with Brimble, SAWEA, 2018.

Africa proposed similar procedures for solar power, that industry's association, the South African Photovoltaic Industry Association (SAPVIA), made a preemptively vehement objection to extending the approach (BirdLife 2016).

As already discussed for Brazil, patterns of land ownership and land-tenure policies may become part of the backdrop for community responses to wind and solar projects. Separatist land policies like the 1913 Natives' Land Act moved Black African populations to rural Bantustans and restricted their movement and legal right to own land afterwards. A systematic land survey completed in South Africa in 2017 shows that the legacies of this Act are still strong. Formal land ownership for black Africans has increased since the end of apartheid government in 1994, although nonblacks continue to control much of the land in areas where wind and solar power have expanded. In two of the three provinces that have the largest number of wind and solar power installations, black Africans owned only 4.9 percent (Western Cape) and 6.4 percent (Northern Cape) of agricultural land in 2016 – up from 0 percent in 1994. In the third province, the Eastern Cape, black Africans owned nearly half of the agricultural land (48.3 percent, up from 28 percent) (Agri SA 2017: 17, 19). Beyond formal land ownership, 2.5 million mostly black Africans moved off farms between 1994 and 2003, 940,000 of those evicted (Cousins and Hall 2014: 172). The population that remains on farms informally is widely dispersed, with little access to state services and less notice (ibid.: 180). Policies to achieve land distribution are in development and being strongly disputed. So far, they have had little direct effect on renewable energy siting.

In conclusion, Brazil and South Africa have both selected auction systems that limit the presence of the community-owned projects that promoted energy democracy in the first generation of adopters. They have also both ended up with fairly similar EIA regimes for renewable energy, despite beginning at opposite points. Brazil began with a very permissive licensing scheme for wind power, but it now offers an accelerated environmental permit for proposed wind power plants that avoid certain problematic locations while full EIAs are demanded in sensitive areas. South Africa does the same, although it began with a system that required full EIAs for all wind and solar plants and now relieves proposed projects in designated zones from that requirement. In both cases, the difference is meant to offer developers incentives to put plants in less sensitive locations without forbidding more sensitive locations outright. The differentiated treatment, in both cases, is meant to address one of the possible causes of mobilized community opposition, which is the physical risks and hazards of the project. In Sections 5.5 and 5.6, I explore whether such risks and hazards have been a driver of varying community responses in the two countries, along with other possible causes.

5.4 Community Responses: Approach and Methodology

Do local communities resist the installations of wind and solar power plants in Brazil and South Africa? If they do, when, why, and how do they do so? This section begins to answer those questions by taking a panoramic view of all the renewable power installations that have won auctions to supply the national grid in each country. For both countries, I conducted internet searches to find reports of community-based contestation directed either at individual power plants or at cities that host multiple plants. I then analyzed the resulting patterns to see whether and how physical sensitivities, political opportunity factors, and/or environmental justice considerations helped to account for the community responses.

The internet searches were conducted through Google using the name in quotation marks of each of the individual wind and solar projects that won auctions to supply the respective national electrical grids before 2017. South Africa had 34 wind farms and 45 solar PV installations, while Brazil had 600 and 94, respectively.[26] I read through as many as ten pages of results for each, although many projects had fewer. Since Brazilian regulatory incentives result in large numbers of ostensibly separate 30 MW plants that are placed right next to each other,[27] summing to much larger collective installations of wind power in particular, I then grouped the Brazilian wind plants by the towns in which they were located. This resulted in

---

[26] These lists exclude a small number of additional plants in each country that supply their electricity to individual consumers directly as well as the projects of Brazil's early feed-in tariff plan for wind power, Proinfa. While the additional projects could have been included here, these lists match the primary focus of Chapters 2 and 3 on the projects secured through auctions for the national grid for general consumers.

[27] Projects with an installed capacity of 30 MW or less have lower tax rates and receive a discount on transmission connections (Chapter 4).

seventy-seven city cases. I conducted additional searches in quotation marks on the word "wind" in its male and female forms (*eólico, eólica*) and the names of the towns, to reflect the possibility of community objections to the plants as a group. In fact, most of the Brazilian wind conflicts were found by searching on town names rather than the names of individual plants.

In addition to newspaper articles and social media pages that report the community resistance of interest here, the search results often included reports from local and regional newspapers about the opening of the plants, suggesting that the searches found many local news sources. The fact that the search methodology encountered local news sources and social media pages counteracts some of the known biases of collective action research based on national media reports, as national media tend to cover only very large or violent protests (Earl, Martin, McCarthy, and Soule 2004). The largest number of the search results was links to firms and individuals announcing their involvement with the projects or to various listings of Brazilian or South African electricity projects. There were also many videos and photographs of the plants, especially the wind power plants.

5.5 Community Responses to Wind Power

Between the two countries, there is considerably less contestation of wind power in South Africa, where I found reports of local contestation for just three of thirty-four wind plants (8.8 percent). The wind farms are quite large individually and they are concentrated further in the Cookhouse area in the Eastern Cape, in St Francis Bay and neighboring small towns along the Southern Ocean coast west of Port Elizabeth, and in a cluster of small towns north of Cape Town. Two of the three reports of community mobilization were in the St Francis Bay area and this is the only location in South Africa where there are sustained and ongoing community efforts to monitor current and prospective wind farms and their socioenvironmental impacts. I will discuss this mobilization in more detail later in this section.

Rates of contestation were higher in Brazil, with communities objecting to wind power plants in nineteen of seventy-seven cities that hosted them (24.7 percent). The conflict was located in four Brazilian states: Bahia, Ceará, Piauí, and Rio Grande do Norte. All of these are in the Northeastern region, a poor, dry part of the country. There were no conflicts reported in

Rio Grande do Sul in the wealthy Southern region, the other major location of wind power in Brazil. Instead of provoking conflict, wind farms in Rio Grande do Sul often feature their own well-liked Facebook pages and are promoted as sites of tourism and student visits.

The grievances and concerns that motivate communities to mobilize against wind plants in the two countries are even more strikingly different, as are the strategies they use to raise them. In South Africa, almost all of the contestation around wind plants is in the neighboring coastal locations of St Francis Bay, Oyster Bay, Van Stadens, and Jeffreys Bay, just west of Port Elizabeth in the Eastern Cape province. The St Francis Bird Club and the Kromme Enviro-Trust St Francis led the community response to the plants and have worked continuously since 2011 to ensure that they caused the least possible harm. Both were long-standing organizations that saw threats to their traditional concerns with birds and community development initiatives, respectively.[28] Although early community meetings heard angry denunciations of dropping property values, aesthetic and quality of life losses, and threats to the local tourist industry,[29] ongoing community engagement has focused on very specific impacts, especially on birdlife. A particular set of turbines on the Kromme River itself was abandoned and no turbines are allowed close to the nesting areas of key bird species. About twenty community members do bird counts on the existing wind farms every six weeks. All prospective wind farm proposals are carefully scrutinized and birders interact with developers to ensure that they can support the projects as proposed.

Outside of this remarkably well-organized community, owners of game reserves and occasional farmers who use small aircraft for farming are the most likely to register what are usually individual comments on an EIA and occasional legal challenges.[30] Communities remain largely outside the siting process, especially as organized groups. The fraught history of land ownership in South Africa, with black South Africans dispossessed during apartheid and evicted from informal land access even post-apartheid (Cousins and Hall 2014: 172), would seem

[28] Interview with a representative of Kromme Enviro-Trust, by Skype, 2017. See also http://stfranciskrommetrust.co.za.
[29] https://stfrancischronicle.com/2011/07/21/feature-st-francis-residents-to-fight-the-kromme-wind-farm/.
[30] Interviews with Brimble, SAWEA, 2018; CSIR scientists, 2014; Fischer, DEA, 2018; and Ralston-Paton, BirdLife South Africa, 2017.

to make conflict around large wind farms likely (McEwan 2017). Instead, with many possible sites available, developers have chosen locations where mostly white farmers can sell or lease land individually, as described in Section 5.3. Just one wind farm, Tsitsikamma, is located on communally held land in the Eastern Cape, where an amaFengu community was expelled during apartheid but has recovered its land and now owns 9 percent of the plant (McEwan 2017: 5).[31] Industry actors do not see land claims as likely sources of conflict for their installations. Farmers have typically been on their land for generations and land rights are secure.[32]

The best-known cases of community opposition in Brazil look very different, except for also taking place in coastal communities. The most emblematic case, covered in five of eight known published case studies of Brazilian community responses to wind farms (Araujó 2016; Brower Brown 2011; Pinto, Joventino do Nascimento, Ferreira Bringel, and de Andrade Meireles 2014; Porto, Finamore, and Ferreira 2013; Viana, Joventino do Nascimento, and de Andrade Meireles 2016), is the Aracati municipality. As these articles detail, some of the wind farms in Aracati were planned for locations in moving dunes and estuaries, with obviously problematic environmental implications. They also significantly disrupted economic and cultural practices of local subsistence communities of African slave descent. Communities that resisted wind farm installation in coastal Ceará and Rio Grande do Norte (e.g., Galinhos) frequently faced this combination of direct environmental and social impacts (see also Brannstrom et al. 2017; Gorayeb and Brannstrom 2016; Moreira, de Almeida Bizarria, Schilling Marqueson, and Sampaio Barbosa 2017). A participatory mapping exercise dotted the coast of Ceará with a wide variety of negative impacts on communities (Viana et al. 2016: 75). Off the coasts, community conflicts tended to focus on land claims as well as concerns about environmental issues like incursions into protected areas and impacts on birds and bats (e.g., Pacheco and dos Santos 2013). A final set of conflicts focused on the disruptions of construction itself, often involving complaints about roads and dust but sometimes developing into larger worries about land speculation and in-migration of young,

---

[31] www.energy.org.za/news/177-tsitsikamma-community-wind-farm-sod-turning -celebrations.
[32] Interview with Brimble, SAWEA, 2018.

male workforces – the latter leaving a legacy of *"filhos do vento"* or children of the wind (e.g., Viana et al. 2016).

Turning to the possible explanations of the patterns of community opposition to wind projects, the *level of objective risk* appears to play some role. There is no simple association of size of the wind installation and community resistance in either country, even when the clustering of plants is taken into account. Some large individual plants and clusters of plants faced opposition while others did not; conversely, residents also resisted a few small plants.

Beyond size, online reports showed that communities in Brazil resisted at least four wind plants that were installed in moving dunes and estuaries and a fifth blamed land speculation related to wind plants for incursions on dunes, primarily in Ceará. The impact of fixed wind turbines on such local ecologies and associated communities was severe and one of the most problematic features of wind farm siting in Brazil (Araújo 2016; Pinto et al. 2014). Online reports also showed that eight wind farms were built in conservation areas in Brazil, especially in Bahia; half of these generated community opposition while others faced scrutiny from conservation agencies.[33] These were among the types of site officially discouraged through more-extensive licensing requirements after 2014. Even the licensing specialist of the wind industry association ABEEólica acknowledged that wind farms should no longer be licensed for dunes now that there is "a broader vision of the process" rather than one focused only on wind potential.[34]

In South Africa, community resistance also focused on objective levels of risk, although the first concern was with impact on bird life, with other environmental and socioeconomic concerns following. As described in Section 5.3, bird impacts have become something of a veto point for potential wind farms, with developers choosing to have bird impact studies of potential sites done before advancing to further impact studies, since they expect mobilized resistance to follow projections of significant impacts on birds.[35] While bird impact was considered low on the list of environmental threats from wind farms in Brazil, it is worth noting that no winning projects in South Africa

---

[33] For example, http://geografiadopiemonte.blogspot.co.uk/2012/02/licencas-para-parques-eolicos-da-ba.html. On the Sento Sé area, see Pacheco and dos Santos 2013).

[34] Interview with technical analyst for licensing, ABEEólica, 2014.

[35] Interview with representative of Kromme Enviro-Trust, 2017.

planned to site their wind farms in protected areas or in very sensitive ecosystems like moving dunes and estuaries. Wind farms there were subject to normal EIA processes throughout, which limited siting choices.

Political opportunities, and especially the ability to find allies, supported the community mobilization that developed in both countries. In the single mobilized South African community, activists could draw on two different strands of past local organization. Residents created the St Francis Kromme Enviro-Trust in 1982 to monitor proposed development projects for their environmental and community impacts,[36] so it formed a receptive home for those who wanted closer scrutiny of proposed wind farms. As a long-time local organization, it also gave credibility to their efforts.[37] Local birders were also able to draw on the expertise and assistance of the national organization BirdLife South Africa, although the St Francis Bay area was the only wind site where BirdLife South Africa worked closely with a local ally.[38]

The lack of broader national support for mobilizations against wind farms in South Africa is not because environmental organizations are inactive in the politics of siting projects. In Durban, the combination of dirty growth (refineries and other heavy industry) and a "history of forced removals based on environmental racist planning" has led to significant site-based activism (Scott and Barnett 2009: 373). A network of fourteen NGOs reported contributing to hundreds of EIAs in the process (ibid.: 379). One of those fourteen, groundWork, worked closely with EarthLife Africa in trying to block the large coal plants Medupi and Kusile, even coordinating with community members to ask for and secure a World Bank Inspection Panel on the bank's support for the projects (see Chapter 2). In the case of nuclear power, the Kromme Enviro-Trust also mobilized against the possibility of a nuclear power plant in local Thyspunt and other local communities organized against local plants without larger coordination.[39] Yet outside of BirdLife South Africa, no national activist organizations appear to have developed significant concerns about wind power sites, and

---

[36] http://stfranciskrommetrust.co.za/about-us/our-origins/.
[37] Interview with representative of Kromme Enviro-Trust, 2017.
[38] Interview with Ralston-Paton, Birdlife South Africa, 2017.
[39] http://stfranciskrommetrust.co.za/thyspunt-report-for-agm-jan-2017/; interview with Peter Becker, Koeberg Alert Alliance, Cape Town, 2013.

BirdLife South Africa is oriented toward shifting the locations of wind farms and turbines to locations with lower bird impacts rather than wanting to block them altogether.[40] The CER, which supports legal strategies to challenge coal plants, explicitly approved of the REDZ as having identified locations where electricity can be generated with minimal environmental costs and with socioeconomic benefits for the whole country.[41]

In Brazil, in contrast, local communities could draw on diverse allies to support their mobilizations against wind power. In the Galinhos municipality in Rio Grande do Norte, for example, five individuals directly involved with tourism led the opposition movement, contacting a journalist friend from the state capital Natal who wrote an article that gained national media attention.[42] The journalist also helped build a dossier for the Ministério Público office in Natal, by providing photos, documents, and interviews that someone in the office hinted could be useful. Another movement leader advised the local Ministério Público of the schedule of public audiences and sent cars to pick up the local prosecutor. One of the movement leaders worked closely with the non-PT mayor and convinced him to stall the process while the community organized. Two active citizens reported their impression that the state environmental agency and IBAMA were clearly in favor of the project, but individuals within these agencies provided advice on how to bolster opposition claims. Citizens organized a large protest called "A Hug for the Dunes," joined by professors and students of the Federal University of Rio Grande do Norte. Protest signs clearly stated the position of residents: "Wind Park Yes, On the Dunes, No."[43] Other mobilizations also reflected this kind of dense networking with individuals

[40] Interview with Ralston-Paton, Birdlife South Africa, 2017.
[41] Interview with Loser, CER, 2018. See also www.csir.co.za/national-wind-solar-sea.
[42] http://noticias.uol.com.br/cotidiano/ultimas-noticias/2012/09/08/moradores-debatem-sobre-instalacao-de-aerogeradores-em-dunas-no-rio-grande-do-norte.htm. This summary of local conditions and mobilization is based on interviews with seven community residents, the journalist-activist Paulo Francisco, and officials in the Secretariat of Tourism, the state MP, and the state university, all in Galinhos or Natal, July 2014. J. Ricardo Tranjan conducted the interviews and wrote this paragraph.
[43] www.tjrn.jus.br/index.php/comunicacao/noticias/1211-revogada-suspensao-para-instalacao-de-parque-eolico-em-galinhos.

and institutions that were willing to help local communities block or reshape wind farms.

The Ministério Público was an ally for activists in many locations, as it has been for environmental and social issues across Brazil for several decades (McAllister 2008). Communities that questioned wind farms in their midst could also draw on long-standing activist networks that have worked for decades in Brazil on related issues. The Pastoral Land Commission of the Catholic Church (CPT) has been the anchor of many land-based claims since it was created in 1975, joining with well-known organizations like the Landless Rural Workers' Movement (MST) (Ondetti 2008). The wind farms drew their attention for aggravating conflicts over land ownership and use, especially the incentives that wind farm siting gave for asserting private control over land that previously served collective uses of marginal rural people.[44] The Instituto Terramar was another organization that supported local communities resisting wind power plants in coastal zones, building on earlier mobilizations related to mass tourism and shrimp farming. Terramar closely monitors developments across the Northeastern region and moves to educate and organize local communities early.[45]

In 2012 and 2017, the CPT organized meetings of local residents that already had or expected wind farms, to exchange information and experiences about the impacts of wind farms and strategies for successfully countering them.[46] The 2012 meeting brought together twenty-nine organizations, some of which were themselves broader networks, like the Environmental Justice Network (*Rede Brasileira de Justiça Ambiental*). Meetings like this were instrumental for introducing larger framings about impacts, with participants in 2012 noting that the social and environmental impacts "go far beyond the, already recognized, death of migratory birds."[47] The summary verdict was that wind farms created environmental injustice by supporting national development strategies in imposing those

---

[44] For example, http://cptjuazeiroba.blogspot.co.uk/2012/10/energia-eolica-uma-analise-dos-impactos.html.

[45] Interview with official at Instituto Terramar, Fortaleza, 2014 (JRT).

[46] www.irpaa.org/noticias/1713/seminario-regional-debateu-sobre-impactos-dos-parques-de-energia-eolica-no-nordeste.

[47] https://acervo.racismoambiental.net.br/2012/12/03/parques-de-energia-eolica-conflitos-e-injusticas-ambientais-na-zona-costeira-carta-das-comunidades-e-organizacoes-da-sociedade-civil/.

significant local costs.[48] Academic analysts in the region agreed, and added their own support for community activism (Viana et al. 2016).

Other national environmental organizations offered more general support for wind power. An energy campaigner for Greenpeace Brasil, for example, was still recommending wind power in 2012 for allowing simultaneous alternative uses like agriculture and cattle raising (Baitelo 2012: 72). While noting that too many plants had been placed in inappropriate sites or caused problems related to land-use claims, Baitelo also pointed out that no energy sources of electricity are free of such problems in Brazil (ibid.: 74). In 2014, the organization stressed that its support for different kinds of energy depended on how specific projects were carried out. It had also switched to lobbying for distributed rather than grid generation and now focused more on solar power.[49]

Community activists and their more institutionalized allies agreed that they rarely were able to find allies among local and state governments and that environmental licensing processes seemed designed to accelerate permits rather than to fully consider impacts.[50] Indeed, most of the projects were licensed under the pre-2014 accelerated process of Simplified Environmental Reports. A representative of the Instituto Terramar, for example, gave a lengthy list of wind plant impacts and noted in particular that the EIAs "hide [*invisibilizam*] the way people live."[51] This was literally the case in the EIA report for the Praia Formosa wind farm, where a small local community called Xavier with historical use of a coastal area was simply left off the maps used by the firm and the municipality for the permitting process for the wind farm (Gorayeb et al. 2018).

The Brazilian environmental justice critiques raise the third possible explanation of community response, which is the question of whether *community characteristics* explain either where wind farms are located or when communities resist them. Clearly, many Brazilian wind farms are placed in poor communities where vulnerable populations may lack land tenure security and have livelihood

---

[48] https://acervo.racismoambiental.net.br/2012/12/03/parques-de-energia-eolica-conflitos-e-injusticas-ambientais-na-zona-costeira-carta-das-comunidades-e-organizacoes-da-sociedade-civil/.
[49] Interview with Baitelo, Greenpeace Brasil, 2014.
[50] Interviews with Instituto Terramar, 2014; Janny Lima and Ana Luiza of the Ministêrio Público of RN, Natal, 2014 (JRT); Chesma Alves Marina, former secretary of tourism of Galinhos, Galinhos, 2014 (JRT).
[51] Interview with Instituto Terramar, 2014.

strategies that are challenged by infrastructure projects. Proponents of the wind farms – often local city councils as well as developers – frequently cited the poverty of their communities as a reason for welcoming the new projects. The director general of Voltalia for Brazil, Robert Klein, captured this point of view: "Someone made the world very well, putting the wind in an area that still needed to be developed."[52] Challengers argued that their same poverty made them a target, especially since economically disenfranchised populations often lacked the documentation for their historic use and even ownership of the lands used for some wind farms. Communities were sometimes able to use the institutions set up for *quilombolos* to raise claims, and sometimes protect, their historic land uses.

These complexities mean that environmental injustice or environmental racism are potent frames for understanding the location of some wind farms and local community resistance in Brazil, but not all. In addition, many wind farms are also located in the Southern state Rio Grande do Sul, which is comparatively wealthy. This area is free of conflict, and wind farms have even become tourist attractions and subjects for Instagram feeds. Thus, unlike the usual expectation that environmental injustice means that projects are sited in poor communities that will be unable to organize to resist and reform them (Aldrich 2010), contention around wind power is highest in very poor communities. It is not surprising that it is difficult to find a statistical correlation between community characteristics and instances of resistance in the communities that host electricity projects in Brazil (Hochstetler and Tranjan 2016).

The South African experiences present a strikingly different picture. The only community that has had significant resistance to wind farms is the comparatively wealthy, mostly white community around the St Francis Bay area. Wind farms in other, similar communities did not face organized resistance, nor did quite different communities. Developers do seem to have chosen sites that minimize the risk of community opposition. They developed few projects in the former black homelands, often communally owned and therefore seen as risky, although the Chaba project secured support from traditional leaders and has been fully operational since 2015.[53] A World Bank

[52] http://g1.globo.com/rn/rio-grande-do-norte/noticia/2016/06/rn-ganha-com plexo-de-energia-eolica-em-serra-do-mel-na-costa-branca.html.
[53] www.engineeringnews.co.za/article/renewable-energy-edges-closer-to-the-former-homelands-2014-10-24.

review of six of the projects in the data set here indicated that all are "located in rural and remote areas far away from community centers, residential, and commercial areas and the Projects sites will be developed within privately owned farms" (World Bank 2016: 10). Cheryl McEwan argues that conditions for community-based conflict over land and territory seem to be present in many locations in South Africa (McEwan 2017), but they have largely not yet emerged around wind infrastructure. As discussed earlier in this section, that is not from a lack of mobilization against other kinds of electricity infrastructure or from insensitivity to environmental justice issues.

The possible explanations considered so far to explain when and where community-based conflict is present have focused on the costs of wind plants and the ability of communities to organize themselves to limit those costs. The other side of community impact is, of course, potential benefits, and those may also help to understand the patterns of community response.

In the auctions that select specific electricity projects for long-term purchasing power agreements for the national grid, Brazil considers only the bid cost of providing the electricity (see Chapter 3). Any additional benefits for local communities are ad hoc, both in defining the affected community and in determining benefits to be offered to them. EIA has been the most common institution for defining both impact and compensation, but it was abbreviated for wind projects until 2014, as discussed in Section 5.3.1, and so offered little to host communities. In addition, while other energy installations like hydropower and oil and gas production pay royalties to the states and municipalities where they are located (Pulice, Paiva, and Moretto 2017),[54] only Rio Grande do Sul has had a small 0.5 percent environmental compensation charge for wind, adding one for solar in 2018.[55] Most local jobs are construction jobs (Brower Brown 2011). The wind energy association ABEEólica estimates that just some 4,000 landowners are compensated for hosting wind farms, with a total payment of R$10 million (roughly US$2.5 million) per month.[56] The direct local beneficiaries of a new plant are therefore limited.

---

[54] The article finds few measurable improvements in development outcomes from the increased municipal revenues associated with hydroelectric dams.

[55] "RS quer compensação ambiental de projeto solar," *Valor Econômico*, December 6, 2018, p. A2.

[56] www1.folha.uol.com.br/mercado/2017/12/1945898-energia-traz-bilhoes-para -nordeste-mas-beneficio-fica-na-mao-de-poucos.shtml.

The Brazilian National Economic and Social Development Bank (BNDES) funded many of these projects, and it requires loan recipients to include plans to address the impacts of their projects, which it will finance.[57] Developers are asked to generally approach these issues through a posture of corporate social and environmental responsibility, but BNDES's guidelines do not require even consultation with local communities. While firms must seek what it calls strategic interlocutors, these can come from any of a set of possible social agents: the list includes financial agents, nonprofit organizations, the set of professional organizations known as *Sistema S*, educational and research organizations, workers, *or* civil society organizations, none of which are required to be local. In this regulatory context, concrete benefits for local communities that host wind farms are at best unpredictable and may be minimal. There is also no central registry of compensatory promises made, making it difficult for communities to hold developers responsible for outcomes that might come years after wind farms are built.

Firms in the sector expressed frustration with the demands of local communities. An official of CPFL Renováveis, one of the largest firms in Brazilian alternative renewable electricity, described "a social movement infiltrating some municipalities. We encounter communities that are already opposed to the parks and start out from the very beginning with absurd demands."[58] Representatives of Bons Ventos (now acquired by CPFL Renováveis and renamed Bons Ventos da Serra), which had placed early wind farms in the contentious Aracati region, declined to criticize the licensing process but said that the firm now has a long list of qualities to avoid in potential sites. These include communities primed to protest against any change or that have tourism as a major industry. They also noted that investors are asked to take on numerous tasks – schools, leisure areas, job generation – that should be state responsibilities and that bring administrative costs to 12–15 percent of project costs.[59]

Developers did make big promises of benefits to come for local communities in Brazil, often amplified by local politicians. Yet there could be misfits between what developers offered and what communities demanded, as seen in the Serra do Mel region of Rio Grande do

[57] www.bndes.gov.br/wps/portal/site/home/quem-somos/responsabilidade-social-e-ambiental/o-que-nos-orienta/politicas/politica-entorno-integra.
[58] Interview with official of CPFL Renováveis, São Paulo, 2014 (JRT).
[59] Interview with two officials of Bons Ventos da Serra, Fortaleza, 2014 (JRT).

Norte where twelve wind farms had an installed capacity of almost 400 MW. On the one side, developers paid for sports, health, quality of life, water supply, and income generation programs, as well as rebuilding a road used during construction. For just one wind farm, sixty property owners in a village all received payments, whether or not they actually had a wind turbine on their land.[60] Despite these benefits, a broad coalition of artists, environmentalists, university actors, the CPT, and local community members was continuing to protest against the wind farms in 2016. In addition to objecting to wind turbines on beaches that had historically been open leisure and livelihood areas, they argued that the turbines had contributed to a wave of land speculation and land grabs (*grilhagem*, in Brazilian Portuguese terms) in a place with overlapping land claims. If money is to be paid for possibly hosting a turbine, the value of documented ownership of that land increases. In one example that shows the complexity of these arrangements, three of the wind farms were originally meant to be located on land also claimed by the Comunidade Quilombola Maambira. That community secured an agreement with developers to build elsewhere in 2014 and was eventually granted formal land title in 2016.[61] While the disputes in this location focused on land, other locations spotlighted jobs. In the Serra da Babilônia project, community members closed a road, claiming that they had agreed to allow access to their lands in exchange for jobs that had not appeared.[62]

In South African auctions, in contrast, developers win contracts according to a formula that weights the cost of the electricity at 70 percent of the competition, while the other 30 percent is based on specific social promises made by the developer. Developers are asked to consider a set impact area of 50 km around the proposed plant, developing commitments relating to the numbers of jobs that will be offered to residents within the impact area – and especially to Black Africans. In addition, 2.5–5 percent of the ownership of the plant is to be placed in a community trust and 1–1.5 percent of project revenue should be spent

[60] http://g1.globo.com/rn/rio-grande-do-norte/noticia/2016/06/rn-ganha-complexo-de-energia-eolica-em-serra-do-mel-na-costa-branca.html.
[61] https://marsemfim.com.br/especulacao-em-areia-branca-provoca-reacao/; www.politicaemfoco.com/decretos-desapropriam-areas-para-reforma-agraria-e-regularizacao-de-territorio-quilombola-no-rn/.
[62] http://leoricardonoticias.com.br/dia-a-dia/manifestacao-de-moradores-de-tabua-de-varzea-nova-fecha-estrada-de-eolica/.

on socioeconomic development (Tait et al. 2013: 8). In the first two procurement auctions, developers simply needed to make some promise of community benefits, but in the final two rounds they were evaluated on the basis of their comparative generosity. This has meant an ever-increasing number of jobs promised in operations and maintenance (Chapter 3). In the South African case, the promises from developers are contractual so that their fulfillment can be better tracked over time. All of this is part of an explicit social contract that trades private profits for participating firms in exchange for jobs and other community benefits.[63] The reporting and obligations for those benefits are negotiated between the firm and the national government, skipping local governments and, often, the communities themselves.[64]

South Africa's more activist environmental organizations have their doubts about the success of that social contract and some industry participants agreed in confidential discussions. GroundWork called the overall approach "development by lottery" and worried that it asked private developers to step in to promote development while the government stepped out. The resulting promises were doubted: "Amenities and opportunities of variable quality will be created but, as with corporate social responsibility, they are in the gift of the corporation (however reluctant) and are not the rights of citizens" (Hallowes 2015: 114). GroundWork and its partner organizations like EarthLife Africa criticize the choice to have private firms build and supply renewable energy instead of the energy parastatal Eskom – although Eskom comes in for heavy criticism over its own social and environmental practices as well (Hallowes 2015). The small number of academic analyses agree, noting the difficulty in defining communities within that arbitrary 50 km boundary to be part of a "passive beneficiary model" (McEwan, Mawdsley, Banks, and Scheyvens 2017: 43). The processes do not call for any coordination of the renewable energy programs with governmental planning processes (McEwan et al. 2017: 41–42). And all of these programs are well outside the expertise of most wind and solar power developers (Tait et al. 2013). The Department of Energy tracks developers' social spending closely but only to tally the

[63] Interview with Fabricius, Eskom, 2014.
[64] Interview with Fumani Mthembi, managing director of Knowledge Pele, by Skype, 2018. Knowledge Pele is a social enterprise that researches, consults on, and helps design and implement the social and enterprise programs that form 30 percent of the bid for private contracts to build wind and solar power.

number of rands spent, not development outcomes. Perhaps most tellingly, when Eskom refused to sign contracts for two years, delaying project starts, there was no mobilization by local communities demanding that the projects advance.[65]

Experimental research suggests that compensation can affect public response to a local wind farm, with respondents preferring the kind of community (versus individual) compensation offered through the South African system (García et al. 2016). Without extended research in each of the communities that host wind farms in South Africa, it is difficult to know whether such promises of benefits accompanying wind farms have helped to dampen opposition. However, the industry associations for wind and solar power have created permanent boards to provide guidance to firms on the social development requirements, trying to address the lack of expertise. In 2016, they also held a series of roundtables that suggested that there have been both failures and successes with respect to those requirements (Wlokas and Soal 2016a, 2016b).

An initial workshop was well attended by developers, many of whom "had experienced threats, strikes and conflict in the context of their work" and now needed strategies to avoid being pulled into violence and partisanship around local elections (Wlokas and Soal 2016a: 5–6). This suggests a level of community dissatisfaction that may have been present but too low to be picked up by the media-based research strategy used here. The second roundtable, focused on the mandatory community trusts, could not accommodate all those who wanted to attend. There, a representative of the Cookhouse Windfarm Community Trust (in a community that hosts multiple plants) explained how it had successfully overseen community nomination and selection of trustees who were all Black African and 40 percent female. After training and mentorship, the trustees carried out comprehensive planning for their community trust, choosing to focus on education and holding monthly social dialogues with local residents (Wlokas and Soal 2016b: 11–12). Notwithstanding this apparently positive outcome, the facilitators later wrote that little of South Africa's rich history of community development traditions had made its way into the renewable energy program; developers could comply with the regulations with little on-the-ground impact

---

[65] Interview with Mthembi, Knowledge Pele, 2018.

and little oversight or guidance from any level of government (Wlokas, Westoby, and Soal 2017: 41; see also Sovacool, Burke, Baker, Katikalapudi, and Wlokas 2017: 685). More effective programs would depend on deeper knowledge of the specific project locations, which was hard for private energy firms to develop (Wlokas et al. 2017: 42).

5.6 Community Responses to Solar Power

Writing about community responses to solar power installations is a much smaller task. Similar searches on the ninety-four plants (at least three of which had contracts revoked for not meeting the construction timelines) in thirty Brazilian municipalities found very little organized community opposition. This was true even in cities like Bom Jesús de Lapa (Bahia), Ribeira and São Jõao do Piauí, and Pirapora (Minas Gerais), with large installations. In the Intuverava (Bahia) and Coremas (Pernambuco) complexes, there were minor complaints about dust during construction, but the public record finds little else of note. Most of the records were, again, in lists of projects and government documents. The searches on city names often turned up courses being offered for training in solar installation and a remarkable number of proud announcements that the new solar installation would be the biggest in a state, the region, or the country. Local news sources spoke of jobs, of new revenue for municipalities, and new sources of electricity, and occasionally noted the contribution to reducing GHG emissions. Notwithstanding the fears of observers that solar plants would also attract opponents (Frate and Brannstrom 2017), that does not seem to be the case so far.

In South Africa, too, there was no reported community opposition to solar plants or to solar power in the towns where the plants are located. This was true even in the area around De Aar, Upington, and Kimberley in the Northern Cape, which has many plants. Reports on the solar plants leaned toward the strongly positive, with many stories about the social spending that accompanied the plants as well as praise for the accompanying jobs. In De Aar, Solar Capital's plant was called the "saving grace" for "ailing towns." The firm had provided free Wi-Fi for the town, entrepreneurial programs that supported local enterprises from recycling to ostrich farming, and programs for fetal alcohol syndrome, among other projects.[66] The social spending of other plants also drew local media praise. As evidence begins to slowly accumulate about the impact of solar installation on birdlife there (Visser et al. 2019), these patterns may change.

5.7 Conclusion

Unlike the other chapters, this one began with theoretical uncertainty about the structure of interests in the policy arena of siting renewable energy projects in particular locations. Are there many local benefits from these projects that should incentivize the expansion of wind and solar power? Economists and energy scholars often propose that there are, especially with greater local control. Alternatively, anthropologists and geographers worry that wind and solar installations bring unacceptable economic, social, and environmental costs to host communities, especially poor ones. If these do not block the projects and limit new renewable energy's prospects, it is only because of problems that the communities have in sustaining collective action. The chapter does not resolve these issues because the outcomes for wind and solar power in the two countries are different. In addition, the outcomes are directly opposed to the relative success of wind and solar power more generally – the rates of opposition to Brazilian wind power are highest, while it is also far more advanced than the others – suggesting that the siting logic is not very influential to overall outcomes in either.

Brazil adopted an auction system for most of its procurement of wind and solar power, which favors selection of large, cost-efficient firms and installations to build the projects. Its EIA regulatory structure for wind power was highly permissive, leading to an early generation of plants that were sometimes sited in areas where they would have large environmental and socioeconomic effects. Those regulations were changed in 2014 to encourage developers to avoid particularly sensitive sites. There are no systematic benefits that come to local community hosts, unlike with other kinds of electricity project, so any benefits are the economic benefits of the projects themselves.

Systematic research on Brazil's 600 wind farms in 77 cities found mobilized community resistance to them in nearly one-quarter of the

[66] www.moneyweb.co.za/news/industry/solar-farm-project-saving-grace-de-aar-community/.

cities. (This means, of course, that three-quarters of the cities did not have mobilized community resistance.) Resistance often occurred in cities that were in environmentally or socially sensitive locations, such as moving dunes in historic fishing or tourism locations. Others, however, avoided opposition despite similar conditions. Mobilized resistance in communities, many of which were poor, also benefited from significant links to elite actors including the Catholic Church, other NGOs, journalists, university academics, and others. Past and future host communities in the poor Northeast region began to share mostly negative experiences with each other, creating a regional network that was skeptical of wind power. Against expectations, there were very few mobilizations in wealthy communities in Rio Grande do Sul, which also hosted large numbers of wind farms. In broad terms, this experience supports the environmental justice storyline, although poor communities were more able to overcome collective action problems and mobilize than expected. It is worth noting that the project-level research design used here is not able to assess this storyline's broader structural arguments, but conflict is not as widespread and inevitable as the environmental injustice arguments can imply.

Conversely, the nonmobilization around solar power in both countries is consistent with the storyline that sees renewable energy as a win–win opportunity to achieve environment and development aims together. Even very large solar installations clustered in a few cities generated little community reaction. While the outcomes are consistent with that storyline, all that is actually documented in the chapter is the absence of conflict. It could conceivably be due to collective action problems for local communities as well as to actual benefits and costs. However, this seems unlikely as community activists in both countries are able to mobilize around their incumbent fuels (hydropower in Brazil and coal in South Africa) as well as organizing against many wind power installations in Brazil.

Finally, South African responses to wind power broadly fit the environmental conservation storyline, where activists recognize the climate benefits of wind power but seek to keep it out of locations where it is harmful to birds as well as having related secondary issues. There is only one community that has sustained community organization around wind power, a comparatively wealthy tourist community. The national organization BirdLife South Africa is highly engaged, working with this one community or on its own to closely monitor exactly where whole wind farms and even particular turbines are located. It has been able to demand that wind farm developers do bird and bat impact studies that go beyond those required in the formal EIA process. Neither BirdLife nor host communities have developed the kind of generalized mistrust of all wind power that is appearing in some communities in Northeast Brazil.

Beyond the ambiguous conclusions on the storylines, there is also little evidence that community and site-based mobilizations have directly affected the overall trajectory of wind and solar power development in the two countries. The highest levels and rates of contestation, with the thorniest claims, are over Brazilian wind power – but this is the form of renewable energy infrastructure that has expanded at the fastest rates to the highest levels of wattage and is continuing to grow. Conversely, the lack of contestation over solar power has not, so far, helped to pull it out of a very slow start there. Similarly, there is more contestation over wind than solar power installations in South Africa, but the two have moved in close step, with wind power, if anything, a bit ahead of solar power in installed capacity. The evidence here is supported by a comparative study of project completion rates, which found a 100 percent completion rate for South African wind and solar plants and the fewest delays. While Brazil, in the same study, showed the highest delays (only 14 percent of wind projects were completed on time), the vast majority of the plants were completed and the delays were attributed to transmission connections and supplier problems (Bayer, Schäuble, and Ferrari 2018: 308–309).

Siting decisions and community responses are part of the broader political economy of the expansion of wind and solar power, and clearly contribute to the legitimacy or lack of it of renewable energy. If they do not appear to have shaped the overall outcomes to this point, that may be because other electricity siting choices also face similar scenarios. Essentially all kinds of electricity infrastructure in Brazil have contentious licensing and community mobilization processes, with hydropower and nuclear power leading the way and fossil fuels the least contentious (Hochstetler and Tranjan 2016). In South Africa, the small numbers of coal and nuclear plants face much larger opposition coalitions than the BirdLife-led efforts to influence wind power plant sites. In addition, industry interviews in both countries suggest that local opposition may move projects from one location to another rather than blocking them altogether. The lack of an observed impact on outcomes so far does not mean that opposition to wind plants in both countries will never affect outcomes. However, the ongoing opposition to some wind power indicates a failure to lay down path dependencies of future support for the sector in this policy arena (Roberts et al. 2018: 306).

The political economy of siting sits quite separately from the other political economies in this book, although choices made for them, like the use of auctions to select projects, have consequences here. Eskom and its status quo coalition are notably absent here after dominating the other chapters. It is not building the projects or licensing them for local impacts – or inserting itself in unrelated arenas, as it did with industrial policy. That absence may contribute to surprisingly quiet dynamics around siting in South Africa, where a technical orientation dominates for once. For Brazil, we are back to a set of actors that last appeared in Chapter 2, on climate change, the Ministry of Environment and environmental and human rights activists. While they historically shared a vision and worked together to control deforestation, they divided here on impact assessment of wind power plants. As a result, conflict and contestation were at their highest for any of the political economies. Most host communities already had electricity (Chapter 4), so they could not find a benefit in that, and industrial policy aims (Chapter 3) were achieved at regional or national rather than local levels. As a result, conflict was not limited or exacerbated by the political economies of other chapters and there was a partial exception to the technical character of the Brazilian approach.

6 Political Economies of Energy Transition

This book began with the question of why there are very different outcomes for wind and solar power in Brazil, with further differences in the fates of these electricity sources in South Africa. I have examined four policy arenas, each with a different configuration of interests and policy coalitions, and asked if the resulting political economies can account for the outcomes observed. In this conclusion, I first briefly review the theoretical framework of the book. I then put the stories of the four policy arenas together for each country, showing the distinct national political economy of energy transition that emerged out of the interactions of the four. I present and analyze the important difference between the politicized nature of the South African energy transition versus the bureaucratically grounded Brazilian experience. I conclude with reflections on what these countries show about whether and how the four political economies are likely to be important for other middle-income and developing economies.

6.1 A Brief Review of Political Economies of Energy Transition

The primary theoretical claim in this book is that "an" energy transition is actually a series of political economy transitions. The prospect of energy transition convokes actors and disputes in at least four policy arenas. Each of them has a different basic interest structure that should generate the participation of particular, different actors and institutions of the state and of society. These interact with more conjunctural features of the country and coalitional struggles to produce the actual dynamics of each political economy. The four may not push in the same direction; nor are they necessarily moving at the same pace. As a result, it is also necessary to set them together, to see where one may exaggerate or undermine the outcomes of another policy sphere.

This is a marked departure from many studies of energy transition that focus only on the motivations and dynamics that come from the dilemma of climate change. The climate change political economy does receive special treatment here too. It comes first (Chapter 2) because it is the only rationale for energy transition that also explicitly calls for sunsetting fossil fuels. As a result, the interest structure involves not only the broad and diffuse interest in taking action to prevent climate change but also the sharp and concentrated interests of any fossil fuel actors involved in electricity provision. This political economy acknowledges the fundamental difference in the two cases considered here, which is that South Africa had such a coal-dominated electricity structure as the country contemplated climate action while Brazil's electricity structure was based on non-fossil fuel sources instead. I argue that this set the two countries down different tracks from the beginning. I also propose that the presence of strong actors defending the use of fossil fuels in electricity generation sets the stage for a much more conflictual and politicized energy transition debate, as appears in South Africa, while situations like Brazil's leave open the possibility of a more bureaucratic and measured response.

The other three political economies are all more focused on economic interests that might be linked to energy transition and the development of wind and solar power in particular. They potentially provide "cobenefits," that is, economic advantages that may be valued regardless of their climate impact. As such, they may be especially important for those middle-income and developing countries that will be next to take up the possibility of energy transition. Chapter 3 on industrial policy sees an interest structure where some state and private actors have concentrated interests in developing a new national industry in wind and solar power. The aims of economic growth, new jobs, and the possibility of innovation in a major new economic sector are set against industrial policy concerns of managing economic rents. There is also the prior question of whether public or private actors are chosen to play the industrial development roles. Localization of a new industry can be costly, meaning that it directly interacts with the next political economy of costs and distribution. Chapter 4 examines the role of the state as service provider with citizens and businesses as consumers and asks how wind and solar power might either complicate or ease the state's efforts to provide electricity for all consumers at affordable costs. The political economy of Chapter 5, which views wind and solar power through the lens of siting an infrastructure project in a local community, does not settle on a single summary of the interests involved. The academic literature itself is divided on whether such projects should offer net costs or benefits to hosting communities.

As already said, each of these policy arenas is operating simultaneously, to potentially different ends. Therefore, the final analytical task is to set the political economies together, to see how they may interact and create, in the end, a holistic national political economy of energy transition. That may come together in a big, reinforcing sweep or it may be a national political economy of contradictions and disjunctures. In other words, the whole energy transition may be more or less than the sum of its four political economy parts. That putting-together is the aim of the rest of this chapter, along with initial observations about what the Brazilian and South African cases show for other middle-income and developing countries.

6.2 South Africa

6.2.1 A National Political Economy of Energy Transition

After nearly a decade of development, wind and solar power in South Africa still show few signs of really taking off, as they have been caught in highly politicized and contentious energy transition debates. Support for their deployment actually seemed to go backwards after a promising start in 2011, as the electricity parastatal Eskom refused to sign contracts for projects that had won competitive national elections from 2016 to 2018. Repeated efforts to update electricity build plans after 2011 were notable mostly for the inconsistency of their preferred electricity sources and for the unwillingness of political leaders to formally adopt any of them. Coal or renewables or nuclear power? What will come next?

The political economy at the heart of these debates is the climate political economy. This is not to say that climate concern drives South African energy policy. Instead, the climate political economy recognizes that a long-term and diffuse interest in climate action will be paired with strong opposition when the incumbent electricity type is a fossil fuel that will now be shut down or at least not allowed to expand. Eskom, the electricity parastatal that has historically generated almost all of South Africa's electricity from coal, was the heart of that pro-status quo opposition. It and its allies in the government, the industrial sector, and the labor unions were powerful opponents against an incipient coalition in favor of climate action and energy transition. The pro-transition coalition had the new renewable energy industry at its core, but it also counted on allies in government and civil society. The latter gained some unexpected space from electricity supply shortages in 2008 and then-president Zuma's unexpected international commitment for climate action in Copenhagen in 2009. While the status quo coalition did not openly resist climate policy itself, it concentrated on blocking the turn to wind and solar power as a result. This could be expected in a situation of existential threat, but the status quo coalition also strongly favored nuclear power as a low-carbon option – for reasons that increasingly appear to come from the private interests of Zuma and a few cronies in "state capture" relations. As such, there are both systematic reasons based on the structure of interests for the climate political economy developments and more particular national reasons.

The political economy of industrial policy motivated a parallel fight, with many of the same actors reappearing in the same coalitions and some artificiality in separating them for analysis. Eskom had refused earlier directives to build wind and solar power, and the Ministry of Energy eventually gave the task to private firms chosen through auctions. That again posed an existential threat, this time to Eskom's monopoly role in the sector. The battles over the balance between public and private roles were public and called everyone to take a side. The African National Congress (ANC) itself was divided and even Zuma, president from 2009 to 2018, changed the stances he took publicly. The association of a public utility with all the coal-based generation and of private firms with nearly all the wind and solar power generation meant an interlocking and reinforcing cleavage through the sector. Labor unions, initially favorable toward wind and solar power and climate action, could not accept that private firms would take them on, and so moved onto Eskom's side. Their genuine concerns with a just transition reinforced this choice, as existing coal jobs and communities depend on Eskom. In addition, the starts and stops to renewable energy demand meant minimal industrial development and new jobs in the emerging sector.

Already in high conflict, the same coalitions spilled over into the political economy of cost and distribution, this time arguing about whether wind and solar power or nuclear power were cheaper. Over time, wind and solar power had clearly become cheaper, but the state's capture for nuclear power reappeared here as Eskom and others insisted on the opposite facts. The backdrop of electricity service provision in South Africa was deep electricity inequality from decades of an apartheid government that would not recognize its Black African citizens as citizens and provide them services. After the democratizing transition in 1994, the ANC made significant efforts to bring those Black Africans onto the national electricity grid, eventually using grid-scale wind and solar power to try to meet demand. But neither the state nor many citizens can afford to pay for the expanding service, nor to reach the last millions without service. While distributed solar power is often touted as a solution for those who do not yet have access, South Africa finds that comparatively wealthy citizens who do have access are increasingly using distributed solar to opt out of the costly, low-quality public service.

The presence of a strong, well-resourced actor like Eskom fighting an existential threat clearly drove the emergence of these counter-coalitions and their battles. The absence of coalitional conflict in Chapter 5 is plausibly traced to the fact that Eskom has no particular presence in the mostly remote towns that host wind and solar power installations. There are still familiar conflicts between wind power plants and defenders of nesting and migratory birds, but the tone is quieter without the broader fight. Eskom has been diminished through these years, not least from the way it was systematically looted and from its difficulties building new coal. Facing possible bankruptcy and probable division into smaller parts, it is less likely to be able to play the same organizing role in conflicts over energy transition in the future. But in the first two decades of the twenty-first century, Eskom and its allies drove a disruptive, politicized transition process, where the same actors in multiple policy arenas simultaneously fought to a draw that is not yet a green spiral or a fully negative one.

6.2.2 *A Political Story*

Electricity has been headline news for more than a decade in South Africa. The electricity utility Eskom is always somewhere at the center of breaking stories about rising tariffs, looming service cuts, state capture, and much more. Wind and solar power plants and the private firms that build them are a perennial theme. Eskom and the wind and solar firms form the core of two opposing coalitions who have battled in nearly every policy arena, whether it is nominally climate change, industrial policy, or electricity distribution and service. Neither has definitively won, and the stops and starts of wind and solar power reflect that overall stalemate in their struggles in three of the political economies.

The heat of their battle emanates more from Eskom, for whom it has been an existential battle – based on the climate logic – to protect existing roles and resources, rather than from what is still quite a small group of industry actors whose resources and skills are not well designed for such a politicized debate. Other actors picked sides between them, with the shifts of the labor movement (to Eskom) and the Energy Intensive Users Group (EIUG) (away from Eskom) being some of the most important alignments and realignments. Not all politicized transitions will extend into corruption and state capture stories like South Africa's does, but the open and sometimes dishonest opposition to energy transition seems likely.

It is important to note that the openly politicized opposition coalitions took the headlines but never were the whole story in South Africa. Eskom has many experienced and capable technical staff employees, as do the industry firms. During these years, they kept the lights on (at least most of the time), built and operated new plants, learned new technologies and skills, connected new consumers, and so on. Even so, they have been largely sidelined in direct policy-making as the political appointees at Eskom, together with ANC allies, intervened to squelch, among other things, electricity build plans that included wind and solar power instead of the nuclear power they favored. The overall mode of transition in South Africa is clearly the politicized mode, developing from the existential threat that Eskom and its allies faced as climate politics proposed a life beyond coal.

6.3 Brazil

6.3.1 *A National Political Economy of Energy Transition*

The development of wind and solar power in Brazil is frankly puzzling at first glance. As Figure 1.1 showed, wind procurement began quite early, in 2002, and then began to take off quickly in 2009, reaching nearly 20 GW a decade later with more coming. Solar power, in contrast, joined the national electricity grid only in 2014, with distributed solar production appearing suddenly in 2016 to begin a vertiginous climb. Both wind and solar electricity resources are abundant in Brazil, so the difference must lie in politics and policy. In fact, routine bureaucratic functioning can account for most of the outcomes, culminating in a very different mode of energy transition from the South African one. The absence of an electricity sector actor like Eskom, dependent on fossil fuels, set the stage for this development.

As is often the case (Aklin and Urpelainen 2018: 12), an electricity supply crisis in 2001 opened the door for an alternative to Brazil's usual hydropower. In turn, modelers in the Ministry of Mines and Energy set the course of wind and solar power by using cost and industrial policy considerations to prioritize wind but not solar power. By their calculations, the wind power technology of 2002 was comparatively cheap (relative to solar power) and its higher cost (relative to the incumbent hydropower) could be offset by developing a national industry of suppliers and manufacturers. As Chapter 3 shows, they turned out to be too optimistic about how quickly that national industry could grow, but once greater state demand was joined with supportive policies from the Brazilian National Economic and Social Development Bank (BNDES) and other economic agencies, wind power installation and manufacturing began an accelerated climb after 2009 that proved self-reinforcing, as industry representatives worked with supportive but rent-disciplining state actors.

Grid-scale solar power had to wait to begin the same process, but, once global solar prices fell, it also began the climb in 2014. The later start – attributable to differential costs – meant a less hospitable industrial policy context, as a change in government in 2016 removed many of the supportive policies. Most solar manufacturing beyond simple assembly of solar cells and brackets is still delayed. If industrial policy (Chapter 3) and cost considerations (Chapter 4) help account for the late start for solar power, Chapter 4 also tells the story of a small group of bureaucrats in the energy regulator ANEEL (National Electricity Agency) who instigated a series of regulatory changes that they kept deliberately off the partisan agenda as long as possible. Their 2012 regulations removed certain barriers to distributed generation, while the 2015 regulations opened the floodgates for household-level installations beginning in 2016.

The other two chapters (Chapters 2 and 5), on climate change and siting of wind and solar installations, tell us little directly about the Brazilian outcomes of interest. Brazil has an unusual GHG emissions profile, with most historical emissions coming from deforestation and an electricity system based on hydropower. Climate debates were heated, as Chapter 2 shows, but they had relatively little to do with wind and solar power. If Brazil is to take meaningful climate action, it will need to take on Petrobras, its domestic oil production, and the way it is threaded through national transport and industry. There will be substantial just transition challenges in doing so. But this energy is mostly not used in the electricity sector and so is not itself a major part of the political economy of wind and solar power.

The fact that effective climate action does not require reducing emissions in the electricity sector has an important indirect effect on the Brazilian case: it removes an important source of opposition and conflict in the form of an incumbent fossil fuel source of electricity. This allows the more bureaucratic solutions observed in the other political economies. Electricity planners in Brazil's Energy Research Enterprise (EPE) added climate considerations to their optimization models, but cost considerations mattered far more for expanding wind and solar power. In any event, climate concerns would not call for adding wind but not solar power. The small role of climate policy in shaping wind and solar outcomes means that President Bolsonaro's much-reported opposition to ambitious climate action is unlikely to have much effect on wind and solar power, for which he has stated support.

With regards to siting issues, Chapter 5 shows that about a quarter of local communities resisted the installation of a wind power facility in their towns, while there was no reported resistance to solar installations. Little in Brazil's institutions created specific benefits for local communities for hosting a plant, while loose regulations allowed harmful site selection for over a decade before 2014. Still, the link to outcomes is weak, as wind power in Brazil is the more successful of the two types of renewable energy. Siting difficulties, if anything, kept wind from an even faster rollout, but they cannot account for its having earlier and larger success than solar power. This is the only one of the four political economies where Brazilian citizens mobilized to make just transition claims related to wind or solar power.

This summary shows that the political economies of industrial policy and the cost of electricity service discussed in the development-oriented chapters shaped wind and solar outcomes in Brazil much more than did the political economies of the environment-oriented chapters. The politics of energy transition was also notably muted. Wind and solar power have had cross-partisan support from presidents from four different parties even as the rest of the national political system passed through some of its most polarized and antagonistic years. With no strong opponent, much decision-making around wind and solar power took place in bureaucracies of various kinds, filling regulatory bulletins but not usually news sites. Those bureaucrats and societal actors differ from one policy arena to another, so there is an overall lack of coordination, with the direction and level of ambition on renewable energy differing from one arena to another.

6.3.2 A Bureaucratic Story

Every chapter's discussion of Brazil includes a national ministry and sometimes a large national political initiative or policy shift. Yet the decisions that affected the outcomes in the policy arena most often came from bureaucratic actors acting within their existing regulatory spaces, using standard operating procedures to take the next steps that make sense. Thus, the Ministry of Environment launched a major climate policy in the 2000s, but, because that policy was focused on reducing Brazil's GHG emissions from deforestation, it fell to EPE to be responsible for incrementally adding more and more wind and then solar power to the annual grid plans. Climate emissions were just one of a set of parameters in its routine optimization models that pushed this outcome. The Ministry of Energy initiated a small feed-in tariff program for wind power, but it procures most electricity through auctions. These deliberately exclude industrial policy for the sector, but BNDES introduced local content requirements when it financed auction winners, following its statutory mandate to promote jobs. The Workers' Party's (PT's) marquee program of Light for All led to just 3,500 installations of distributed solar power, while a small group of technocrats in ANEEL made regulatory changes that are expected to motivate at least 1.35 million of them by 2027 and perhaps twice that. Finally, routine environmental impact assessments (EIAs) shaped the local-level conflicts around siting.

As these Brazilian examples show, renewable energy may be disruptive, but renewable energy policies can reflect technical rather than

openly disruptive and politicized forces. They may be all the more
effective at promoting wind and solar power in that event. While
different in almost all of its details, the Brazilian pattern is similar to
what Jonas Meckling and Jonas Nahm call bureaucratic policy design,
where legislators set the broad policy aims and bureaucrats design the
implementation (Meckling and Nahm 2018: 742). They suggest – and
find – that bureaucracy-driven policies are more likely to be effective in
achieving their policy goals since bureaucracies are less vulnerable to
regulatory capture. Their alternative type, legislative policy design,
identifies legislatures as the actor designing implementation and
doing so subject to strong pressures from interest groups that result in
state capture. This obviously does not describe South Africa, where the
legislature is only a bit player, but it is compatible with a broader view
of the complications and ineffectiveness that arise when partisan and
political actors play a major role in energy and climate policy. Thus,
a similar contrast appears in a comparison of Brazil and South Africa as
in the California and Germany cases that Meckling and Nahm study,
otherwise very different cases.

6.4 Four Political Economies: Generalizable Drivers of Wind and Solar Power?

Moving on from the two core cases, this book is organized around four
policy sectors, or political economies, that oriented the expansion of
wind and solar power in early adopter countries. In this section, I take
them up in the order of the book's chapters, reflecting on how likely
they are to be relevant for promoting renewable energy transitions in
a larger set of countries. Since most countries in that larger set are
middle-income and developing countries, the Brazilian and South
African experiences may be more informative than those of earlier
developed country innovators. The policy outcomes of wind and
solar power will continue to vary between countries, however, as
countries apply very different, preexisting industrial and economic
strategies even to the same new industry (see also Lachapelle,
MacNeil, and Patterson 2017; Nahm 2017).

The need to address climate change (Chapter 2) can be a motivator
for building more wind and solar power capacity in countries around
the world. As the Intergovernmental Panel on Climate Change (IPCC)
has said, decarbonization is more feasible, faster in the electricity sector

than in any other sector, and the rapid development of wind and solar power production capacity is key to that (Intergovernmental Panel on Climate Change 2014: 20). There is little that is competitive about this process – wind and solar power expansion in one country does not reduce the capacity of others to also expand. Using wind and solar power to mitigate climate change also improves an important environmental justice outcome: future generations of humans and future ecosystems could face somewhat less global warming and have fewer adaptations to make to a problem that current and past generations are creating. The presence or absence of a strong actor(s) committed to a model of electricity generation based on fossil fuels will set a baseline expectation for how hard or easy it will be to realize these gains.

The two countries discussed here offer different caveats on how much to expect wind and solar power to help reduce GHG emissions. The South African case provides evidence that fossil fuel incumbents may now fight harder against a low-carbon transition than they did in the early-adopter European countries. In this, they would be more like their US counterparts (Hess 2014). It should be noted that Eskom is near the expected theoretical maximum in terms of the strength and motivation of such an actor. Few countries would have a large state-owned enterprise (SOE) that is a vertically controlled monopoly utility and almost entirely dependent on coal. In addition, it had developed deep and wide capacity in the electricity sector and was once considered an island of bureaucratic excellence. The Brazilian hydro-based system offers the seemingly unlikely possibility that expanding intermittent wind and solar power may actually increase GHG emissions from the electricity sector as gas and other thermal electric plants are added to balance the supply – at least until storage is cheaper and more readily available. This could also be true for other countries that are largely building out their grids now, even if wind and solar power are their primary sources of electricity.

Many countries cite the possibility of industry development as a key motivator for building wind and solar power (Chapter 3). They are rarely aiming for only an installation industry; they are also hoping for manufacturing jobs and even to be on the cutting edge of innovation (Aggarwal and Evenett 2012; Hess 2012; Pegels 2014b). Logically, only a small number of countries could ever have achieved a strong manufacturing position for export. The actual experiences of Brazil and South Africa, the most industrialized countries in their regions, also suggest that these ambitions are set too high. Only Brazilian wind power has achieved much localization at all, and it did so only by building on an established industrial and financial base. The prospects are even lower for most developing countries. The wind and solar industries require significant existing industrial capabilities (Schmidt and Huenteler 2016). As wind and solar power have developed, firms are increasingly drawn into global production networks that have little place for newcomers (Baker and Sovacool 2017; Meckling and Hughes 2018). Countries are actively protecting their national industries' positions through a growing number of challenges at the World Trade Organization (WTO) (Lewis 2014). Since jobs and related economic opportunities are a key component of addressing just transition claims, the weakness of the industrial policy political economy foreshadows significant transition upheavals with less compensation than hoped. In fact, proponents might be better served by lowering the expectations of labor and national capital for unlikely outcomes.

Writers on industrial policy generally assume, and even argue directly, that business opportunities in wind and solar power will widen support coalitions for energy transition (e.g., Meckling, Kelsey, Biber, and Zysman 2015). That appears to be true only when there is already strong support for market forces and private capital. In South Africa, introducing private power producers brought extra opposition, not support, to the renewable energy program. Brazil's labor unions also resisted bringing private firms into the electricity sector, although not as strongly. Mexico is yet another country where a market-skeptical president is now questioning wind and solar power because of the role of private capital and firms in the sector. Manuel Lopez Obrador raised the issue in his inauguration speech and canceled a procurement auction.[1] The appeal of private industrial growth is more of a variable than is often assumed.

For all countries, expanding wind and solar power generation looks more viable as generation costs are dropping (Chapter 4). Globally, average solar power prices dropped 80 percent between 2008 and 2017 while wind power prices fell by more than half (Bischof-Niemtz and Creamer 2019: 38). The global cost tipping point for renewables happened in around 2014, when they began to be competitive with

---

[1] www.windpowermonthly.com/article/1524666/mexico-cancels-clean-energy-auction-updated.

many other forms of new electricity generation (Bischof-Niemtz and Creamer 2019: 40). These cost developments followed from the willingness of countries like Germany to invest in and develop the technology at a time when their costs greatly exceeded measurable benefits. Those higher costs had made wind and solar power seem untenable for developing countries, creating a just transition dilemma with their unaffordability (Márquez and Rufín 2011). The falling costs were a major consideration for both Brazil and South Africa and are potentially widely relevant. This motivation even has a possible virtuous circle, as there appear to be substantial economies of scale for both production and installation that will further bring down prices.

It is worth noting, however, that the global averages are not the actual prices in most countries. Many of the political economies discussed in this book affect the costs of wind and solar power. The local content requirements in Chapter 3 and the taxes and subsidies discussed in Chapter 4 both tend to increase the costs of wind and solar power, or at least to affect their prices compared to prices of other sources of electricity. Both Brazil and South Africa chose to use auctions, which help to lower the costs of wind and solar power while working against the participation of local and small-scale producers (Leiren and Reimer 2018). Feed-in tariffs would yield higher prices. Other factors also affect costs, such as the availability and cost of appropriate land, the balance between grid-scale and off-grid generation, and whether wind and solar power themselves internalize the costs of just transition for phasing out fossil fuels. It also matters what the costs of the incumbent fuels and other alternatives are. So, in general, the steep drop in average generation costs provides a global stimulus to wind and solar power, but the details matter a great deal and there may be trade-offs between cost and other aims.

The development of wind and solar power has the potential to expand the consumer and self-generation options of populations around the world (Chapter 4). The ability to generate especially solar power at a small scale makes distributed generation possible in ways it has not been before. As others have noted, this is especially important for populations that still lack electricity, especially when they are in remote locations that distribution lines do not easily reach (Sovacool and Drupady 2012). Brazil and South Africa underline the potential limits to the quality of the resulting electricity provision, however. The rural electrification programs in both offer at best just a few hours of daily light, television or radio, and cell phone charging. South African consumers and analysts have been particularly vocal about that service being so inadequate that it is an environmental injustice (Monyei, Adewumi, and Jenkins 2018). Both countries also show the possibility that comparatively wealthy, urban consumers may be opting out of supporting consumer grids, and both are considering regulatory changes to address this possible utility death spiral.

Local communities often resist local grid-scale wind installations in early-adopter countries, even when they support renewable energy in principle (Chapter 5). Since their reasons are often objections about aesthetics, birdlife, and quality of life issues, it has not been clear whether developing country host communities will follow their lead. Brazil and South Africa provide rather mixed evidence, as communities resist many wind power plants in Brazil but rarely mobilize against solar power there; South Africa sees little mobilization of any kind from host communities. Certainly, scholars and advocates should not expect community opposition to necessarily pose a major brake on industry development. At the same time, both of these are comparatively large countries with low population density. They have large areas that are appropriate for wind and solar power development. If communities resist deployment in one location, there are plenty of others with good wind or solar resources. Smaller and denser countries with fewer siting options may see much more stress over siting plants, especially since wind and solar power require much more land than other alternatives (Scheidel and Sorman 2012). In addition, where land claims are informal or contested – including in Northeast Brazil – expanding wind and solar power may introduce significant new energy injustices and deepen the just transition challenge. Some scholars see community ownership or control as key to managing this dilemma (e.g., Bode 2013), but these two countries do not offer any direct evidence on this point.

On the interlocking national political economies, the dividing line seen between more bureaucratic and more partisan or politicized policy approaches could be a useful starting point for characterizing the variations in outcomes for energy transition more generally. The contrast between South Africa's powerful coal-committed utility Eskom, which is able to organize an active and combative coalition to support its opposition to the renewable energy program, and Brazil's more diverse and dispersed set of actors offers a possible analytical starting point for evaluating which outcome should be expected. I have suggested that this polarized model stems from the logic of the climate political economy, where the need to block and dismantle electricity from fossil fuels galvanized the opposition of its defenders. The presence of a powerful resister like Eskom, plausibly, is a necessary condition for that.

In policy terms, wind and solar power proponents in countries with an actor like Eskom should prepare for its resistance and the complex politics that follow, while those without can take advantage of the less polarized opportunities to explore technocratic solutions. More broadly, this book's focus on multiple political economies of energy transition points to the need to develop transition approaches like those in the emerging Green New Deal.[2] Sometimes criticized for raising contentious issues "unrelated" to climate change, the Green New Deal is actually also recognizing that multiple policy arenas and interest structures are engaged in building a broad-based coalition that will support extensive and quick transformations that will address climate change.

Finally, to return to academic agendas, this book's close focus on wind and solar power should not hide that it raises wider themes about national political economies. Scholars of energy and electricity in the advanced industrialized countries have shown that these sectors are integral to comparative investigations of regulatory models, innovation, sociotechnical systems and transitions between them, taxation systems, and a whole array of climate and environmental topics (e.g., Ansolabehere and Konisky 2014; Jacobsson and Lauber 2006; Stokes 2016; Valentine 2014; Verbong and Geels 2007). In contrast, studies of energy and electricity in the developing world have tended to restrict themselves to a small set of questions like utility privatization or the pathologies of oil and gas dependency. While these topics are important, the studies understate the influence of energy and electricity on many comparative political economy questions in middle-income and developing countries, and these sectors will be even more important in a world with a changing climate. This book should be just a first step toward investigating those impacts.

---

[2] https://ocasio-cortez.house.gov/sites/ocasio-cortez.house.gov/files/Resolution%20on%20a%20Green%20New%20Deal.pdf.

References

Aamodt, Solveig. 2018. The Ability to Influence: A Comparative Analysis of the Role of Advocacy Coalitions in Brazilian Climate Politics. *Review of Policy Research* 35(3): 372–397.

Aberbach, Joel D., and Rockman, Bert A. 2002. Conducting and Coding Elite Interviews. *PS: Political Science and Politics* 35(4): 673–676.

Abers, Rebecca. 2018. Conflitos, Mobilizações e a Participação Institucionalizada: A Relação entre a Sociedade Civil e a Construção de Grandes Obras de Infraestrutura. In *Governança da Política da Infraestrutura: Condicionantes Institucionais ao Investimento*, eds. Alexandre de Ávila Gomide and Ana Karine Pereira. Brasília: IPEA. 349–376.

Abers, Rebecca Naera, and Oliveira, Marília Silva de. 2015. Nomeações Políticas no Ministério do Meio Ambiente (2003–2013): Interconexões Entre ONGs, Partidos e Governos. *Opinião Pública* 21(2): 336–364.

ABINEE. 2012. *Propostas para Inserção da Energia Solar Fotovoltaico na Matriz Elétrica Brasileira*. Online at www.abinee.org.br/informac/arqui vos/profotov.pdf.

Abromovay, Ricardo. 2010. Decarbonizing the Growth Model of Brazil: Addressing Both Carbon and Emissions Intensity. *Journal of Environment and Development* 19(3): 358–374.

Abromovay, Ricardo. 2014. Innovations to Democratize Energy Access without Boosting Emissions. *Ambiente e Sociedade* 17(3): 1–18.

Acende Brasil and PricewaterhouseCoopers. 2016. *Estudo sobre a Carga Tributária & Encargos do Setor Elétrico Brasileiro, Ano Base 2015*. São Paulo: Acende Brasil.

Agência Brasileira de Desenvolvimento Industrial. 2014. *Mapping of Brazil's Wind Power Industry Productive Chain*. Brasília: Ministério de Desenvolvimento, Indústria e Comércio, Associação Brasileiro de Desenvolvimento Industrial.

Agência Brasileira de Desenvolvimento Industrial. 2018a. *Propostas de Aproveitamento do Potencial Brasileiro no Mercado da Energia Solar Fotovoltaica*. Brasília: Agência Brasileira de Desenvolvimento Industrial.

Agência Brasileira de Desenvolvimento Industrial. 2018b. *Plano Nacional de Desenvolvimento Setorial em Energia Eólica na Perspectiva da Industria.* Brasília: Agência Brasileira de Desenvolvimento Industrial.

Aggarwal, Vinod K., and Evenett, Simon J. 2012. Industrial Policy Choice During the Crisis Era. *Oxford Review of Economic Policy* 28(2): 261–283.

Agri, S.A. 2017. *Land Audit: A Transactions Approach.* Online in Archive at www.agrisa.co.za/coes.

Aitken, Mhairi, McDonald, Seonaidh, and Strachen, Peter. 2008. Locating "Power" in Wind Power Planning Processes: The (Not So) Influential Role of Local Objections. *Journal of Environmental Planning and Management* 51(6): 777–799.

Aitken, Robert, Thorne, John, Thorne, Steve, and Kruger, Wikus. n.d. *Sustainability of Decentralised Renewable Energy Systems Report.* Pretoria: Department of Environmental Affairs. Online at www.environment.gov.za/sites/default/files/reports/decentralised_renewableenergysystems_report.pdf.

Aklin, Michaël, Bayer, Patrick, Harish, S. P., and Urpelainen, Johannes. 2017. Does Basic Energy Access Generate Socioeconomic Benefits? A Field Experiment with Off-Grid Solar Power in India. *Science Advances* 3(5): e1602153.

Aklin, Michaël, and Urpelainen, Johannes. 2018. *Renewables: The Politics of a Global Energy Transition.* Cambridge, MA: MIT Press.

Aklin, Michaël, and Urpelainen, Johannes. 2013. Political Competition, Path Dependence, and the Strategy of Sustainable Energy Transitions. *American Journal of Political Science* 57(3): 643–658.

Aldrich, Daniel P. 2010. *Site Fights: Divisive Facilities and Civil Society in Japan and the West.* Ithaca: Cornell University Press.

Alexander, Peter. 2013. Marikana, Turning Point in South African History. *Review of African Political Economy* 40(138): 605–619.

Alexander, Peter, and Ffath, Peter. 2014. Social Relationships to the Means and Ends of Protest in South Africa's Ongoing Rebellion of the Poor: The Balfour Insurrections. *Social Movement Studies* 13(2): 204–221.

Amsden, Alice. 2001. *The Rise of "The Rest": Challenges to the West from Late-Industrializing Economies.* Oxford: Oxford University Press.

Ansolabehere, Stephen, and Konisky, David M. 2014. *Cheap and Clean: How Americans Think about Energy in the Age of Global Warming.* Cambridge, MA: MIT Press.

Araujó, Júlio César Holanda. 2016. Entre Expropriações e Resistências: A Implementação de Parques Eólicos na Zona Costeira do Ceará, Brasil. *Cadernos do CEAS* 237: 327–346.

Aronoff, Kate, Battistoni, Alyssa, Cohen, Daniel Aldana, and Riofrancos, Thea. 2019. *A Planet to Win: Why We Need a Green New Deal.* London and New York: Verso.

Aroun, Woodrajh. 2013. South Africa's Local Content Requirements: Are They Adequate for Creation of Local Manufacturing Capacities? Presentation at World Wind Energy Conference and Renewable Energy Exhibition, Havana, Cuba, June 3–5.

Aroun, Woodrajh. 2012. Climate Jobs and Manufacturing in South Africa. *International Journal of Labour Research* 4(2): 231–248.

Arruda de Almeida, Monica, and Zagaris, Bruce. 2015. Political Capture in the Petrobras Corruption Scandal: The Sad Tale of an Oil Giant. *Fletcher Forum of World Affairs* 39(2): 87–99.

Atwell, William. 2013. Broad-Based BEE? HCI's Empowerment Model and the Sindicalist Tradition. In *New South African Review 3: The Second Phase – Tragedy or Farce?* eds. J. Daniel, P. Naidoo, D. Pillay, and R. Southall. Johannesburg: Wits University Press. 138–153.

Avila, Sofia. 2018. Environmental Justice and the Expanding Geography of Wind Power Conflicts. *Sustainability Science* 13: 599–616.

Bäckstrand, Karin, and Kronsell, Annica. 2015. The Green State Revisited. In *Rethinking the Green State: Environmental Governance Toward Climate and Sustainability Transitions*, eds. K. Bäckstrand and A. Kronsell. London: Earthscan and Routledge. 1–23.

Baer, Werner. 1976. The Brazilian Growth and Development Experience: 1964–1975. In *Brazil in the Seventies*, ed. R. Roett. Washington, DC: American Enterprise Institute. 41–62.

Baitelo, Ricardo. 2012. Energias Renováveis: Eólica e Solar. In *O Setor Elétrico Brasileiro e a Sustentabilidade no Século 21: Oportunidades e Desafios*, 2nd edition, ed. Paula Franco Moreira. Brasília: International Rivers Network. 71–79.

Baker, Lucy. 2015a. Renewable Energy in South Africa's Minerals-Energy Complex: A "Low Carbon" Transition? *Review of African Political Economy* 42(144): 245–261.

Baker, Lucy. 2015b. The Evolving Role of Finance in South Africa's Renewable Energy Sector. *Geoforum* 64: 146–156.

Baker, Lucy, Newell, Peter, and Phillips, Jon. 2014. The New Political Economy of Energy Transitions: The Case of South Africa. *New Political Economy* 19(6): 791–818.

Baker, Lucy, and Phillips, Jon. 2018. Tensions in the Transition: The Politics of Electricity Distribution in South Africa. *Environment and Planning C: Politics and Space* 37(1): 177–196.

Baker, Lucy, and Sovacool, Benjamin. 2017. The Political Economy of Technological Capabilities and Global Production Networks in South Africa's Wind and Solar Photovoltaic (PV) Industries. *Political Geography* 60: 1–12.

Barbier, Edward B. 2010. *A Global Green New Deal: Rethinking the Economic Recovery*. Cambridge: Cambridge University Press and UNEP.

Barros, N., Cole, J. J., Tranvik, L. J., Prairie, Y. T., Bastviken, D., Huszar, V. L. M., Del Giorgio, P., and Roland, F. 2011. Carbon Emission from Hydroelectric Reservoirs Linked to Reservoir Age and Latitude. *Nature Geoscience* 4(9): 593–596.

Bayer, Benjamin. 2018. Experience with Auctions for Wind Power in Brazil. *Renewable and Sustainable Energy Reviews* 81: 2644–2658.

Bayer, Benjamin, Berthold, Lennart, and de Freitas, Bruno Moreno Rodrigo. 2018. The Brazilian Experience with Auctions for Wind Power: An Assessment of Project Delays and Potential Mitigation Measures. *Energy Policy* 122: 97–117.

Bayer, Benjamin, Schäuble, Dominik, and Ferrari, Michele. 2018. International Experiences with Tender Procedures for Renewable Energy: A Comparison of Current Developments in Brazil, France, Italy, and South Africa. *Renewable and Sustainable Energy Reviews* 95: 305–327.

Bayer, Patrick, and Urpelainen, Johannes. 2016. It Is All about Political Incentives: Democracy and the Renewable Feed-In Tariff. *Journal of Politics* 78(2): 603–619.

Beckmann, M. N., and Hall, R. L. 2013. Elite Interviewing in Washington, DC. In *Interview Research in Political Science*, ed. L. Mosley. Ithaca and London: Cornell University Press. 196–208.

Beresford, Alexander. 2012. Organised Labour and the Politics of Class Formation in Post-Apartheid South Africa. *Review of African Political Economy* 39(134): 569–589.

Berry, William D. 1984. An Alternative to the Capture Theory of Regulation: The Case of State Public Utility Commissions. *American Journal of Political Science* 28(3): 524–558.

Bersch, Katherine, Praça, Sérgio, and Taylor, Matthew M. 2017. State Capacity, Bureaucratic Politicization, and Corruption in the Brazilian State. *Governance* 30(1): 105–124.

Bezerra, M. H. M., Melo, C. S. M., Nunes, M. M. A., and Mesquita, T. P. N. 2013. Estudo Analítico do Processo Liciatório Ambiental para Empreendimentos Eólicos no Estado do Rio Grande do Norte. *HOLOS* 29(2): 34–49.

Bezerra, Paula, da Silveira, Borges, Callegari, Camila Ludovique, Ribas, Aline, Lucena, André F. P., Portugal-Pereira, Joana, Koberle, Alexandre, Szklo, Alexandre, and Schaeffer, Roberto. 2017. The Power of Light: Socio-economic and Environmental Implications of a Rural Electrification Program in Brazil. *Environmental Research Letters* 12: 1–14.

BirdLife. 2016. Birds and Solar Energy Best Practice Guidelines: Comments and Response Table. No longer available online; PDF in possession of this volume's author.

Bischof-Niemtz, Tobias, and Creamer, Terence. 2019. *South Africa's Energy Transition: A Roadmap to a Decarbonised, Low-Cost and Job-Rich Future*. New York and London: Routledge.

Blimpo, Moussa P., and Cosgrove-Davies, Malcolm. 2019. *Electricity Access in Sub-Saharan Africa: Uptake, Reliability, and Complementary Factors for Economic Impact*. Washington, DC: International Bank for Reconstruction and Development / The World Bank.

BNDES. 2018. *Green Bond: Relatório Anual 2018*. Rio de Janeiro: BNDES.

Böckler, Liss, and Pereira, Marcio Giannini. 2018. Consumer (Co-) Ownership in Renewables in Brazil. In *Energy Transition: Financing Consumer Co-Ownership in Renewables*, ed. Jens Lowitzsch. Cham: Palgrave Macmillan. 535–557.

Bode, Christiaan César. 2013. *An Analysis of Collective Ownership Models to Promote Renewable Energy Development and Climate Justice in South Africa*. Thesis presented in partial fulfillment of the requirements for the degree Master of Development and Management at the Potchefstroom campus of the North-West University.

Booysen, Susan. 2011. *The ANC and the Regeneration of Political Power*. Johannesburg: Witwatersrand University Press.

Booysen, Susan. 2007. With the Ballot and the Brick: The Politics of Attaining Service Delivery. *Progress in Development Studies* 7(1): 21–32.

Borland, Ralph, Morrell, Robert, and Watson, Vanessa. 2018. Southern Agency: Navigating Local and Global Imperatives in Climate Research. *Global Environmental Politics* 18(3): 47–65.

Bortscheller, Mary J. 2009–2010. Equitable but Ineffective: How the Principle of Common but Differentiated Responsibilities Hobbled the Global Fight Against Climate Change. *Sustainable Development Law and Policy* 10(2): 49–69.

Bouckaert, Geert, Peters, B. Guy, and Verhoest, Koen. eds. 2010. *The Coordination of Public Sector Organizations: Shifting Patterns of Public Management*. Basingstoke: Palgrave Macmillan.

Boyer, Véronique. 2014. Misnaming Social Conflict: "Identity," Land and Family Histories in a *Quilombola* Community in the Brazilian Amazon. *Journal of Latin American Studies* 46: 527–555.

Braathen, Einar. 2015. Passive Revolution? Social and Political Struggles Surrounding Brazil's New-Found Oil Reservoirs. In *Contested Powers: The Politics of Energy and Development in Latin America*, eds. J. McNeish, A. Borchgrevink, and O. Logan. London: Zed Books. 195–215.

Bradshaw, Amanda L. 2018. Electricity Market Reforms and Renewable Energy: The Case of Wind and Solar in Brazil. New York: PhD Dissertation, Columbia University Program in Urban Planning.

Bragagnolo, C., Lemos, C., Ladle, R. J., and Pellin, A. 2017. Streamlining or Sidestepping? Political Pressure to Revise Environmental Licensing and EIA in Brazil. *Environmental Impact Assessment Review* 65: 86–90.

Brannstrom, Christian, Gorayeb, Adryane, de Souza Mendes, Jocicléa, Loureiro, Caroline, de Andrade Meireles, Antonio Jeovah, da Silva, Edson Vicente, Ribeiro de Freitas, Ana Larissa, and de Oliveira, Rafael Fialho. 2017. Is Brazilian Wind Power Development Sustainable? Insights from a Review of Conflicts in Ceará State. *Renewable and Sustainable Energy Reviews* 67: 62–71.

Brass, Jennifer N., Carley, Sanya, MacLean, Lauren M., and Baldwin, Elizabeth. 2012. Power for Development: A Review of Distributed Generation Projects in the Developing World. *Annual Review of Environment and Resources* 37: 107–136.

Bratman, Eve Z. 2014. Contradiction of Green Development: Human Rights and Environmental Norms in Light of Belo Monte Dam Activism. *Journal of Latin American Studies* 46(2): 261–289.

Breetz, Hanna, Mildenberger, Matto, and Stokes, Leah. 2018. The Political Logics of Clean Energy Transitions. *Business and Politics* 20(Special Issue4): 492–522.

Brower Brown, Keith. 2011. Wind Power in Northeastern Brazil: Local Burdens, Regional Benefits and Growing Opposition. *Climate and Development* 3: 344–360.

Brown, David S., and Mobarak, Ahmed Mushfiq. 2009. The Transforming Power of Democracy: Regime Type and the Distribution of Electricity. *American Political Science Review* 103(2): 193–213.

Brown, Jason P., Pender, John, Wiser, Ryan, Lantz, Eric, and Hoen, Ben. 2012. Ex Post Analysis of Economic Impacts from Wind Power Development in U.S. Counties. *Energy Economics* 34: 1743–1754.

Buhlungu, Sakhela, and Bezuidenhuit, Andrïes. 2008. Union Solidarity Under Stress: The Case of the National Union of Mineworkers in South Africa. *Labor Studies Journal* 33(3): 262–287.

Bulkeley, Harriet, Andonova, Liliana B., Betsill, Michele M., Compagnon, Daniel, Hale, Thomas, Hoffmann, Matthew J., Newell, Peter, Paterson, Matthew, Roger, Charles, Vandeveer, Stacy D. 2014. *Transnational Climate Change Governance*. Cambridge: Cambridge University Press.

Burke, Matthew J., and Stephens, Jennie C. 2018. Political Power and Renewable Energy Futures: A Critical Review. *Energy Research and Social Sciences* 35: 78–93.

Burrier, Grant. 2016. The Developmental State, Civil Society, and Hydroelectric Politics in Brazil. *Journal of Environment and Development* 25(3): 332–358.

Caldecott, Ben. 2017. Introduction to Special Issue: Stranded Assets and the Environment. *Journal of Sustainable Finance and Investment* 7(1): 1–13.

Campbell, Maléne, Nel, Verna, and Mphambukeli, Thulisile. 2017. A Thriving Coal Mining City in Crisis? The Governance and Spatial Planning Challenges at Witbank, South Africa. *Land Use Policy* 62: 223–231.

Carter, Miguel. 2015. Social Inequality, Agrarian Reform, and Democracy in Brazil. In *Challenging Social Inequality: The Landless Rural Workers Movement and Agrarian Reform in Brazil*, ed. M. Carter. Durham: Duke University Press. 1–41.

Carter, Miguel, and de Carvalho, Horacio Martins. 2015. The Struggle on the Land: Source of Growth, Innovation, and Constant Challenge for the MST. In *Challenging Social Inequality: The Landless Rural Workers Movement and Agrarian Reform in Brazil*, ed. M. Carter. Durham: Duke University Press. 229–273.

Carvalho, Fernanda Viana de. 2012. The Brazilian Position on Forests and Climate Change from 1997 to 2012: From Veto to Proposition. *Revista Brasileira de Política Internacional* 55(Special Edition): 144–169.

Castaneda, Monica, Franco, Carlos J., and Dyner, Isaac. 2017. Evaluating the Effect of Technology Transformation in the Electricity Utility Industry. *Renewable and Sustainable Energy Reviews* 80: 341–351.

Castro, Camila Moreira de. 2013. Public Hearings as a Tool to Improve Participation in Regulatory Policies: Case Study of the National Agency of Electric Energy. *Revista de Administração Pública* 47(5): 1069–1087.

CEBDS. 2018. *Financiamento a Energia Renovável: Entraves, Desafios e Oportunidades*. Rio de Janeiro: Conselho Empresarial Brasileiro para o Desenvolvimento Sustentável.

Centre for Environmental Rights. 2017. *Broken Promises: The Failure of the Highveld Priority Area*. South Africa: Centre for Environmental Rights, Groundwork, and the Highveld Environmental Justice Network. Online at cer.org.za/wp-content/uploads/2017/09/Broken-Pro mises-full-report_final.pdf.

Centro de Gestão e Estudos Estratégicos. 2015. *Programa Demonstrativo para Inovação em Cadeia Produtiva Selecionada: Energia Eólica*. Brasília: Centro de Gestão e Estudos Estratégicos.

Chandrashekeran, Sangeetha, Morgan, Bronwen, Coetzee, Kim, and Christoff, Peter. 2017. Rethinking the Green State Beyond the Global North: A South African Climate Change Case Study. *WIREs Climate Change* e473: 1–14.

Chen, Geoffrey C., and Lees, Charles. 2016. Growing China's Renewables Sector: A Developmental State Approach. *New Political Economy* 21(6): 574–584.

Chipkin, Ivor, and Swilling, Mark. 2017. *Shadow State: The Politics of State Capture*. Johannesburg: Wits University Press.

Cingolani, Luciana, Thomsson, Kaj, and de Crombrugghe., Denis. 2015. Minding Weber More than Eve? The Impacts of State Capacity and Bureaucratic Autonomy on Development Goals. *World Development* 72: 191–207.

Cloete, Karl. 2018. Coal Jobs, Independent Power Producers (IPPs) and Energy Sovereignty: A Numsa Perspective. *South African Labour Bulletin* 42(3): 4–6.

Cock, Jacklyn. 2012. South African Labour's Response to Climate Change: The Threat of Green Neoliberal Capitalism. In *Labour in the Global South: Challenges and Alternatives for Workers*, eds. S. Mosoetsa and M. Williams. Geneva: International Labour Office.

Conrad, Björn. 2012. China in Copenhagen: Reconciling the "Beijing Climate Revolution" and the "Copenhagen Climate Obstinacy." *The China Quarterly* 210: 435–455.

Copena, Damián, and Simón, Xavier. 2018. Wind Farms and Payments to Landowners: Opportunities for Rural Development for the Case of Galicia. *Renewable and Sustainable Energy Reviews* 95: 38–47.

COSATU. 2017. Notice to NEDLAC about Possible Protest Action, MRA Form 4.4, 21 June 2017. Online at www.ee.co.za/wp-content/uploads/20 17/07/LPC-Circular-No.38.2017-Attachment-Cosatu-S77-Notice.pdf.

Cosbey, Aaron. 2013. Green Industrial Policy and the World Trading System. ENTWINED Issue Brief 17, 10/30/2013. Online at www .iisd.org/pdf/2013/entwined_brief_green_industrial.pdf.

Costa, Márcio Macedo da, Cohen, Claude, and Schaeffer, Roberto. 2007. Social Features of Energy Production and Use in Brazil: Goals for a Sustainable Energy Future. *Natural Resources Forum* 31: 11–20.

Cousins, Ben, and Hall, Ruth. 2014. Rural Land Tenure: The Potential and Limits of Rights-Based Approaches. In *Socio-economic Rights in South Africa: Symbols or Substance?* eds. M. Langford, B. Cousins, J. Dugard, and T. Madlingozi. New York: Cambridge University Press. 157–186.

Da Silva, Gardenio Diogo Pimental, Magrini, Alessandra, Tolmasquim, Maurício Tiomno, and Castelo Branco, David Alves. 2019. Environmental Licensing and Energy Policy Regulating Utility-Scale Solar

Photovoltaic Installations in Brazil: Status and Future Perspectives. *Impact Assessment and Project Appraisal* 37(6): 503–515.

Dear, Michael. 1992. Understanding and Overcoming the NIMBY Syndrome. *Journal of the American Planning Association* 58(3): 288–300.

Death, Carl. 2016. *The Green State in Africa*. New Haven: Yale University Press.

Death, Carl. 2014. Environmental Movements, Climate Change, and Consumption in South Africa. *Journal of Southern African Studies* 40(6): 1215–1234.

Deedat, Hameda. 2018. Climate Change, the Just Transition and Life Beyond Coal. *South African Labour Bulletin* 42(3): 10–12.

De Kadt, Daniel, and Lieberman, Evan S. 2020. Nuanced Accountability: Voter Responses to Service Delivery in Southern Africa. *British Journal of Political Science* 50(1): 185–215.

Delina, Laurence L. 2017. *Accelerating Sustainable Energy Transition(s) in Developing Countries: The Challenges of Climate Change and Sustainable Development*. New York: Routledge.

Department of Energy. 2019b. Integrated Resource Plan for Electricity (IRP) 2010–2030, October 2019. Pretoria: Department of Energy.

Department of Energy. 2019a. Integrated Resource Plan for Electricity (IRP) 2010–2030, March 2019. Pretoria: Department of Energy.

Department of Energy. 2018. Integrated Resource Plan for Electricity (IRP) 2010–2030, August 2018. Pretoria: Department of Energy.

Department of Energy. 2017. Integrated Resource Plan for Electricity (IRP) 2010–2030, November 2017. Pretoria: Department of Energy.

Department of Energy. 2016. Integrated Resource Plan Update, November 2016. Pretoria: Department of Energy.

Department of Energy. 2015. Renewable Energy IPP Procurement Programme, Bid Window 4, Preferred Bidders' Announcement. Online at www.sapvia.co.za/wp-content/uploads/2015/04/Renewables_IPP_Procur ementProgramme_WindowFourAnnouncement-Apr-2015.pdf.

Department of Energy. 2013. Integrated Resource Plan for Electricity (IRP) 2010–2030 Update Report 2013, November 2013. Pretoria: Department of Energy.

Department of Energy. 2012. Non Grid Electrification Policy Guidelines. Online at www.energy.gov.za/files/policies/electrification/Non-Grid-Policy-Guidelines-for-INEP.pdf.

Department of Energy. 2011. Integrated Resource Plan for Electricity, 2010–2030, May 2011. Pretoria: Department of Energy.

Department of Environmental Affairs. 2018. Climate Change Bill, 2018 [Draft]. *Government Gazette* 8 June 2018, No. 41689: 4–39.

Department of Environmental Affairs. 2015. Strategic Environmental Assessment for wind and solar photovoltaic energy in South Africa. Stellenbosch: CSIR Report Number: CSIR/CAS/EMS/ER/2015/0001/B.

Department of Environmental Affairs. 2014. GHG Inventory for South Africa 2000–2010. Pretoria: Department of Environmental Affairs.

Department of Environmental Affairs. 2011. National Climate Change Response White Paper. Pretoria: Department of Environmental Affairs.

Department of Environmental Affairs and Tourism. 2010. Review of Efficiency and Effectiveness of EIA in South Africa. Online at www.environment.co.za/environmental-laws-and-legislation-in-south-africa/review-of-the-effectiveness-and-efficiency-of-eia.html.

Department of Minerals and Energy. 1998. White Paper on the Energy Policy of the Republic of South Africa. Pretoria: Department of Minerals and Energy.

Department of Planning, Monitoring and Evaluation. 2017. Final Impact Assessment (Phase 2) Climate Change Bill. Pretoria: Department of Planning, Monitoring and Evaluation.

DIEESE – Departamento Intersindical de Estatística e Estudos Socioeconômicos. 2015. Comportamento das Tarifas de Energia Elétrica no Brasil, Nota Técnica 147. São Paulo: DIEESE.

Downie, Christian. 2018. Ad Hoc Coalitions in the US Energy Sector: Case Studies in the Gas, Oil, and Coal Sectors. *Business and Politics* 20(Special Issue4): 643–668.

Downie, Christian and Williams, Marc. 2018. After the Paris Agreement: What Role for the BRICS in Global Climate Governance? *Global Policy* 9 (3): 398–407.

Duarte, C. G., Dibo, A. P. A., and Sánchez, Luis E. 2017. What Does the Academic Research Say about Impact Assessment and Environmental Licensing in Brazil? *Ambiente e Sociedade* 20(1): 261–292.

Dubash, Navroz K. 2013. The Politics of Climate Change in India: Narratives of Equity and Cobenefits. *WIRES: Climate Change* 4: 191–201.

Dugard, Jackie. 2014. Urban Basic Services: Rights, Reality, and Resistance. In *Socio-economic Rights in South Africa: Symbols or Substance?* eds. M. Langford, B. Cousins, J. Dugard, and R. Madlingozi. Cambridge: Cambridge University Press. 275–309.

Duit, Andreas. 2016. The Four Faces of the Environmental State: Environmental Governance Regimes in 28 States. *Environmental Politics* 25(1): 69–91.

Dunlap, Alexander. 2019. *Renewing Destruction: Wind Energy Development, Conflict and Resistance in a Latin American Context.* London: Rowman & Littlefield International.

Dutra, Ricardo Marques, and Szklo, Alexandre Salem. 2008. Incentive Policies for Promoting Wind Power Production in Brazil: Scenarios for the Alternative Energy Sources Inventive Program. *Renewable Energy* 33 (1): 65–76.

Earl, Jennifer, Martin, Andrew, McCarthy, John D., and Soule, Sarah A. 2004. The Use of Newspaper Data in the Study of Collective Action. *Annual Review of Sociology*, 30: 65–80.

Eberhard, Anton. 2007. The Political Economy of Power Sector Reform in South Africa. In *The Political Economy of Power Sector Reform: The Experiences of Five Major Developing Countries*, eds. D. Victor and T. C. Heller. Cambridge: Cambridge University Press. 215–253.

Eberhard, Anton, Kolker, Joel, and Leigland, James. 2014. South Africa's Renewable Energy IPP Procurement Program: Success Factors and Lessons. Washington, DC: World Bank Group, Public-Private Infrastructure Advisory Facility Report, May 2014.

Economic Development Department. 2011. *New Growth Path: Accord 4 Green Economy Accord*. Online at www.economic.gov.za/communica tions/publications/green-economy-accord.

Edomah, Norbert. 2020. *Electricity and Energy Transition in Nigeria*. London: Routledge.

Electricity Governance Initiative of South Africa. 2013. *Smart Electricity Planning Report*. Cape Town: Electricity Governance Initiative of South Africa.

Eletrobras. 2017. Especificações Técnicas dos Programas para Atendimento as Regiões Remotas dos Sistemas Isolados no Ambito do Programa Luz para Todos. Brasília: Ministério de Minas e Energia.

Empresa de Pesquisa Energética. 2006. A Questão Socioambiental no Planejamento da Expansão da Oferta de Energia Elétrica. Rio de Janeiro: Empresa de Pesquisa Energética.

Empresa de Pesquisa Energética. 2012a. Análise da Inserção da Geração Solar na Matriz Elétrica Brasileira. Rio de Janeiro: Empresa de Pesquisa Energética, EPE Nota Técnica, May 2012.

Empresa de Pesquisa Energética. 2012b. Metodologia para a Análise Socioambiental Integrada, Nota Técnica DEA 19/12, Série Estudos do Plano Decenal de Expansão de Energia. Rio de Janeiro: Empresa de Pesquisa Energética.

Empresa de Pesquisa Energética. 2014a. *Leilão de Energia de Reserva de 2014: Participação dos Empreendimentos Solares Fotovoltaicos: Visao Geral*. Rio de Janeiro: Empresa de Pesquisa Energética, Nota EPE-DEE-NT-150/2014-r0. Online at www.epe.gov.br/leiloes/Documents/Leil_es% 202014/NT_EPE-DEE-NT-150_2014.pdf.

Empresa de Pesquisa Energética. 2014b. *Demanda da Energia 2050, Série Estudos de Demanda da Energia, Nota Técnica dea [sic] 13/14*. Rio de Janeiro: Empresa de Pesquisa Energética, August 2014.

EScience Associates, Urban-Econ, and Ahlfeldt, Chris. 2013. *The Localisation Potential of Photovoltaics (PV) and a Strategy to Support Large Scale Roll-Out in South Africa, Integrated Report Draft Final v1.2*. Johannesburg: SAPVIA. Online at https://resources.solarbusinesshub.co m/solar-industry-reports/item/photovoltaic-electricity-the-localisation-po tential-of-photovoltaics-and-a-strategy-to-support-the-large-scale-roll-ou t-in-south-africa.

Esping-Andersen, Gøsta. 1990. *The Three Worlds of Welfare Capitalism*. Princeton: Princeton University Press.

Esposito, Alexandre Siciliano. 2010. Contexto e Panorama dos Investimentos no Setor Elétrico Brasileiro. In *Perspectivas do Investimento 2010–2013*, ed. BNDES. Rio de Janeiro: BNDES. Online at www.bndes.gov.br/SiteBNDES/export/sites/default/bndes_pt/Galerias/Ar quivos/conhecimento/liv_perspectivas/07_Perspectivas_do_Investiment o_2010_13_SETOR_ELETRICO.pdf.

Evans, Peter. 1979. *Dependent Development: The Alliance of Multinational, State, and Local Capital in Brazil*. Princeton: Princeton University Press.

Evans, Peter. 1995. *Embedded Autonomy: States and Industrial Transformation*. Princeton: Princeton University Press.

Evans, Peter B., Rueschemeyer, Dietrich, and Skocpol, Theda. eds. 1985. *Bringing the State Back In*. Cambridge: Cambridge University Press.

Fakir, Saliem. 2017. Transition Realism: The Implications of Rent-Seeking to Achieve South Africa's Low-Carbon Technology Ambition. Cape Town: WWF South Africa. Online at www.wwf.org.za/energy/report/tran sition-realism.

Fearnside, Phillip. 2002. Greenhouse Gas Emissions from a Hydroelectric Reservoir (Brazil's Tucuruí Dam) and the Energy Policy Implications. *Water, Air, and Soil Pollution* 133(1–4): 69–96.

Ferreira, Wilinton Conte. 2017. *Política de Conteúdo Local e Energía Eólica: A Experiência Brasileira*. PhD Dissertation, Universidade Federal Fluminese, Centro de Estudos Sociais Aplicados, Faculdade de Economia.

Fine, Ben, and Rustomjee, Zavareh. 1996. *The Political Economy of South Africa: From Minerals Complex to Industrialisation*. London: C. Hurst & Co.

Frankfurt School-UNEP Centre/BNEF. 2019. *Global Trends in Renewable Energy Investment 2019*. Online at wedocs.unep.org/bitstream/handle/20 .500.11822/29752/GTR2019.pdf?sequence=1&isAllowed=y.

Frate, Claudio Albuquerque, and Brannstrom, Christian. 2017. Stakeholder Subjectivities Regarding Barriers and Drivers to the Introduction of Utility-Scale Photovoltaic Power in Brazil. *Energy Policy* 111: 346–352.

French, Jan Hoffman. 2009. *Legalizing Identities: Becoming Black or Indian in Brazil's Northeast*. Chapel Hill: University of North Carolina Press.

Gallagher, Kelly Sims. 2013. Why & How Governments Support Renewable Energy. *Daedalus, the Journal of the American Academy of Arts and Sciences* 142(1): 59–77.

Gallagher, Kelly Sims, Anadon, Laura Diaz, Kempener, Ruud, and Wilson, Charlie. 2011. Trends in Investments in Global Energy Research, Development, and Demonstration. *WIREs Climate Change* 2 (May/June): 373–396.

Garcez, Catherine Aliana Gucciardi. 2015. Políticas de Geração Distribuida e Sustentabilidade do Sistema Elétrico. PhD Dissertation. Universidade de Brasília: Centro de Desenvolvimento Sustentável.

García, Jorge H., Cherry, Todd L., Kallbekken, Steffen, and Torvanger, Asbjørn. 2016. Willingness to Accept Local Wind Energy Development: Does the Compensation Mechanism Matter? *Energy Policy* 99: 165–173.

Gay, Robert. 1990. Neighborhood Associations and Political Change in Rio de Janeiro. *Latin American Research Review* 25(1): 102–118.

Geels, Frank W. 2014. Regime Resistance Against Low-Carbon Transitions: Introducing Politics and Power into the Multi-level Perspective. *Theory, Culture & Society* 31(5): 21–40.

Geels, Frank W. 2004. From Sectoral Systems of Innovation to Socio-technical Systems: Insights about Dynamics and Change from Sociology and Institutional Theory. *Research Policy* 33(6–7): 897–920.

Geels, Frank W. 2002. Technological Transitions As Evolutionary Reconfiguration Processes: A Multi-level Perspective and a Case-Study. *Research Policy* 31(8–9): 1257–1274.

George, Alexander, and Bennett, Andrew. 2005. *Case Studies and Theory Development in the Social Sciences*. Cambridge, MA: MIT Press.

Gibbs, Holly K., Munger, Jacob, L'Roe, Jessica, Barreto, Paulo, Pereira, Ritaumaria, Christie, Matthew, Amaral, Ticiana, and Walker, Nathalie F. 2016. Letter: Did Ranchers and Slaughterhouses Respond to Zero-Deforestation Agreements in the Brazilian Amazon? *Conservation Letters* 9(1): 32–42.

Gibbs, Holly K., Rausch, L., Munger, J., Schelly, I., Morton, D. C., Noojipady, P., … Walker, N. F. 2015. Brazil's Soy Moratorium. *Science* 347(6220): 377–378.

Gilley, Bruce. 2012. Authoritarian Environmentalism and China's Response to Climate Change. *Environmental Politics* 21(2): 287–307.

Giordano, Thierry, Hall, Leonie, Gilder, Andrew, and Parramon, Marie. 2011. *Governance of Climate Change in South Africa*. Pretoria: Department of Environmental Affairs. Online at www.environment.gov.za/sites/default/file s/docs/climate_change_governance.pdf.

Glasson, John, Therivel, Riki, and Chadwick, Andrew. 2012. *Introduction to Environmental Impact Assessment*, 4th edition. London and New York: Routledge.

Goldemberg, José. 1998. Leapfrog Energy Technologies. *Energy Policy* 26 (10): 729–741.

Golden, Miriam A., and Min, Brian. 2013. Distributive Politics Around the World. *Annual Review of Political Science* 16: 73–99.

Gorayeb, Adryane, and Brannstrom, Christian. 2016. Toward Participatory Management of Renewable Energy Resources (Wind-Farm) in Northeastern Brazil. *Mercator* 15(1): 101–115.

Gorayeb, Adryane, Brannstrom, Christian, de Andrade Meireles, Antonio Joevah, and de Souza Mendes, Josicléa. 2018. Wind Power Gone Bad: Critiquing Wind Power Planning Processes in Northeastern Brazil. *Energy Research and Social Science* 40: 82–88.

Government of South Africa. 2000. Initial National Communication under the United Nations Framework Convention on Climate Change. Online at unfccc.int/resource/docs/natc/zafnc01.pdf.

Governo do Brasil. 2003. *Diretrizes de Política Industrial, Tecnológico e de Comércio Exterior*. Brasília: Governo Luiz Inácio Lula da Silva.

Graffy, Elisabeth, and Kihm, Steven. 2014. Does Disruptive Competition Mean a Death Spiral for Electric Utilities? *Energy Law Journal* 35: 1–44.

Grashof, Katherina. 2019. Are Auctions Likely to Deter Community Wind Projects? And Would This Be Problematic? *Energy Policy* 125: 20–32.

Gratwick, Katharine Nawaal, and Eberhard, Anton. 2008. Demise of the Standard Model for Power Sector Reform and the Emergence of Hybrid Power Markets. *Energy Policy* 36 (10): 3948–3960.

Greenpeace Brasil. 2016a. *Damning the Amazon: The Risky Business of Hydropower in the Amazon*. Online at www.researchgate.net/publica tion/335330392_Damning_the_Amazon_The_Risky_Business_of_Hydro power_in_the_Amazon.

Greenpeace Brasil. 2016b. *Alvorada: Como o Incentivo a Energia Solar Fotovoltaica pode Transformar o Brasil*.

groundWork. 2018. *Coal Kills: Research and Dialogue for a Just Transition*. Pietermaritzburg: groundWork.

Hadden, Jennifer. 2015. *Networks in Contention: The Divisive Politics of Climate Change*. Cambridge: Cambridge University Press.

Haggard, Stephan, and Kaufman, Robert R. 2008. *Development, Democracy, and Welfare States: Latin America, East Asia, and Eastern Europe*. Princeton: Princeton University Press.

Hallowes, David. 2015. *The groundWork Report 2015: Climate and Energy, Part three of the Peoples' Power Series*. Online at www .groundwork.org.za/reports/gW%20Report%202015.pdf.

Harris, Tom, Collinson, Mark, and Wittenberg, Martin. 2017. Aiming for a Moving Target: The Dynamics of Household Electricity Connections in a Developing Context. *World Development* 94(9): 14–26.

Healy, Noel, and Barry, John. 2017. Politicising Energy Justice and Energy System Transitions: Fossil Fuel Divestment and a "Just Transition." *Energy Policy* 108: 451–459.

Heller, Patrick. 2019. Divergent Trajectories of Democratic Deepening: Comparing Brazil, India, and South Africa. *Theory and Society* 48(3): 351–382.

Henisz, Witold J., and Zelner, Bennet A. 2006. Interest Groups, Veto Points, and Electricity Infrastructure Deployment. *International Organization* 60 (1): 263–286.

Henrique, Artur. 2012. *CUT: Um Olhar de 2006 a 2012*. Online at www .spbancarios.com.br/Uploads/PDFS/251_livro_artur_cut.pdf.

Hess, David J. 2018. Energy Democracy and Social Movements: A Multi-coalition Perspective on the Politics of Sustainability Transitions. *Energy Research and Social Science* 40: 177–189.

Hess, David J. 2014. Sustainability Transitions: A Political Coalition Perspective. *Research Policy* 43: 278–283.

Hess, David J. 2012. *Good Green Jobs in a Global Economy: Making and Keeping New Industries in the United States*. Cambridge, MA: MIT Press.

Hochstetler, Kathryn. 2018. Environmental Impact Assessment: Evidence-Based Policy-Making in Brazil. *Contemporary Social Science* 13(2): 100–111.

Hochstetler, Kathryn. 2017. Tracking Presidents and Policies: Environmental Policies from Lula to Dilma. *Policy Studies* 38(3): 262–276.

Hochstetler, Kathryn. 2012. Climate Rights and Obligations for Emerging States: The Cases of Brazil and South Africa. *Social Research* 79(4): 957–982.

Hochstetler, Kathryn. 2008. Organized Civil Society in Lula's Brazil. In *Democratic Brazil Revisited*, eds. P. Kingstone and T. Power, Pittsburgh: University of Pittsburgh Press. 33–53.

Hochstetler, Kathryn, and Keck, Margaret E. 2007. *Greening Brazil: Environmental Activism in State and Society*. Durham: Duke University Press.

Hochstetler, Kathryn, and Kostka, Genia. 2015. Wind and Solar Power in Brazil and China: Interests, State-Business Relations, and Policy Outcomes. *Global Environmental Politics* 15(3): 74–94.

Hochstetler, Kathryn, and Montero, Alfred P. 2013. The Renewed Developmental State: The National Development Bank and the Brazil Model. *Journal of Development Studies* 49(11): 1484–1499.

Hochstetler, Kathryn, and Ricardo Tranjan J. 2016. Environment and Consultation in the Brazilian Democratic Developmental State. *Comparative Politics* 48(4): 497–516.

Hochstetler, Kathryn, and Viola, Eduardo. 2012. Brazil and the Politics of Climate Change: Beyond the Global Commons. *Environmental Politics* 21 (5): 753–771.

Huber, Evelyne, and Stephens, John D. 2012. *Democracy and the Left: Social Policy and Inequality in Latin America*. Chicago: University of Chicago Press.

Huberty, Mark. 2014. Motivating Green Growth: The Political Economy of Energy Systems Transformation. In *Can Green Sustain Growth: From the Religion to the Reality of Sustainable Prosperity*, eds. J. Zysman and M. Huberty. Stanford: Stanford Business Books.

Huesca-Pérez, María Helena, Sheinbaum-Pardo, Claudia, and Köppel, Johann. 2016. Social Implications of Siting Wind Energy in a Disadvantaged Region: The Case of the Isthmus of Tehuantepec, Mexico. *Renewable and Sustainable Energy Reviews* 58: 952–965.

Hughes, Llewelyn, and Lipscy, Phillip Y. 2013. The Politics of Energy. *Annual Review of Political Science* 16: 449–469.

Hughes, Llewelyn, and Urpelainen, Johannes. 2015. Interests, Institutions, and Climate Policy: Explaining the Choice of Policy Instruments for the Energy Sector. *Environmental Science and Policy* 54: 52–63.

Hunter, Wendy. 2014. Making Citizens: Brazilian Social Policy from Getúlio to Lula. *Journal of Politics in Latin America* 6(3): 15–37.

Hunter, Wendy. 2010. *The Transformation of the Workers' Party in Brazil, 1989–2009*. Cambridge: Cambridge University Press.

ICMBio (Instituto Chico Mendes de Conservação da Biodiversidade). 2016. *Relatório Anual de Rotas e Áreas de Concentração de Aves Migratórios no Brasil 2016*. Brasília: ICMBio.

ICMBio (Instituto Chico Mendes de Conservação da Biodiversidade). 2014. *Relatório Anual de Rotas e Áreas de Concentração de Aves Migratórios no Brasil 2014*. Brasília: ICMBio.

INESC. 2018. *Subsídios aos Combustíveis Fósseis no Brasil: Conhecer, Avaliar, Reformar*. Brasília: INESC.

Instituto Clima e Sociedade. 2018. Relatório Anual 2017. Online at http://ics .climaesociedade.org/relatorio2017/.

Instituto Energia e Meio Ambiente. 2018a. A Termoeletricidade no Novo Contexto do Setor Elétrico: A Importância da Avaliação de Impactos Ambientais. São Paulo: Instituto Energia e Meio Ambiente.

Instituto Energia e Meio Ambiente. 2018b. Acesso aos Serviços de Energia Elétrica nas Comunidades Isoladas da Amazônia: Mapeamento Jurídico-Institucional. São Paulo: Instituto Energia e Meio Ambiente.

Instituto Escolhas. 2018. *What Are the Real Costs and Benefits of Electric Power Generation Sources in Brazil?* São Paulo: Institute Escolhas.

Intergovernmental Panel on Climate Change. 2000. *Emissions Scenarios.* Cambridge: Cambridge University Press. Online at www.ipcc.ch/site/asse ts/uploads/2018/03/emissions_scenarios-1.pdf.

Intergovernmental Panel on Climate Change. 2014. Summary for Policymakers. In *Climate Change 2014: Mitigation of Climate Change. Contribution of Working Group III to the Fifth Assessment Report of the Intergovernmental Panel on Climate Change*, eds. O. Edenhofer, R. Pichs-Madruga, Y. Sokona, E. Farahani, S. Kadner, K. Seyboth, A. Adler, I. Baum, S. Brunner, P. Eickemeier, B. Kriemann, J. Savolainen, S. Schlömer, C. von Stechow, T. Zwickel, and J. C. Minx. Cambridge and New York: Cambridge University Press. Online at www.ipcc.ch/site/assets/uploads/2018/02/ipcc_wg3_ar5_summary-for-policymakers.pdf.

Intergovernmental Panel on Climate Change. 2018. *Special Report on Global Warming of IPCC 1.5°C.* Online at www.ipcc.ch/sr15/.

International Energy Agency. 2018. *World Energy Outlook 2018.* Paris: OECD and International Energy Agency.

International Renewable Energy Agency (IRENA). 2018. *Renewable Energy and Jobs: Annual Review 2018.* Online at www.irena.org/publications/2 018/May/Renewable-Energy-and-Jobs-Annual-Review-2018.

International Renewable Energy Agency (IRENA). 2017. *Renewable Energy and Jobs: Annual Review 2017.*

International Renewable Energy Agency (IRENA). 2016a. *IRENA 2014–2015: At a Glance.* Online at www.irena.org/menu/index.aspx? mnu=Subcat&PriMenuID=36&CatID=141&SubcatID=689.

International Renewable Energy Agency (IRENA). 2016b. *Renewable Energy and Jobs: Annual Review 2016.*

International Renewable Energy Agency (IRENA). 2015. *Renewable Energy and Jobs: Annual Review 2015.*

Jacobi, Pedro R. 1987. Movimentos Sociais Urbanos numa Época de Transição: Limites e Potencialidades. In *Movimentos Sociais na Transição Democrática*, ed. E. Sader. São Paulo: Cortez Editora. 11–23.

Jacobsson, Staffan, and Lauber, Volkmar. 2006. The Politics and Policy of Energy System Transformation: Explaining the German Diffusion of Renewable Energy Technology. *Energy Policy* 34: 256–276.

Johnson, O., Altenburg, T., and Schmitz, H. 2014. Rent Management Capabilities for the Green Transformation. In *Green Industrial Policy in Emerging Countries*, ed. A. Pegels. London: Routledge. 9–38.

Jucá, Ivan Chaves, Renno, Lúcio, and Melo, Marcus André. 2016. The Political Cost of Corruption: Scandals, Campaign Finance, and Reelection in the Brazilian Chamber of Deputies. *Journal of Politics in Latin America* 8(2): 3–36.

Just Transition Research Collaborative. 2018. *Mapping Just Transition(s) to a Low-Carbon World*. Geneva: United Nations Research Institute for Social Development (UNRISD) and the University of London Institute in Paris (ULIP).

Kambule, Njabulo, Yessoufou, Kowiyou, Nwulu, Nnamdi, and Mbohwa, Charles. 2019. Temporal Analysis of Electricity Consumption for Prepaid Metered Low- and High-Income Households in Soweto, South Africa. *African Journal of Science, Technology, Innovation and Development* 11(3): 375–382.

Karapin, Roger. 2016. *Political Opportunities for Climate Policy: California, New York, and the Federal Government*. Cambridge: Cambridge University Press.

Keefer, Phillip, and Khemani, Stuti. 2005. Democracy, Public Expenditures, and the Poor: Understanding Political Incentives for Providing Public Services. *World Bank Research Observer* 20(1): 1–27.

Kelsey, Nina, and Zysman, John. 2014. The Green Spiral. In *Can Green Sustain Growth? From the Religion to the Reality of Sustainable Prosperity*, eds. J. Zysman and M. Huberty. Stanford: Stanford Business Books.

Khan, Mushtaq H., and Blankenburg, Stephanie. 2009. The Political Economy of Industrial Policy in Asia and Latin America. In *Industrial Policy and Development: The Political Economy of Capabilities Accumulation*, eds. M. Cimoli, G. Dosi, and J. E. Stiglitz. Oxford: Oxford University Press. 336–377.

Kim, Sung-Young, and Thurbon, Elizabeth. 2015. Developmental Environmentalism: Explaining South Korea's Ambitious Pursuit of Green Growth. *Politics and Society* 43(2): 213–240.

Kingstone, Peter. 1999. *Crafting Coalitions for Reform: Business Preferences, Political Institutions, and Neoliberal Reform in Brazil*. University Park: Pennsylvania State University Press.

Kohli, Atul. 2004. *State-Directed Development: Political Power and Industrialization in the Global Periphery*. Cambridge: Cambridge University Press.

Kramon, Eric, and Posner, Daniel N. 2013. Who Benefits from Distributive Politics? How the Outcome One Studies Affects the Answer One Gets. *Perspectives on Politics* 11(2): 461–474.

Kroth, Verena, Larcinese, Valentino, and Wehner, Joachim. 2016. A Better Life for All? Democratization and Electrification in Post-Apartheid South Africa. *Journal of Politics* 78(3): 774–791.

Krüger, L. P. 2011. The Impact of Black Economic Empowerment (BEE) on South African Businesses: Focusing on Ten Dimensions of Business Performance. *Southern African Business Review* 15(3): 207–233.

Kurtz, Marcus J. 2013. *Latin American State Building in Comparative Perspective: Social Foundations of Institutional Order*. Cambridge: Cambridge University Press.

Lachapelle, Erick, MacNeil, Robert, and Paterson, Matthew. 2017. The Political Ecology of Decarbonisation: From Green Energy "Race" to Green "Division of Labour." *New Political Economy* 22(3): 311–327.

Leiren, Merethe Dotterud, and Reimer, Inken. 2018. Historical Institutionalist Perspective on the Shift from Feed-in Tariffs Towards Auctioning in German Renewable Energy Policy. *Energy Research and Social Science* 43: 33–40.

Leite, Antonio Dias. 2009. *Energy in Brazil: Towards a Renewable Energy Dominated System*. London: Earthscan.

Leonard, Llewellyn. 2014. Participatory Justice Against Industrial Risks: Environmental Justice in Durban, South Africa. *Politikon: South African Journal of Political Studies* 41(2): 311–329.

Levin, Kelly, Cashore, Benjamin, Bernstein, Steven, and Auld, Graeme. 2012. Overcoming the Tragedy of Super Wicked Problems: Constraining Our Future Selves to Ameliorate Global Climate Change. *Policy Science* 45 (2): 123–152.

Lewis, Joanna I. 2014. The Rise of Renewable Energy Protectionism: Emerging Trade Conflicts and Implications for Low-Carbon Development. *Global Environmental Politics* 14(4): 10–35.

Lewis, Joanna I. 2013. *Green Innovation in China: China's Wind Power Industry and the Global Transition to a Low-Carbon Economy*. New York: Columbia University Press.

Lewis, Joanna I., and Wiser, Ryan H. 2007. Fostering a Renewable Energy Technology Industry: An International Comparison of Wind Industry Support Mechanisms. *Energy Policy* 35(3): 1844–1857.

Lieberman, Evan S. 2003. *Race and Regionalism in the Politics of Taxation in Brazil and South Africa*. Cambridge: Cambridge University Press.

Lima-de-Oliveira, Renato, and Libby, Martin. 2017. Fueling Development? Assessing the Impact of Oil and Soybean Wealth on Municipalities in Brazil. *Extractive Industries and Society* 4: 576–585.

Lisboa, Marijane Vieira. 2002. Em Busca de Uma Política Externa Brasileira de Meio Ambiente: Três Exemplos e uma Exceção a Regra. *São Paulo em Perspectiva* 16(2): 44–54.

Lockwood, Matthew, Kuzemko, Caroline, Mitchell, Catherine, and Hoggett, Richard. 2016. Historical Institutionalism and the Politics of Sustainable Energy Transitions: A Research Agenda. *Environment and Planning C: Politics and Space* 35(2): 312–333.

Lombard, Andrew, and Ferreira, Sanette. 2014. Residents' Attitudes to Proposed Wind Farms in the West Coast Region of South Africa: A Social Perspective from the South. *Energy Policy* 66(C): 390–399.

Lucas, Hugo, Ferroukhi, Rabia, and Hawila, Diala. 2013. *Renewable Energy Auctions in Developing Countries*. IRENA (International Renewable Energy Agency) Online at www.irena.org/Publications.

Lyon, Thomas P., and Yin, Haitoo. 2010. Why Do States Adopt Renewable Portfolio Standards? An Empirical Investigation. *Energy Journal* 31(3): 133–157.

MacNeil, Robert, and Paterson, Matthew. 2012. Neoliberal Climate Policy: From Market Fetishism to the Developmental State. *Environmental Politics* 21(2): 230–247.

Malvestio, Anne Caroline, and Montaño, Marcelo. 2013. Effectiveness of Strategic Environmental Assessment Applied to Renewable Energy in Brazil. *Journal of Environmental Assessment Policy and Management* 15 (2): 1340007.

Manuel, Viola. 2013. Eskom's Deals Leave Us in the Dark. *Mail & Guardian*, April 26. https://mg.co.za/article/2013-04-26-00-eskoms-deals-leave-us-in-the-dark/.

Margato, Vítor, and Sánchez, Luis E. 2014. Quality and Outcomes: A Critical Review of Strategic Environmental Assessment in Brazil. *Journal of Economic Assessment Policy and Management* 16(2): 1–32.

Marquart, Jens. 2017. *How Power Shapes Energy Transitions in Southeast Asia*. Routledge Series in Energy Transitions. New York: Routledge.

Márquez, Patricia, and Rufín, Carlos, eds. 2011. *Private Utilities and Poverty Alleviation: Market Initiatives at the Base of the Pyramid*. Cheltenham: Edward Elgar.

Marx, Antony W. 1998. *Making Race and Nation: A Comparison of South Africa, the United States, and Brazil*. Cambridge: Cambridge University Press.

Masters, Lesley. 2011. Sustaining the African Common Position on Climate Change: International Organisations, Africa and COP17. *South African Journal of International Affairs* 18(2): 257–269.

Matsuo, Tyeler, and Schmidt, Tobias S. 2019. Managing Tradeoffs in Green Industrial Policies: The Role of Renewable Energy Policy Design. *World Development* 122: 11–26.

Mazzucato, Mariana. 2015. *The Entrepreneurial State: Debunking Public vs. Private Sector Myths*. London: Anthem Press.

McAdam, Doug, and Boudet, Hilary Schaffer. 2012. *Putting Social Movements in Their Place: Explaining Opposition to Energy Projects in the United States, 2000–2005*. Cambridge: Cambridge University Press.

McAdam, Doug, McCarthy, John D., and Zald, Mayer N. 1996. *Comparative Perspectives on Social Movements: Political Opportunities, Mobilizing Structures, and Cultural Framings*. Cambridge: Cambridge University Press.

McAllister, Lesley K. 2008. *Making Law Matter: Environmental Protection and Legal Institutions in Brazil*. Stanford: Stanford Books.

McCarthy, James, and Thatcher., Jim 2019. Visualizing New Political Ecologies: A Critical Data Studies Analysis of the World Bank's Renewable Energy Resource Mapping Initiative. *Geoforum* 102: 242–254.

McDonald, David A. 2011. Electricity and the Minerals-Energy Complex in South Africa. *Africa Review* 3(1): 65–87.

McEwan, Cheryl. 2017. Spatial Processes and Politics of Renewable Energy Transition: Land, Zones, and Frictions in South Africa. *Political Geography* 56: 1–12.

McEwan, Cheryl, Mawdsley, Emma, Banks, Glenn, and Scheyvens, Regina. 2017. Enrolling the Private Sector in Community Development: Magic Bullet or Sleight of Hand? *Development and Change* 48(1): 28–53.

Meadowcroft, James. 2009. What About the Politics? Sustainable Development, Transition Management, and Long Term Energy Transition. *Policy Science* 42: 323–340.

Meckling, Jonas. 2017. The Developmental State in Global Regulation: Economic Change and Climate Policy. *European Journal of International Relations* 24(10): 58–81.

Meckling, Jonas. 2011. *Carbon Coalitions: Business, Climate Politics, and the Rise of Emissions Trading*. Cambridge, MA: MIT Press.

Meckling, Jonas, and Hughes, Llewelyn. 2018. Global Interdependence in Clean Energy Transitions. *Business and Politics* 20(4): 467–491.

Meckling, Jonas, and Hughes, Llewelyn. 2017. Globalizing Solar: Global Supply Chains and Trade Preferences. *International Studies Quarterly* 61 (2): 225–235.

Meckling, Jonas, Kelsey, Nina, Biber, Eric, and Zysman, John. 2015. Winning Coalitions for Climate Policy: Green Industrial Policy Builds Support for Carbon Regulation (Perspectives). *Science* 349(6253): 1170–1171.

Meckling, Jonas, and Nahm, Jonas. 2018. The Power of Process: State Capacity and Climate Policy. *Governance* 31: 741–757.

Melo, Elbia. 2013. Fonte Eólica de Energia: Aspectos de Inserção, Tecnologia e Competitividade. *Estudos Avançados* 27(77): 125–142.

Mey, Franziska, and Diesendorf, Mark. 2018. Who Owns an Energy Transition? Strategic Action Fields and Community Wind Energy in Denmark. *Energy Research and Social Science* 35: 108–117.

Meyer, David, and Minkoff, Debra C. 2004. Conceptualizing Political Opportunity. *Social Forces* 82(4): 1457–1492.

Min, Brian. 2015. *Power and the Vote: Elections and Electricity in the Developing World*. Cambridge: Cambridge University Press.

Ministério de Minas e Energia. 2018. Plano Decenal de Expansão de Energia 2027 [draft for comment]. Brasília: Ministério de Minas e Energia and Empresa de Pesquisa Energética.

Ministério de Minas e Energia. 2017. Plano Decenal de Expansão de Energia 2026. Brasília: Ministério de Minas e Energia and Empresa de Pesquisa Energética.

Ministério de Minas e Energia. 2015. Plano Decenal de Expansão de Energia 2024. Brasília: Ministério de Minas e Energia and Empresa de Pesquisa Energética.

Ministério de Minas e Energia. 2014. Plano Decenal de Expansão de Energia 2023. Brasília: Ministério de Minas e Energia and Empresa de Pesquisa Energética.

Ministério de Minas e Energia. 2013. Plano Decenal de Expansão de Energia 2022. Brasília: Ministério de Minas e Energia and Empresa de Pesquisa Energética.

Ministério de Minas e Energia. 2012. Plano Decenal de Expansão de Energia 2021. Brasília: Ministério de Minas e Energia and Empresa de Pesquisa Energética.

Ministério de Minas e Energia. 2011. Plano Decenal de Expansão de Energia 2020. Brasília: Ministério de Minas e Energia and Empresa de Pesquisa Energética.

Ministério de Minas e Energia. 2010. Plano Decenal de Expansão de Energia 2019. Brasília: Ministério de Minas e Energia and Empresa de Pesquisa Energética.

Ministério de Minas e Energia. 2009. Pesquisa Quantitativa Domiciliar de Avaliação da Satisfação e de Impacto do Programa Luz para Todos: Principais Resultados. Brasília: Ministério de Minas e Energia and Empresa de Pesquisa Energética.

Ministério de Minas e Energia. 2008. Plano Decenal de Expansão de Energia 2017. Brasília: Ministério de Minas e Energia and Empresa de Pesquisa Energética.

Ministério de Minas e Energia. 2007. Plano Nacional de Energia 2030. Brasília: Ministério de Minas e Energia and Empresa de Pesquisa Energética.

Ministério de Minas e Energia. 2006. Balanço Energético Nacional 2006: Ano Base 2005. Brasília: Ministério de Minas e Energia and Empresa de Pesquisa Energética.

Mitchell, Timothy. 2011. *Carbon Democracy: Political Power in the Age of Oil*. London: Verso.

Mitnick, Barry M. 2011. Capturing "Capture": Definition and Mechanisms. In *Handbook on the Politics of Regulation*, ed. D. Levi-Faur. Cheltenham: Edward Elgar.

Moe, Espen. 2015. *Renewable Energy Transformation or Fossil Fuels Backlash: Vested Interests in the Political Economy*. London: Palgrave McMillan.

Montero, Alfred. 2014. *Brazil: Reversal of Fortune*. Cambridge and Malden: Polity Press.

Monyei, C. G., Adewumi, A. O., and Jenkins, K. E. H. 2018. Energy (In) justice in Off-Grid Rural Electrification Policy: South Africa in Focus. *Energy Research & Social Science* 44: 152–171.

Moore, Sharlissa. 2018. *Sustainable Energy Transformations, Power, and Politics*. Routledge Studies in Energy Transitions. New York: Routledge.

Moreira, Roseilda Nunes, de Almeida Bizarria, Fabiana Pinto, Schilling Marqueson, Fábio Freitas, Sampaio Barbosa, Flávia Lorenne. 2017. Sustentabilidade e Energia Eólica: Percepções Comunitárias no Interior do Ceará-Brasil. *Colóquio – Revista de Desenvolvimento Regional* 14(1): 79–97.

Morgado, Naeeda Crishna, Taşkın, Özlem, Lasfargues, Bérénice, and Sedemund, Jens. n.d. *Scaling Up Climate-Compatible Infrastructure: Insights from National Development Banks in Brazil and South Africa*. Report. Paris: Organisation for Economic Co-operation and Development.

Morgan, Courtney, and Domingo, Aaisha. 2018. SAFTU's Working-Class Summit: Building Solidarity to Address the Climate Crisis. *South African Labour Bulletin* 42(3): 12–14.

Morgan, Richard K. 2012. Environmental Impact Assessment: The State of the Art. *Impact Assessment and Project Appraisal* 30(1): 5–14.

Morris, Craig, and Jungjohann, Arne. 2016. *Energy Democracy: Germany's ENERGIEWENDE to Renewables*. Switzerland: Palgrave Macmillan and Springer Nature.

Morris, Mike, and Martin, Lucy. 2015. Political Economy of Climate-Relevant Policies: The Case of Renewable Energy in South Africa. Sussex: Institute of Development Studies and Cape Town: University of Cape Town, Evidence Report No 128, Rising Powers in International Development.

Morrison-Saunders, Angus, and Retief, François. 2012. Walking the Sustainability Assessment Talk: Progressing the Practice of Environmental Impact Assessment (EIA). *Environmental Impact Assessment Review* 36: 34–41.

Mottiar, Shanna. 2013. From "Popcorn" to "Occupy": Protest in Durban, South Africa. *Development and Change* 44(3): 603–619.

Mulvaney, Dustin. 2017. Identifying the Roots of Green Civil War over Utility-Scale Solar Energy Projects on Public Lands across the American Southwest. *Journal of Land Use Science* 12(6): 493–515.

Mulvaney, Dustin. 2013. Opening the Black Box of Solar Energy Technologies: Exploring Tensions Between Innovation and Environmental Justice. *Science as Culture* 22(2): 230–237.

Murillo, Maria Victoria. 2009. *Political Competition, Partisanship, and Policy Making in Latin American Public Utilities*. Cambridge: Cambridge University Press.

Murillo, Maria Victoria. 2001. *Labor Unions, Partisan Coalitions, and Market Reforms in Latin America*. Cambridge: Cambridge University Press.

Nahm, Jonas. 2017. Renewable Futures and Industrial Legacies: Wind and Solar Sectors in China, Germany, and the United States. *Business and Politics* 19(1): 68–106.

Naidoo, Suvania. 2015. An Assessment of the Impacts of Acid Mine Drainage on Socio-economic Development in the Witswatersrand: South Africa. *Environment, Development and Sustainability* 17: 1045–1063.

Naqvi, Ijlal. 2016. Pathologies of Development Practice: Higher Order Obstacles to Governance Reform in the Pakistani Electrical Power Sector. *Journal of Development Studies* 52(7): 950–964.

Naqvi, Natalya, Henow, Anne, and Chang, Ha-Joon. Forthcoming. Kicking Away the Financial Ladder? German Development Banking under Economic Globalisation. *Review of International Political Economy*.

Nasser de Oliveira, Ana Leonardo. 2015. Forests and Climate Change: Strategies and Challenges for Brazilian Civil Society Organizations between 2005 and 2010. *Review of European Community and International Environmental Law* 24(2): 182–193.

National Energy Regulator of South Africa. 2017. Decision and Reasons for Decision: Eskom Holdings SOC Limited: Eskom's Revenue Application for 2018/19. Pretoria: NERSA.

National Planning Commission. 2018. NPC Economy Planning Series: Energy 1.0. Pretoria: National Planning Commission.

National Planning Commission. 2012. National Development Plan 2030: Our Future – Make It Work. Pretoria: National Planning Commission.

Nattrass, Nicoli. 2014. A South African Variety of Capitalism? *New Political Economy* 19(1): 56–78.

Nattrass, Nicoli. 1994. Economic Restructuring in South Africa: The Debate Continues. *Journal of Southern African Studies* 20(4): 517–531.

Ndletyana, Mcebisi. 2013. Policy Incoherence: A Function of Ideological Contestation? In *State of the Nation: South Africa 2012–2013*, eds. U. Pillay, G. Hagg, and F. Nyamnjoh with J. Jansen. Cape Town: HSRC Press. 51–71.

Newell, Peter, and Mulvaney, Dustin. 2013. The Political Economy of the "Just Transition." *The Geographical Journal* 179(2): 132–140.

Newell, Peter, and Paterson, Matthew. 2010. *Climate Capitalism: Global Warming and the Transformation of the Global Economy.* Cambridge: Cambridge University Press.

Nugent, Daniel, and Sovacool, Benjamin K. 2014. Assessing the Lifecycle Greenhouse Gas Emissions from Solar PV and Wind Energy: A Critical Met-Survey. *Energy Policy* 65: 229–244.

NUMSA. 2012. Motivations for a Socially-Owned Renewable Energy Sector in South Africa. Online at www.numsa.org.za/article/motivations-for-a-s ocially-owned-renewable-energy-sector-2012-10-15/.

NUMSA. 2011. Towards a Socially-Owned Renewable Energy Sector. No longer available online; PDF in possession of this volume's author.

Nugent, Daniel, and Sovacool, Benjamin J. 2014. Assessing the Lifecycle Greenhouse Gas Emissions from Solar PV and Wind Energy: A Critical Meta-Survey. *Energy Policy* 65: 229–244.

Observatório do Clima. 2018. *Emissões de GEE no Brasil e suas Implicações para Políticas Públicas e a Contribuição Brasileira para o Acordo de Paris, 2018 Documento de Analise.* Online at http://seeg.eco.br/wp-content/upl oads/2018/08/Relatorios-SEEG-2018-Sintese-FINAL-v1.pdf.

Observatório do Clima. 2008. Elementos para Formulação de um Marco Regulatório em Mudanças Climáticas no Brasil: Contribuições da Sociedade Civil.

Ogilvie, Matthew, and Rootes, Christopher. 2015. The Impact of Local Campaigns Against Wind Energy Developments. *Environmental Politics* 24(6): 875–893.

Oliveira, Adilson de. 2007. Political Economy of the Brazilian Power Industry Reform. In *The Political Economy of Power Sector Reform: The Experiences of Five Major Developing Countries*, eds. D. Victor and T. C. Heller. Cambridge: Cambridge University Press. 31–75.

Oliveira, Marília Silva de. 2016. Movimento para as Instituições: Ambientalistas, Partidos Políticos e a Liderança de Marina Silva. Brasília: PhD Dissertation at the Instituto de Ciência Política, Universidade de Brasília.

Ondetti, Gabriel. 2008. *Land, Protest, and Politics: The Landless Movement and the Struggle for Agrarian Reform in Brazil.* University Park: Penn State University Press.

Oye, Kenneth A., and Maxwell, James H. 1994. Self-Interest and Environmental Management. *Journal of Theoretical Politics* 6(4): 593–624.

Pacheco, Clecia Simone Gonçalves Rosa, and dos Santos, Reinaldo Pacheco. 2013. Parques Eólicos e Transformações Espaciais: Uma Análise dos Impactos Socioambientais na Região de Sento Sé/BA. *Revista Brasileira de Geografia Física* 5: 1243–1258.

Patel, Zarina. 2014. South Africa's Three Waves of Environmental Policy: (Mis)Aligning the Goals of Sustainable Development, Environmental Justice and Climate Change. *Geography Compass* 8(3): 169–181.

Patel, Zarina. 2009. Environmental Justice in South Africa: Tools and Trade-offs. *Social Dynamics* 35(1): 94–110.

Pearson, Joel, Pillay, Sarita, and Chipkin, Ivor. 2016. State-Building in South Africa After Apartheid: The History of the National Treasury. Johannesburg: Working Paper, Public Affairs Research Institute, 19.02.2016.

Pearson, Peter J. G., and Foxon, Timothy J. 2012. A Low Carbon Industrial Revolution? Institutions and Challenges from Past Technology and Economic Transformations. *Energy Policy* 50: 117–127.

Pegels, Anna. 2014a. Why We Need a Green Industrial Policy. In *Green Industrial Policy in Emerging Countries*, ed. A. Pegels. London: Routledge. 1–8.

Pegels, Anna. ed. 2014b. *Green Industrial Policy in Emerging Countries.* London: Routledge.

Pegels, Anna. 2014c. The Politics of South African Renewable Energy Support. In *Green Industrial Policy in Emerging Countries*, ed. A. Pegels. London: Routledge. 126–147.

Pegels, Anna, and Becker, Bastian. 2014. Implementing Green Industrial Policy. In *Green Industrial Policy in Emerging Countries*, ed. A. Pegels. London: Routledge. 38–68.

Perlman, Janice E. 2006. The Metamorphosis of Marginality: Four Generations in the Favelas of Rio de Janeiro. *Annals of the American Academic of Political and Social Sciences* 606: 154–177.

Peterson, Tarla Rae, Stephens, Jennie C., and Wilson. Elizabeth J. 2015. Public Perception of and Engagement with Emerging Low-Carbon Energy Technology: A Literature Review. *MRS Energy and Sustainability: A Review Journal* 2(e11): 1–14.

Petrova, Maria A. 2013. NIMBYism Revisited: Public Acceptance of Wind Energy in the United States. *WIREs Climate Change* 4(6): 575–601.

Pettifor, Ann. 2019. *The Case for the Green New Deal*. London: Verso.

Pinto, Marcia Freire, Joventino do Nascimento, João Luís, Ferreira Bringel, Paulo Cunha, and de Andrade Meireles, Antônio Jeovah. 2014. Quando os Conflitos Socioambientais Caracterizam um Territorio? *Gaia Scientia* 2014 Special Issue on Populações Tradicionais: 271–288.

Porto, Marcelo Firpo de Souza, Finamore, Renan, and Ferreira, Hugo. 2013. Injustiças da Sustentabilidade: Conflitos Ambientais Relacionados à Produção de Energia Limpa no Brasil. *Revista Crítica de Ciências Sociais* 100: 37–64.

Post, Alison E. 2014. *Foreign and Domestic Investment in Argentina: The Politics of Privatized Infrastructure*. Cambridge: Cambridge University Press.

Power, Marcus, Newell, Peter, Baker, Lucy, Bulkeley, Harriet, Kirshner, Joshua, and Smith, Adrian. 2016. The Political Economy of Energy Transitions in Mozambique and South Africa: The Role of the Rising Powers. *Energy Research and Social Science* 17: 10–19.

Prakash, Aseem, and Gugerty, Mary Kay. 2010. Advocacy Organizations and Collective Action: An Introduction. In *Advocacy Organizations and Collective Action*, eds. A. Prakash and M. K. Gugerty. Cambridge: Cambridge University Press. 1–28.

Presidência da República. 2002. *Brasil 1994–2002: The Era of the Real*. Brasília: Secretaria de Estado de Comunicação de Governo.

Princen, Thomas, Manno, Jack P., and Martin, Pamela L. eds. 2015. *Ending the Fossil Fuel Era*. Cambridge, MA: MIT Press.

Public Protector. 2016. *State of Capture: Report No: 6 of 2016/17*. Pretoria: Office of Public Protector of South Africa.

Pulice, Sérgio, Paiva, Mantovani, and Moretto, Evandro Mateus. 2017. A Compensação Financeira e o Desenvolvimento dos Municípios Brasileiros Alagados por Usinas Hidrelétricas. *Ambiente e Sociedade* 20 (4): 107–130.

Ralston-Paton, Samantha, Smallie, Jon, Pearson, Andrew, and Ramalho, Ricardo. 2017. Wind Energy's Impacts on Birds in South Africa: A Preliminary Review of the Results of the Renewable Energy Independent Power Produce Procurement Programme in South Africa, BirdLife South Africa Occasional Report Series No. 2. Johannesburg: BirdLife South Africa.

Rennkamp, Britta. 2019. Power, Coalitions and Institutional Change in South African Climate Policy. *Climate Policy* 19(6): 756–770.

Rennkamp, Britta, and Boyd, Anya. 2015. Technological Capability and Transfer for Achieving South Africa's Development Goals. *Climate Policy* 15(1): 12–29.

Rennkamp, Britta, and Marquand, Andrew. 2018. South Africa's Multiple Faces in Current Climate Clubs. *South African Journal of International Affairs* 27(4): 443–461.

Rennkamp, Britta, Hauss, Sebastian, Wongsa, Kridtyaporn, Ortega, Araceli, and Casamadrid, Erika. 2017. Competing Coalitions: The Politics of Renewable Energy and Fossil Fuels in Mexico, South Africa, and Thailand. *Energy Research and Social Science* 34: 214–223.

Republic of South Africa. 2018. *South Africa's Greenhouse Gas Report 2000–2015* (Draft for Public Comments).

Retief, François, Welman, Coert N. J., and Sandheim, Luke. 2011. Performance of Environmental Impact Assessment (EIA) Screening in South Africa: A Comparative Analysis Between the 1999 and 2006 EIA Regimes. *South African Geographical Journal* 93(2): 154–171.

Richards, Peter, Arima, Eugenio, VanWey, Leah, Cohn, Avery, and Bhattarai, Nishan. 2017. Are Brazil's Deforesters Avoiding Detection? *Conservation Letters* 10(4): 470–476.

Ritchkin, Edwin, and Zadeck, Simon. 2010. *Unlocking South Africa's Green Growth Potential: South African Renewables Initiative*. Pretoria: Department of Trade and Industry.

Roberts, Cameron, and Geels, Frank W. 2019. Conditions for Politically-Accelerated Transitions: Historical Institutionalism, the Multi-level Perspective, and Two Historical Case Studies in Transport and Agriculture. *Technological Forecasting and Social Change* 140: 221–240.

Roberts, Cameron, Geels, Frank W., Lockwood, Matthew, Newell, Peter, Schmitz, Hubert, Turnheim, Bruno, and Jordan, Andy. 2018. The Politics of Accelerating Low-Carbon Transitions: Towards a New Research Agenda. *Energy Research and Social Science* 44: 304–311.

Rubini, Luca. 2012. Ain't Wastin' Time No More: Subsidies for Renewable Energy, the SCM Agreement, Policy Space, and Law Reform. *Journal of International Economic Law* 15(2): 525–579.

Rucht, Dieter. 2002. Mobilization Against Large Techno-Industrial Projects: A Comparative Perspective. *Mobilization: An International Journal* 7(1): 79–95.

Runciman, Carin. 2015. The Decline of the Anti-privatisation Forum in the Midst of South Africa's "Rebellion of the Poor." *Current Sociology* 63(7): 961–979.

Sachs, Jeffrey, Woo, Wing Thye, Yoshino, Naoyuki, and Taghizadeh-Hesary, Farhad. eds. 2019. *Handbook of Green Finance: Energy Security and Sustainable Development*. Singapore: Springer and Asian Development Bank.

Sauer, Sérgio, and Mészáros, George. 2016. The Political Economy of Land Struggle in Brazil under Workers' Party Governments. *Journal of Agrarian Change* 17: 397–414.

Schaeffer, Roberto, Lucena, André F. P., Rathmann, Régis, Szklo, Alexandre, Soria, Rafael, and Chavez-Rodriguez, Mauro. 2015. *Who Drives Climate-Relevant Policies in Brazil?* Brighton: IDS Evidence Report 132.

Scharfetter, Beate, and van Dijk, Marco. 2017. Legislation Governing the Implementation of Small-Scale Hydropower Projects for Rural Electrification in South Africa. *Journal of Energy in Southern Africa* 28 (2): 14–28.

Scheidel, Arnim, and Sorman, Alevgul H. 2012. Energy Transitions and the Global Land Rush: Ultimate Drivers and Persistent Consequences. *Global Environmental Change* 22: 588–595.

Schlömer S., Bruckner, T., Fulton, L., Hertwich, E., McKinnon, A., Perczyk, D., Roy, J., Schaeffer, R., Sims, R., Smith, P., and Wiser, R. 2014. Annex III: Technology-Specific Cost and Performance Parameters. In *Climate Change 2014: Mitigation of Climate Change. Contribution of Working Group III to the Fifth Assessment Report of the Intergovernmental Panel on Climate Change*, eds. O. Edenhofer, R. Pichs-Madruga, Y. Sokona, E. Farahani, S. Kadner, K. Seyboth, A. Adler, I. Baum, S. Brunner, P. Eickemeier, B. Kriemann, J. Savolainen, S. Schlömer, C. von Stechow, T. Zwickel, and J. C. Minx. Cambridge and New York: Cambridge University Press.

Schmidt, Tobias S., and Huenteler, Joern. 2016. Anticipating Industry Localization Effects of Clean Technology Deployment Policies in Developing Countries. *Global Environmental Change* 38: 8–20.

Schmitz, Hubert, Johnson, Oliver, and Altenburg, Tilman. 2015. Rent-Management: The Heart of Green Industrial Policy. *New Political Economy* 20(6): 812–831.

Schneider, Ben Ross. 2015. *Designing Industrial Policy in Latin America: Business-State Relations and the New Developmentalism*. New York: Palgrave.

Schneider, Ben Ross. 2004. Organizing Interests and Institutions in the Politics of Market Reform in Latin America. *World Politics* 56(3): 456–479.

Schwarzer, Johannes. 2013. *Industrial Policy for a Green Economy*. Report. Manitoba: International Institute for Sustainable Development. June 2013.

Schwartzman, Stephen, Moutinho, Paulo, and Hamburg, Steven. 2012. Policy Update: Amazon Deforestation and Brazil's Forest Code: A Crossroads for Climate Change. *Carbon Management* 3(4): 341–343.

Scott, Dianne, and Barnett, Clive. 2009. Something in the Air: Civic Science and Contentious Environmental Politics in Post-Apartheid South Africa. *Geoforum* 40: 373–382.

Sebrae. 2017a. *Cadeia de Valor da Energia Eólica no Brasil*. Brasília: Serviço Brasileiro de Apoio as Micro e Pequenas Empresas. Online at https://bibl iotecas.sebrae.com.br/chronus/ARQUIVOS_CHRONUS/bds/bds.nsf/118 8c835f8e432ddd43bc39d27853478/$File/9960.pdf.

Sebrae. 2017b. *Cadeia de Valor da Energia Solar Fotovoltaica no Brasil*. Brasília: Serviço Brasileiro de Apoio as Micro e Pequenas Empresas. Online at www.sebrae.com.br/sites/PortalSebrae/artigos/conheca-mais-sobre-a-cadeia-produtiva-de-energia,17ead6d4760f3610VgnVCM 1000004c00210aRCRD.

Secretaria de Mudanças Climáticas e Qualidade Ambiental. 2009. Pesquisa Sobre Licenciamento Ambiental de Parques Eólicos. Brasília: Ministêrio do Meio Ambiente. Online at www.mma.gov.br/estruturas/164/_publica cao/164_publicacao26022010101115.pdf.

SEEG. 2018a. Emissões de GEE no Brasil e Suas Implicações para Políticas Públicas e a Contribuição Brasileiro para o Acordo de Paris: 2018 Documento de Análise.

SEEG. 2018b. Emissões dos Setores de Energia, Processos Industriais e Uso de Produtos: 2018 Documento de Análise. Online at http://seeg.eco.br/wp-content/uploads/2018/05/Relatórios-SEEG-2018-Energia-Final-v1.pdf.

Seekings, Jeremy, and Nattrass, Nicoli. 2011. State-Business Relations and Pro-Poor Growth in South Africa. *Journal of International Development* 23(3): 338–357.

Seidman, Gay W. 1994. *Manufacturing Militance: Workers' Movements in Brazil and South Africa, 1970–1985*. Berkeley and Los Angeles: University of California Press.

Seyfang, Gill, Park, Jung Jin, and Smith, Adrian. 2013. A Thousand Flowers Blooming? An Examination of Community Energy in the UK. *Energy Policy* 61: 977–989.

Shadlen, Kenneth C. 2017. *Coalitions and Compliance: The Political Economy of Pharmaceutical Patents in Latin America*. Oxford: Oxford University Press.

Sherman, Daniel J. 2011. *Not Here, Not There, Not Anywhere: Politics, Social Movements, and the Disposal of Low-Level Radioactive Waste*. Washington, DC: Resources for the Future Press.

Sikkink, Kathryn. 1991. *Ideas and Institutions: Developmentalism in Brazil and Argentina*. Ithaca: Cornell University Press.

Simas, Moana, and Pacca, Sergio. 2013. Socio-economic Benefits of Wind Power in Brazil. *Journal of Sustainable Development of Energy, Water and Environment Systems* 1(1): 27–40.

Sjöberg, Lennart. 1997. Explaining Risk Perception: An Empirical Evaluation of Cultural Theory. *Risk Decision and Policy* 2(2): 113–130.

Skillings, Jeremy, and Nattrass, Nicoli. 2005. *Class, Race, and Inequality in South Africa*. New Haven: Yale University Press.

Skocpol, Theda. 1985. Bringing the State Back In: Current Research. In *Bringing the State Back In*, eds. P. B. Evans, D. Rueschemeyer, and T. Skocpol. Cambridge: Cambridge University Press.

Slough, Tara, Urpelainen, Johannes, and Yang, Joonseok. 2015. Light for All? Evaluating Brazil's Rural Electrification Progress, 2000–2010. *Energy Policy* 86(C): 315–327.

South African Local Government Association. 2017. Status of Small Scale Embedded Generation (SSEG) in South African Municipalities. Online at www.salga.org.za/SALGA%20Energy%20Summit%202018/Energy%2 0Summit%20Web/Document/Status%20of%20Small%20Scale%20Em bedded%20Generation.pdf.

Southall, Roger. 2016. The Coming Crisis of Zuma's ANC: The Party State Confronts Fiscal Crisis. *Review of African Political Economy* 43(147): 73–88.

Southall, Roger. 2013. The Power Elite in Democratic South Africa: Race and Class in a Fractured Society. In *New South African Review 3: The Second Phase – Tragedy or Farce?* eds. J. Daniel, P. Naidoo, D. Pillay, and R. Southall. Johannesburg: Wits University Press.

Sovacool, Benjamin K., Burke, Matthew, Baker, Lucy, Katikalapudi, Chaitanya Kumar, and Wlokas, Holle. 2017. New Frontiers and Conceptual Frameworks for Energy Justice. *Energy Policy* 105: 677–691.

Sovacool, Benjamin K., Gilbert, Alex, and Nugent, Benjamin. 2014. An International Comparative Assessment of Construction Cost Overruns for Electricity Infrastructure. *Energy Research and Social Science* 3: 152–160.

Sovacool, Benjamin K., and Drupady, Ira Martina. 2012. *Energy Access, Poverty, and Development: The Governance of Small-Scale Renewable Energy in Developing Asia*. Burlington: Ashgate.

Statistics South Africa. 2016. *Community Survey 2016: Statistical Release PO301*. Pretoria: Statistics South Africa.

Stern, Nicolas. 2007. *The Economics of Climate Change: The Stern Report*. Cambridge: Cambridge University Press.

Stevis, Dimitris, and Felli, Romain. 2015. Global Labour Unions and Just Transition to a Green Economy. *International Environmental Agreements* 15(1): 29–43.

Stokes, Leah Cardmore. 2020. *Shortcircuiting Policy: Interest Groups and the Battle Over Clean Energy and Climate Policy in the American States*. Oxford: Oxford University Press.

Stokes, Leah C. 2016. Electoral Backlash Against Climate Policy: A Natural Experiment on Retrospective Voting and Local Resistance to Public Policy. *American Journal of Political Science* 60(4): 958–974.

Stokes, Leah C. 2013. The Politics of Renewable Energy Policies: The Case of Feed-In Tariffs in Ontario, Canada. *Energy Policy* 56: 490–500.

Stone, Christopher D. 2004. Common but Differentiated Responsibilities in International Law. *American Journal of International Law* 98(2): 276–301.

Sustainable Energy Africa. 2014. Tackling Urban Energy Poverty in South Africa. Online at https://za.boell.org/2014/03/20/tackling-urban-energy-poverty-south-africa.

Swilling, Mark, and Annecke, Eve. 2012. *Just Transitions: Exploration of Sustainability in an Unfair World*. Claremont: University of Cape Town Press and New York: United Nations University Press.

Swilling, Mark, Musango, Josephine, and Wakeford, Jeremy. 2016. Developmental States and Sustainability Transitions: Prospects of a Just Transition in South Africa. *Journal of Environmental Policy and Planning* 18(5): 650–672.

Tait, Louise. 2012. *The Potential or Local Community Benefits from Wind Farms in South Africa*. MA Thesis. Cape Town: Energy Research Centre, University of Cape Town.

Tait, Louise, Wlokas, Holle Linnea, and Garside, Ben. 2013. *Making Communities Count: Maximising Local Benefit Potential in South Africa's Renewable Energy Independent Power Producer Procurement Programme*. London: International Institute for Environment and Development.

Tankha, Sunil. 2008. Lessons from Brazilian Power Reforms on the Provision of Public Services. *Policy and Society* 27: 151–162.

Tarrow, Sydney. 2011. *Power in Movement: Social Movements and Contentious Politics*, 3rd edition. Cambridge: Cambridge University Press.

Taylor, Scott D. 2007. *Business and the State in Southern Africa*. Boulder: Lynne Rienner.

Tendler, Judith. 1968. *Electric Power in Brazil: Entrepreneurship in the Public Sector*. Cambridge, MA: Harvard University Press.

Teske, Sven, and Lins, Christine, with Ferrial, Adam, Musana, Fiona, Steele, Melita, and Teule, Rianne. 2011. The Advanced Energy Revolution: A Sustainable Energy Outlook for South Africa. Brussels: Greenpeace International and European Renewable Energy Council.

Thompson, Onah P. 2018. Minority Rights and Environmental Justice in Developing Countries. In *Human Rights Dilemmas in the Developing World: The Case of Marginalized Populations at Risk*, eds. E. Ike Udogu and Sambuddha Ghatek. Lanham: Lexington Books.

Ting, Marie Blanche, and Byrne, Rob. 2020. Eskom and the Rise of Renewables: Regime-Resistance, Crisis, and the Strategy of Incumbency in South Africa's Electricity System. *Energy Research and Social Science* 60: 101333.

Toke, David, Breukers, Sylvia, and Wolsink. Maarten, 2008. Wind Power Deployment Outcomes: How Can We Account for the Differences? *Renewable and Sustainable Energy Reviews* 12: 1129–1147.

Tolmasquim, Mauricio T. ed. 2016. *Energia Renovável: Hidráulica, Biomassa, Eólica, Solar, Oceânica.* Rio de Janeiro: Empresa de Pesquisa Energética.

Tolmasquim, Mauricio T. 2012. *Power Sector Reform in Brazil.* Rio de Janeiro: Synergy / Empresa de Pesquisa Energética.

Torre, Oscar de la. 2013. 'Are They Really *Quilombos*?' Black Peasants, Politics, and the Meaning of Quilombo in Present-Day Brazil. *OFO: Journal of Transatlantic Studies* 3(1 and 2): 99–118.

Trainer, Ted. 2007. *Renewable Energy Cannot Sustain a Consumer Society.* Dordrecht: Springer.

Trollip, Hilton, and Michael Boulle. 2017. Challenges Associated with Implementing Climate Change Mitigation Policy in South Africa. Cape Town: University of Cape Town Energy Research Centre Research Report, March 2017.

Tsikati, M., and Sebitosi, A. B. 2010. Struggling to Wean a Society Away from a Century-Old Legacy of Coal Based Power: Challenges and Possibilities for South African Electric Supply Future. *Energy* 35: 1281–1288.

Unruh, Gregory C. 2000. Understanding Carbon Lock-In. *Energy Policy* 28 (12): 817–830.

Upadhyaya, Prabhat. 2016. Aligning Climate Policy with National Interest: Disengagements with Nationally Appropriate Mitigation Actions in South Africa. *Journal of Environmental Policy and Planning* 18(4): 463–481.

Valentine, Scott Victor. 2014. *Wind Power Politics and Policy.* Oxford: Oxford University Press.

Van Niekerk, Sandra. 2020. Resource Rich and Justice Poor: Securing a Just Transition to Renewables in South Africa. In *Just Transitions: Social Justice in the Shift to a Low-Carbon World,* eds. E. Morena, D. Krause, and D. Stevis. London: Pluto Press. 132–150.

Vasi, Ion Bogdan. 2011. *Winds of Change: The Environmental Movement and the Global Development of the Wind Energy Industry.* Oxford: Oxford University Press.

Verborg, Geert, and Geels, Frank W. 2007. The Ongoing Energy Transition: Lessons from a Socio-technical, Multi-level Analysis of the Dutch Electricity System (1960–2004). *Energy Policy* 35(2): 1025–1037.

Vermeulen, Paul. 2017. Global Electricity Disruption: The South African Parallels. Paper presented at the annual convention of the Association of Municipal Electricity Undertakings (AMEU) in 2017. Online at www .ee.co.za/wp-content/uploads/2017/11/Pages-from-AMEU-2017_-67-74 .pdf.

Vialli, Andrea. 2018. O Que Seu Candidato vai Fazer a Respeito do Aquecimento Global? Online at www.observatoriodoclima.eco.br/o-clim a-nas-eleicoes/.

Viana, Lígia Alves, Joventino do Nascimento, João Luís, and de Andrade Meireles, Antônio Jeovah. 2016. Complexos Eólicos e Injustiças Provocados pela Implantação de Parques Eólicos no Ceará. *Revista Geografar* 11(1): 64–83.

Victor, David, and Heller, Thomas C. 2007a. Major Conclusions. In *The Political Economy of Power Sector Reform: The Experiences of Five Major Developing Countries*, eds. D. Victor and T. C. Heller. Cambridge: Cambridge University Press. 254–306.

Victor, David, and Heller, Thomas C. eds. 2007b. *The Political Economy of Power Sector Reform: The Experiences of Five Major Developing Countries*. Cambridge: Cambridge University Press.

Victor, David, and Heller, Thomas C. 2007c. Introduction and Overview. In *The Political Economy of Power Sector Reform: The Experiences of Five Major Developing Countries*, eds. D. Victor and T. C. Heller. Cambridge: Cambridge University Press. 1–30.

Viglio, José Eduardo, Di Giulio, Gabriela Marques, and da Costa Ferreira, Lúcia. 2017. Not All Glitters in the Black Gold: Uncertainties and Environmental Threats of the Brazilian Pre-salt. *Ambiente e Sociedade* 20(3): 21–38.

Viola, Eduardo, and Franchini, Matías. 2018. *Brazil and Climate Change: Beyond the Amazon*. New York and London: Routledge.

Visser, Elke, Perold, Vonica, Ralston-Paton, Samantha, Cardenal, Alvaro C., and Ryan, Peter G. 2019. Assessing the Impacts of a Utility-Scale Photovoltaic Solar Energy Facility on Birds in the Northern Cape, South Africa. *Renewable Energy* 133: 1285–1294.

Von Schnitzler, Antina. 2016. *Democracy's Infrastructure: Techno-Politics and Protest after Apartheid*. Princeton: Princeton University Press.

Vorster, Shaun, Winkler, Harald, and Jooste, Meagan. 2011. Mitigating Climate Change through Carbon Pricing: An Emerging Policy Debate in South Africa. *Climate and Development* 3: 242–258.

Walker, Chad, and Baxter, Jamie. 2017. Procedural Justice in Canadian Wind Energy Development: A Comparison of Community-based and Technocratic Siting Processes. *Energy Research and Social Science* 29: 160–169.

Waroux, Yann Le Poulain de, Garrett, Rachael D., Graesser, Jordan, Nolte, Christoph, White, Christopher, and Lambin, Eric F. 2019. Restructuring of South American Soy and Beef Production and Trade Under Changing Environmental Regulations. *World Development* 121: 188–202.

Warren, Charles R., Lumsden, Carolyn, O'Dowd, Simone, and Birnie, Richard V. 2005. "Green on Green": Public Perceptions of Wind Power in Scotland and Ireland. *Journal of Environmental Planning and Management* 48(6): 853–875.

Weiss, Linda. 1998. *The Myth of the Powerless State*. Ithaca: Cornell University Press.

Wenzel, Philip. 2007. Public-Sector Transformation in South Africa: Getting the Basics Right. *Progress in Development Studies* 7(1): 47–64.

Willems, Stéphane, and Baumert, Kevin. 2003. Institutional Capacity and Climate Actions. Organisation for Economic Co-operation and Development and International Energy Agency. Online at www .researchgate.net/profile/Kevin_Baumert/publication/228910054_Institut ional_capacity_and_climate_actions/links/573618ad08ae9ace840aef5c/I nstitutional-capacity-and-climate-actions.pdf.

Winkler, Harald. 2010. *Taking Action on Climate Change: Long Term Mitigation Scenarios for South Africa*. Claremont: University of Cape Town Press.

Winkler, Harald. 2009. *Cleaner Energy, Cooler Climate: Developing Sustainable Energy Solutions for South Africa*. Cape Town: HSRC Press.

Wlokas, Holle, and Soal, Sue. 2016a. Economic Development in REIPPPP Managing Community Unrest: Roundtable Report. Cape Town: Transformation Energy Trust.

Wlokas, Holle, and Soal, Sue. 2016b. Economic Development in REIPPPP Supporting Sound Community Trusts – Establishment, Governance, and Operation: Roundtable Report. Cape Town: Transformation Energy Trust.

Wlokas, Holle L., Westoby, Peter, and Soal, Sue. 2017. Learning from the Literature on Community Development for the Implementation of Community Renewables in South Africa. *Journal of Energy in Southern Africa* 28(1): 35–44.

Wolford, Wendy. 2003. Producing Community: The MST and Land Reform Settlements in Brazil. *Journal of Agrarian Change* 3(4): 500–520.

Wood, Geof, and Gough, Ian. 2006. A Comparative Welfare Regime Approach to Global Social Policy. *World Development* 34(10): 1696–1712.

World Bank. 2016. Environmental and Social Review Summary, Lekela Wind Energy Facilities. Online at www.miga.org/sites/default/files/arch

ive/Documents/SPGDisclosures/ESRS_Lekela_SouthAfrica_Cat.A_updat
ed%205%20PM%20Oct%2025%202016.pdf.
World Bank Inspection Panel. 2011. Investigation Report: South Africa:
Eskom Investment Support Project (IBRD Loan No. 78620-ZA.
Washington, DC: World Bank. Online at www.inspectionpanel.org/sites/
www.inspectionpanel.org/files/ip/PanelCases/65-Investigation%20Repor
t%20%28English%29.pdf.
World Commission on Environment and Development. 1987. *Our Common
Future. [Brundtland Report]*. New York: United Nations.
Wright, Christopher. 2012. Global Banks, the Environment, and Human
Rights: The Impact of the Equator Principles on Lending Policies and
Practices. *Global Environmental Politics* 12(1): 56–77.
Wright, Rachel A., and Boudet, Hilary Schaffer. 2012. To Act or Not to Act:
Context, Capability, and Community Responses to Environmental Risk.
American Journal of Sociology 118(3): 728–777.
WWF-Brasil. 2015a. *Desafios e Oportunidades para a Energia Solar
Fotovoltaica no Brasil: Recomendações para Políticas Públicas*. Brasília:
WWF-Brasil.
WWF-Brasil. 2015b. *Desafios e Oportunidades para a Energia Eólica no
Brasil: Recomendações para Políticas Públicas*. Brasília: WWF-Brasil.
Wu, Fuzuo. 2018. *Energy and Climate Policies in China and India*.
Cambridge: Cambridge University Press.
Wu, Mark, and Salzman, James. 2014. The Next Generation of Trade and
Environment Conflicts: The Rise of Green Industrial Policy. *Northwestern
University Law Review* 108(2): 401–474.
Xia, Fang, and Song, Feng. 2017. Evaluating the Economic Impact of Wind
Power Development on Local Economies in China. *Energy Policy* 110:
263–270.
Yonk, Ryan M., Simmons, Randy T., and Steed, Brian C. 2013. *Green vs.
Green: The Political, Legal and Administrative Pitfalls Facing Green
Energy Production*. New York and London: Routledge.
Zhouri, Andrea, and Valencio, Norma. eds. 2014. *Formas de Matar, de
Morrer e de Resistir: Limites da Resolução Negociada de Conflitos
Ambientais*. Belo Horizonte: Editora UFMG.
Zysman, John, and Huberty, Mark. eds. 2014. *Can Green Sustain Growth?
From the Religion to the Reality of Sustainable Prosperity*. Stanford:
Stanford Business Books.

Index

ABEEólica, 68, 97, 100, 102, 191, 205, 211
Absolar, 68, 104, 106, 162, 170, 171
advanced industrialized countries, 1, 17, 59, 81, 178
African National Congress (ANC), 28, 36, 49, 83, 109, 110, 128, 143, 144, 147, 224
Angra 3 nuclear plant, 74
Anti-Privatisation Forum, 147
auctions, 24, 26, 87, 104, 130, 181, 182, 186, 233
  in Brazil, 65, 82, 92, 94, 95, 96, 103, 105, 165, 189, 229
  in South Africa, 48, 52, 111, 114, 115, 118, 121, 124, 128, 150, 195, 213

Belo Monte hydroelectric dam, 74
birdlife, 3, 177, 185, 192, 199, 203, 205, 218
BirdLife South Africa, 25, 179, 198, 199, 206, 218
Black Economic Empowerment (BEE), 112, 115, 119
Bolsonaro, Jair, 28, 33, 58, 63, 77, 190, 228
Brazil
  Amazon Fund, 61
  ANEEL, 65, 66, 71, 91, 162, 163, 171
  Bigger Brazil Plan, 94
  Brazilian Agency of Industrial Development (ABDI), 100, 102, 107
  Brazilian Forum on Climate Change, 59, 64, 68
  carbon tax, 64
  Chico Mendes Institute for Conservation of Biodiversity (ICMBio), 192

deforestation, 23, 33, 57, 60, 62, 63, 64, 77, 228, 229
Energy Research Enterprise (EPE), 66, 92
EPE ten-year energy plans, 66, 68, 69, 71, 74, 77, 164, 167, 193, 228, 229
foreign ministry, 59
hydropower, 7, 17, 20, 33, 57, 65, 66, 69, 70, 74, 77, 93, 158, 160, 219
Industrial, Technology, and Foreign Trade Policy (PITCE), 94
inequality, 5, 137, 139, 165
Inter-ministerial Commission on Climate Change, 59
Inter-ministerial Committee on Climate Change, 61
labor movement, 92, 102
Ministêrio Público, 184, 207, 208
Ministry of Development, Industry, and Foreign Trade (MDIC), 94
Ministry of Energy, 64
Ministry of Environment, 27, 35, 59, 61, 64, 77, 220
Ministry of Finance, 105
Ministry of Mines and Energy, 25, 62, 65, 66, 82, 91, 93, 94, 104, 105
Ministry of Science and Technology (MCT), 59, 61, 101
National Climate Law, 62
National Council on Energy Policy, 66, 68
National Environmental Council (CONAMA), 190, 191
National Plan on Climate Change, 61
National Policy for Sustainable Development of Traditional Peoples and Communities, 194
Plan for Action to Prevent and Control Deforestation in the Legal Amazon, 60

For EU product safety concerns, contact us at Calle de José Abascal, 56–1°,
28003 Madrid, Spain or eugpsr@cambridge.org.